Nazi Economics

Avraham Barkai

Nazi Economics
Ideology, Theory, and Policy

Translated from the German by
Ruth Hadass-Vashitz

Yale University Press
New Haven and London

First published in the United Kingdom 1990 by
Berg Publishers Limited.

First published in the United States 1990 by
Yale University Press.

Printed in Great Britain.

Library of Congress catalog card number: 89–52113
International standard book number: 0–300–04466–6

10 9 8 7 6 5 4 3 2 1

Contents

Preface to the English Edition

In the first German edition of this book published in 1977, I presented my conception of the Nazis' economic policies and institutions as a distinctive and consistent system. Contrary to previous and still prevailing opinions, it is my understanding that during the years 1933 to 1945 the German economy operated on the basis of a unique combination of short-term anticyclical interventions and of ideologically preconceived guidelines utilized to establish a new social and economic order. In the formation of this system, the original contribution of the National Socialist party's leadership, its ideologists and economic experts, was admittedly not very substantive. It was the prevailing depression that, to a large extent, dictated immediate economic measures. The more farsighted concepts that were part of this system were copied or adapted, in large part, from previous and contemporary economic philosophies and theories. But this is unimportant in our present context. What is significant is the fact that, within a very short time after the Nazis achieved power, they had succeeded in establishing an economic framework containing so many newly formulated postulates, methods, and institutions that it can be defined as a unique and distinctive economic system.

When the first German edition of this work appeared, the revolutionary or modernizing impact of the Nazi regime on German society had already been the subject of several previous studies.[1] The authors of these works underscored how National Socialist rule had resulted in the permanent modernization of German society, an effect that, to a large extent, survived the defeat and collapse of the Third Reich. Most of these authors shared the view that these effects, in one form or another, were the lasting but unintentional results of reactionary ideological and political aims but that Nazi

1. Most outstanding are Ralf Dahrendorf, *Gesellschaft und Demokratie in Deutschland* (Munich, 1965); and David Schoenbaum, *Hitler's Social Revolution: Class and Status in Nazi Germany, 1933–1939* (London, 1967).

policies, once set in motion, acted according to their own internal dynamics to move beyond the original intentions of their creators. I still believe this to be a correct and persuasive assessment. However, these studies focused on the sociological and political aspects of modernization. In the economic sphere, it was generally believed, no original or even distinctly definable system existed within the Third Reich, which merely depended on pragmatic improvisation and rearmament as the basis for its economic policies. Scholarly differences dealt mainly with the class character of the regime and drew upon preconceived models. In my introduction to this volume, I therefore focus on reviewing and discussing the major scholarly opinions on this central issue that were presented in earlier studies written up to the mid-1970s.

Since then a number of new books and articles on the same subject have been published, and some important and detailed studies of specific or sectoral aspects of the economy have added significantly to our knowledge of this period. Mainly for technical reasons, however, I have been unable to integrate the themes of these more recent publications into the new German and English editions of my book. Though I may be wrong, I did not feel it necessary to make any essential changes in the central theses and conclusions of my original work. The English translation therefore remains a slightly shortened and revised version of the first and second German editions. Only the bibliography has been updated to include a listing of the more important new works on this topic. The last chapter, which deals with the war economy of 1937 to 1945, has been retained from the German pocketbook edition of 1988. This chapter was added in both the second German and the English editions for the benefit of the general reader, for whom the first edition's interruption of the narrative and analysis at the end of 1936 made little sense. I feel compelled to emphasize, however, that the chapter is merely a short review of the available research by other specialists in the field, without any original contribution on my part.

In recent research the authenticity of some of the sources quoted in the first German edition has also been questioned. In particular, the records of Hitler's conversations with Hermann Rauschning and Richard Breiting have been discredited. Nevertheless, I have decided to retain the few sentences cited from these sources in the new German and English editions because I believe that, like the unpublished Breiting-Hugenberg interview, they are still valid, at least as secondary evidence. It may be true that when presented in the form of alleged verbal monologues by Hitler these were literary falsifications. But even if that is the case, these authors, who were Hitler's contemporaries, demonstrated remarkable insight into his innermost thoughts and intentions, as corroborated by later and uncontested evidence.

For two main reasons, my first edition of this book dealt almost exclusively with the period up to 1936, which is still its main subject. First, the later years of the Third Reich, and especially the war period, had been much more carefully researched by the 1970s, and I felt unable to add much new information. The second and, nevertheless, more decisive reason was that, in my opinion, ideological aims and objectives played a comparatively greater role in the earlier stages of the Nazi regime; later these goals had to yield to the more urgent and pragmatic task of war preparations. As long as large parts of Germany's production capacity were still idle, ideologically motivated economic experimentation in the agricultural sector, for example, could continue without causing great damage. It was only after full employment was achieved, however, that the problem of priorities became urgent. At this stage the leadership gave seemingly temporary preference to the predominantly industrial, short-term goals of war preparation, putting aside fulfillment of its racist *Lebensraum* dreams until after the more urgent need for war victory was satisfied. Later commentators have criticized what they consider to be a rather arbitrary periodization on my part, arguing that war and *Lebensraum*, as components of the Nazi ideology, were just as significant as the state dirigism and the integrative *Volksgemeinschaft* that dominated the first years of Nazi rule.

In my work I have not ignored the ideological dimensions of rearmament and war, and I am heartened to find that the somewhat neglected and underestimated role of ideology has now been revived and developed in the works of a younger generation of scholars.[2] One should nevertheless be cautious in dealing with generalizing concepts such as revolution or even modernization, simply because such ideas convey habitually positive connotations in the minds of many readers. Certainly after a half century of research and many

---

2. See among others: Peter Krüger, "Zu Hitlers 'nationalsozialistischen Wirtschaftserkenntnissen,'" *Geschichte und Gesellschaft* 6 (1980): 263–82; Ludolf Herbst, *Der totale Krieg und die Ordnung der Wirtschaft: Die Kriegswirtschaft im Spannungsfeld von Politik, Ideologie und Propaganda, 1939–1945* (Stuttgart, 1982).

thousands of books on the subject, few people still regard Hitler as an ignorant, eclectic housepainter or a psychopathic demon who somehow succeeded in forcing his terrorist dictatorship on millions of Germans. He may have been eclectic; nevertheless, he became the persuasive promoter of a consistent ideology and of the political program deriving from it, both of which appealed widely to the German people. Within broad strata of German society, the economic and political achievements of the National Socialist regime in its first years contributed even more to reinforcing the initial consensus on and identification with this ideology and program; without this support the Nazis would never have retained control of the government. But this view is still far removed from that of a young German scholar whose recent thought-provoking study presents Hitler as a farsighted and rational revolutionary who intentionally planned and pursued the modernization of the German economy and society.[3]

Some time ago American historians reopened the discussion of the relationship between economic interests and political power in Nazi Germany.[4] The central points of the argument involve the Weimar period up to its end in 1933 and the role of business interests in its destruction and in the Nazi party's rise to power. These issues therefore touch only marginally on the subjects investigated in this book. But since an essential aim of my argument is to prove the "primacy of politics," or rather of ideology, during the twelve years of National Socialist rule, a short comment is unavoidable. Putting aside the important methodological questions regarding the presentation and interpretation of source material that arose as part of this discussion and developed into a somewhat overheated academic dispute, I am surprised to find little real disagreement among these historians about the actual role of German big business in the Nazis' rise to power. According to almost all of these scholars, big business leaders played no significant role in the Nazi seizure of power, either because at that crucial point in time they did not want Hitler to become Reichskanzler or because they had already lost power. There seems to be a consensus that, at the end of 1932, whatever German big business may have actually wanted, in reality it no longer had sufficient political leverage either to install

3. Rainer Zitelmann, *Hitler: Selbstverständnis eines Revolutionärs* (Hamburg, Leamington Spa, and New York, 1987).
4. Most outstanding is Henry A. Turner, Jr., *German Big Business and the Rise of Hitler* (New York and Oxford, 1985).

Hitler as chancellor or to prevent his assuming power. There is little argument about the fact that no united political action could be agreed upon. Scholarly opinion is divided mainly on the issues of explaining the causes for this division and of analyzing the intentions and motivations of the big business interests in terms of differences in economic interests, political convictions, and personal temperaments.[5] In the end, the primacy of politics seems to have gained more or less general recognition, and no serious historian, except perhaps some of the most inveterate orthodox Marxists, still adheres to the concept of Hitler as the mere agent or tool of German capitalism. If scholars agree that this state of affairs existed during the final months of the Weimar Republic, it certainly prevailed during the twelve years of the Third Reich. In my opinion, it was the continuity of this historical process that first turned many of Germany's big business leaders into "sleeping partners" of the Nazi regime and later into accomplices to its atrocious crimes.[6]

The reader should note that chapter 3 of the 1988 German edition appears here as chapters 3 and 4, with the result that there is an additional chapter in the English edition. Furthermore, the term billion is used here in statistics in the American sense, not the British.

I am indebted to my friend, Mrs. Ruth Hadass-Vashitz of Lehavoth Habashan, for her translation of my work and to Dr. Deborah Del Gais Muller for her editing of the English version. I also wish to thank Professor Henry A. Turner, Jr., who encouraged me to have my book translated, and last but not least, my publishers.

A.B.
Kibutz Lehavoth Habashan, July 1989

5. See among others: David Abraham, *The Collapse of the Weimar Republic: Political Economy and Crisis* (Princeton, 1981); Harold James, *The German Slump* (Oxford, 1986); Reinhard Neebe, *Großindustrie, Staat und NSDAP* (Göttingen, 1981).

6. See my article, "Die deutschen Unternehmer und die Judenpolitik im 'Dritten Reich,'" *Geschichte und Gesellschaft* 15 (1989): 227–47.

Abbreviations

ADGB	Allgemeiner Deutscher Gewerkschaftsbund
AEG	Allgemeine Electrizitäts-Gesellschaft
BA	Bundesarchiv, Koblenz
BDC	Berlin Document Center
DAF	Deutsche Arbeitsfront
DIHT	Deutscher Industrie- und Handelstag
DNVP	Deutsch-Nationale Volkspartei
HF	Forschungsstelle für die Geschichte des Nationalsozialismus in Hamburg
IfZ	Institut für Zeitgeschichte, Munich
NA	National Archives, Washington, D.C.
NSBO	Nationalsozialistische Betriebszellen Organisation
NSDAP	Nationalsozialistische Deutsche Arbeiterpartei
RDI	Reichsverband der Deutschen Industrie
RNS	Reichsnährstand
SAP	Sozialistische Arbeiterpartei
SPD	Sozialdemokratische Partei Deutschlands
WPA	Wirtschaftspolitische Abteilung

Introduction

There can be no doubt that the economic crisis of 1929–33 played a major role in strengthening the Nazi movement and facilitated its attainment of power on January 30, 1933. When the Nazis seized power, a third of the German labor force was unemployed and almost half of the country's industrial capacity lay unused. During their first year of government unemployment began to recede considerably and by the end of 1936 – that is, within four years – Germany's economy reached full employment.[1] It was mainly this "economic miracle" that won support for the Nazi regime among a majority of the German people – thus providing its government with a broad popular basis. In the eyes of ordinary Germans the Nazi party was the one that had promised "bread and work" and had kept its promise when it assumed power – while the anguish of unemployment continued to harass other countries.

This rapid economic recovery was the result of the implementation of an active economic policy by state agencies which established deficit spending on a scale unprecedented in a capitalist industrial economy during peacetime. It is therefore only natural that since the thirties this policy has become the subject of a large body of economic literature that describes and analyzes its implementation. After 1945 research in this field could also avail itself of considerable statistical and documentary evidence. It is therefore surprising that to date no convincing explanation has been offered – in regard to the reasons or the theoretical premises – for why the Nazi regime employed an active "countercyclical" economic policy; although today the theoretical foundations of such a policy and its implementation are, in fact, accepted by most states, they were certainly revolutionary at the time. There has been no adequate explanation of why Nazi Germany, of all states, implemented this

---

1. Wolfram Fischer, *Deutsche Wirtschaftspolitik, 1918–1945*, 3d ed. (Opladen, 1968), p. 108.

policy earlier and with greater success than other countries, such as the United States with its New Deal.

One reason for this lack of a satisfactory explanation is no doubt the assumption that in fact no Nazi economic policy ever existed and that the Nazi success was altogether the result of pragmatic improvisation. Some scholars go even further and ascribe this success to the ingenuity and inventiveness of a single man – Hjalmar Schacht, minister of economics and head of the Reichsbank from 1933 to 1939.[2] Others, more moderately inclined, consider the policies the Nazis employed as a large-scale continuation of measures initiated by previous governments.[3] The predominant opinion among scholars is still that the Nazis themselves had no theoretical or practical economic concepts of their own and that there was no relation whatsoever between actual Nazi policies and whatever confused ideas they may have had about economic systems. On the face of it, this approach is confirmed by the fact that Nazi "economic experts" like Gottfried Feder and others soon dropped out of sight, leaving the execution of economic policy to people like Schacht and the top echelons of established departmental bureaucracy. The fact that numerous individuals and organizations outside the Nazi camp retained their former positions in the economic sphere after 1933 also supports the claim that economic policy throughout these years was not dictated by the norms and goals of Nazi ideology. All that actually mattered were short-term political objectives, foremost among which was rearmament in order to prepare for war; here the Nazis found a common denominator with the economic interests of traditional power groups.[4]

Assuming that the economic policy the Nazis employed was in fact not their own, the bulk of research did not consider it necessary to investigate how this policy, in theory or in practice, came into being. Most studies – each one with its own, preconceived point of view – examine the balance of power between classes and interests

2. See W. Treue and G. Frede, *Wirtschaft und Politik, 1933–1945: Dokumente mit verbindendem Text* (Braunschweig, 1953), p. 13; René Erbe, *Die nationalsozialistische Wirtschaftspolitik, 1933–1939, im Lichte der modernen Theorie* (Zurich, 1958), p. 177.

3. Gerhard Kroll, *Von der Weltwirtschaftskrise zur Staatskonjunktur* (Berlin, 1958), pp. 411ff.; Dieter Petzina, "Hauptprobleme der deutschen Wirtschaftspolitik, 1932/33," *Vierteljahreshefte für Zeitgeschichte* 15 (1967): 19–55; Wilhelm Grotkopp, *Die große Krise: Lehren aus der Überwindung der Wirtschaftskrise, 1929–32* (Düsseldorf, 1954).

4. Franz Neumann, *Behemoth: The Structure and Practice of National Socialism* (London, 1942), pp. 187f.

that shaped the Nazis' economic policy or at least influenced it decisively. By definition this kind of research operates on a high level of abstraction: when a "model" of social and political power relations has been designed, empirical research, sometimes detailed and rather exhausting, tries to "fit" the facts into the appropriate squares. In consequence, there is an abundance of studies dealing in a general way with the nature of the Nazi regime and its class structure, while empirical research in many economic sectors suffers neglect. To date we still have no study of the German banking system, of price and wage controls, and of numerous economic branches, national as well as regional.

However, no one can possibly ignore the substantial changes that took place in Germany's economy during this period: active government control over all branches of the economy; massive deficit spending on public works; regulation of foreign trade, prices, wages, and investment. It is quite clear that there was no free market economy in Germany throughout those years, even in comparison with other advanced industrial countries, none of which had operated under conditions of "pure competition" since the beginning of the century. The scope and depth of state intervention in Nazi Germany had no peacetime precedent or parallel in any capitalist country, Fascist Italy included.[5]

In the thirties and during the war years the inclination to ascribe this phenomenon to preparation for war was natural and understandable. Western economists perceived Germany as an organized war economy, planned down to the last detail and created by the Nazis in a conscious and purposeful effort from the time they assumed power:

> With the Nazis in power in Germany a unifying principle was brought to bear on the economic system. They had a predetermined purpose: the creation of a war machine. In subordinating the economic system to that objective they substituted conscious over-all direction for the autonomy

5. In 1940 the economic editor of the *Deutsche Allgemeine Zeitung* compared entrepreneur freedom of action in 1939 to that of 1913. According to him, the German employer of 1939 was "free" only with regard to the internal organization of his enterprise and the choice of its managers. All his other activities – the level of wages and prices, joining cartels, distribution of profits, the use of credit, the choice of markets and the manner of competition and advertising, investment, and development of new products – were fettered (*gebunden*) or at least directed (*gelenkt*) by state agencies. Although the article was written in wartime, it should be noted that all institutional arrangements listed there had already been operative in Germany in 1936, if not earlier (J. Winshuh, *Gerüstete Wirtschaft* [Berlin, 1940], p. 6).

of the market-mechanism . . . a totalitarian system of government control within the framework of private property and private profit. . . . A
vast network of organizations was erected to embrace . . . every factor of
production, distribution and consumption in the country. By domi-
nating this organizational structure, through which orders could be
issued to every businessman in the country, large and small, and by
insisting on strict obedience from all, the government obtained complete
control over the economy without actually owning the means of production. The extent to which the government made use of this extensive
machine in every branch of the economy is a matter for conjecture. . . .
Another matter that must remain obscure for the time being is the
particular agency in which the plans for the various industries and sectors
of the economy were coordinated. Such an agency certainly existed . . .
but there is no explicit reference to it in the literature.[6]

This was written by the American economist Otto Nathan in
1943. He described the institutional structure and constitutional
framework of the German economy with great precision, basing his
work on official German publications. From the data available to
him at the time he concluded that such an economy must have
operated on instructions from a central planning authority – although he did not find documentary evidence that such an authority
existed. Nazi Germany's military successes in the initial stages of
war added credibility to the description of its economy as an
organized, well-oiled war machine – a notion that was invalidated
only by postwar research. It is less understandable that the same
claim appears without qualification in the new, 1971 edition of his
book. In addition, Nathan's description centers mainly on data for
1936–39, leaving the early period of Nazi rule almost completely in
the dark. Consequently, one receives the impression that there was
a single reason for the economic and institutional measures of Nazi
policy and the liquidation of unemployment in Germany – preparation for war.

Marxist authors like Charles Bettelheim (1946) arrive at similar
conclusions.[7] Rather surprisingly, Bettelheim provides an orthodox
Marxist underpinning for the Nazi concept of *Lebensraum* (living
space). He argues that, given scanty domestic markets and no
export outlets, monopoly capital had no way to expand its Euro-

---

6. Otto Nathan, *The Nazi Economic System: Germany's Mobilization for War*
(Durham, 1944), pp. 5f.
7. Ch. Bettelheim, *L'économie allemande sous le Nazisme: Un aspect de la
décadence du capitalisme* (Paris, 1946).

4

pean markets except through war. According to Bettelheim it was impossible to increase production of consumer goods in Germany without lowering prices and profits; the only way out of the capitalist surplus production crisis was to prepare for war, that is, to generate production that did not depend on private consumer demand. "Guided" by the interests of big business, "its" state chose war as the only way out of the crisis. It is therefore natural for Bettelheim to belittle the importance of economic regulation by state agencies: "What 'guides' the economy is still the market – and it is a capitalist market, dominated by profit."[8]

Bettelheim bases his work scrupulously on the Dimitroff definition of fascism, which has informed Soviet and Communist research ever since it was formulated in 1935: "Fascism is the undisguised, terrorist dictatorship by the most reactionary, most chauvinist and most imperialist elements of finance capital."[9] According to this conception, Hitler and the Nazi regime acted as executive agents for monopoly capital, whose role was to crush organized labor in order to secure the continued dominance of capitalism. The economy remained capitalist, based on private ownership and the quest for maximization of profit; such an economy cannot be "planned" unless the aim is war, which also arises from the needs of big business. If we ignore for the moment the discourse concerning the regime's class structure and the argument about "primacy of economics" versus "primacy of politics" (which will be discussed further on), we find that Bettelheim pinpoints rearmament as the principal characteristic of economic policy throughout the Nazi period and as the sole cause for the liquidation of unemployment.

Most modern studies, which could draw on the abundance of available documentary evidence, continue, however, to describe the liquidation of unemployment as just a marginal benefit of rearmament.[10] Today we know for certain that no central planning authority existed – not even after the introduction of the Four-Year Plan in 1936, which was a not entirely successful attempt to impose such planning on some sectors of the economy.[11] The picture that

8. Ibid., p. 273.
9. W. Pieck, G. Dimitroff, and P. Togliatti, *Die Offensive des Faschismus: Referat auf dem VII. Kongress der Kommunistischen Internationale (1935)* (Berlin [East], 1957), p. 87.
10. E.g., Fischer, *Deutsche Wirtschaftspolitik*, p. 66.
11. See D. Petzina, *Autarkiepolitik im Dritten Reich: Der nationalsozialistische Vierjahresplan* (Stuttgart, 1968).

emerges, therefore, depicts an economy regulated exclusively by the demands of rearmament, without central planning and without an attempt to formulate any kind of economic method: "It belongs to the paradoxes of the National Socialist era that the state leadership had no organizing principle to guide its severely strained economy; instead, it experimented for twelve years without rhyme or reason, trying first this and then something else – so that the people involved could never rest."[12]

Many authors draw on an elaborate study by René Erbe, published in 1958.[13] This is an attempt to present a quantitative and generally comprehensive analysis of the German economy under Nazi rule, using the tools provided by the Keynesian model. Erbe believes that the German economy, at least from 1934 onward, was "a war economy in peacetime," and he considers this to be the explanation for the Nazis' economic achievements. Erbe's work remains a major source for research of the period, but it fails almost completely to touch on the system of controls and other institutional measures of regulation within the economy. On the other hand, the discussion is excessively influenced by the rather peculiar desire "to clear Keynes" of a suspected similarity between his theory and practical proposals and the performance of Nazi Germany prior to the final theoretical formulation of his method. Although Erbe admits a certain similarity, he believes it to be limited to fiscal policy, that is, deficit spending – claiming that in all other areas the Nazis acted in contradiction to Keynesian rules: they did not encourage investment and private consumption, and by unequal distribution of income and the promotion of savings they deliberately created a low "multiplier." The impact of their initial injections of capital was thus reduced – in contrast to what could have been achieved by a countercyclical policy aimed at consumer demand instead of war. On the grounds of this analysis Erbe concludes that to compare the Nazis' economic policy with Keynesian theory "appears to us as a gross injustice inflicted on Keynes and an inadmissible interpretation of his thought."[14] Yet, as we will see below, Keynes himself was not at all horrified by such a comparison.[15]

12. Fischer, *Deutsche Wirtschaftspolitik*, p. 77.
13. Erbe, *Nationalsozialistische Wirtschaftspolitik*.
14. Ibid., p. 172.
15. Erbe's argument is opposed to the view of G. Haberler, expressed in a letter quoted by Erbe: "I still think that the Nazi policy can be called Keynesian. Large-scale deficit spending is, after all, the decisive factor. That the objectives of the

The conception of an economy based exclusively on war was first challenged by Burton H. Klein in 1959.[16] The statistics in his book rely mainly on data supplied by the American Strategic Bombing Survey during the war. Klein presents the far-reaching argument that until 1939 Germany's expenditure on defense did not exceed that of England, either in absolute figures or in relation to the gross national product (GNP). Nor did public consumption in Germany increase throughout these years at a higher rate than private investment and consumption. According to Klein, Hitler planned a series of short "piecemeal blitzkriegs," not a lengthy "total" war, and therefore did not consider it necessary to prepare the economy for a prolonged war effort. In addition, conservative economists led by Schacht worried about the possible inflationary impact of accelerated military spending, while the regime itself shied at imposing constraints on private consumption in favor of war preparations.[17] Klein concludes that the picture of a German war economy as presented by Otto Nathan and others was, in fact, a myth: "The German leaders simply did not at this time understand the elementary economic lesson that 'a nation can finance everything which can be produced.'"[18]

There is no doubt today that Klein underestimated the scope of German rearmament. It is rather strange that the author of a book published in 1959 relied primarily on statistical data gathered during and immediately after the war and failed to utilize subsequent research, for example, the aforementioned book by Erbe that had appeared the previous year. Techniques of covert expenditure like the Mefo-bill arrangement (discussed below), although known since the Nuremberg trials and the memoirs of Schacht and the finance minister, Lutz Graf Schwerin von Krosigk, are not even mentioned. Only by ignoring changes in the economic and institutional structure could Klein maintain the position that nothing had basically changed and that the policies employed were, in fact, conventional and conservative.[19]

Nazis were different is something else. You can use Keynesian policies for different purposes" (Erbe, *Die nationalsozialistische Wirtschaftspolitik*, p. 167, n.).

16. B.H. Klein, *Germany's Preparations for War* (Cambridge, Mass., 1959).
17. Ibid., pp. 16ff.
18. Ibid., p. 21.
19. T.W. Mason, "Some Origins of the Second World War," in E.M. Robertson, ed., *The Origins of the Second World War: Historical Interpretations* (London, 1967), pp. 120ff.

However, these shortcomings do not invalidate Klein's merit in being the first to question the previously widespread view of the Nazi economy as an effectively organized war machine, in contrast to the economies of the Western democracies. Alan Milward's 1965 work, which focuses mainly on the war years, utilizes much of Klein's data and sources.[20] But Milward also discusses aspects of the economy Klein had ignored, for example, employment policies and foreign trade. He comes to the conclusion that "the direct control of investment and foreign trade were very much more important . . . [in eliminating unemployment] than the creation of an armament industry with a relatively high production capacity."[21]

We will see further on that this assertion does not stand up under close scrutiny: there is no doubt that a major part of German deficit spending went into rearmament and that foreign trade contributed very little to the liquidation of unemployment. Here again the weakness seems to lie in unrealistically low estimates of German military spending, at least with regard to the initial years of the Nazi regime. Nevertheless, Milward also has a major share in dispelling the myth of the economic and organizational efficiency the Germans demonstrated in preparing for war and in conducting its initial stages. Additional evidence for the inefficiency and faulty organization of the economic war effort is provided by the memoirs of Albert Speer, appointed minister for armament and munitions production in 1942 and afterward convicted at the Nuremberg trials.[22]

Berenice A. Carroll's 1968 book provides a more comprehensive and balanced evaluation.[23] She concludes that the German economy became a real war economy only in 1938, but that its gradual development toward this goal had begun in 1934. However, she rejects the proposition, argued by Nathan, Erbe, and others, that from the very beginning of Nazi rule the German economy was a totalitarian entity cemented by a single guiding principle – preparation of a war machine.[24] Like Milward, Carroll does not deal directly with the question of to what extent rearmament alone explains the liquidation of unemployment in Germany. However,

20. Alan S. Milward, *The German Economy at War* (London, 1965).
21. Ibid., p. 2.
22. A. Speer, *Inside the Third Reich* (London, 1971), pp. 299f.
23. Berenice A. Carroll, *Design for Total War: Arms and Economics in the Third Reich* (The Hague, 1968).
24. Ibid., pp. 179f.

her work implies that the impact of rearmament on employment and production could have become notable only by the end of 1934, when signs of recovery began to surface in all sectors of the economy. This was due to the fact that industry as well as the military needed a period of preparation and warm-up in order to produce or absorb large quantities of military equipment; it was not due to a shift in political or economic objectives at government level.[25] Some German writers, as well as the apologetics of involved officials, present the inadmissible claim that Nazi economic policy falls into two separate periods – a period of *Arbeitsbeschaffung* (works projects), described in a variety of versions as continuing until 1934, which was only then replaced by a period of accelerated rearmament.[26] With regard to political objectives, there can be no doubt that Hitler sought to prepare for war as soon as he assumed power; he also tried to channel employment projects, some of which had already been worked out by previous governments, toward rearmament and the creation of a strategic infrastructure.[27] This does not, however, validate the thesis that rearmament was the single and exclusive factor in the liquidation of unemployment.

Among other reasons, the thesis is inadequate because it does not answer the *economic* question with which this discussion is concerned: what was the source of the economic tools employed by the Nazis in the implementation of their policies and how did they come into existence? Pinpointing the *political* goals these policies served circumvents the problem and fails to provide an answer. Today no one doubts that preparing for war had top political priority for the Nazi regime from its very beginnings. But *economic policy* did not end with the allocation of resources for rearmament, and it was not an inherently indispensable result of the preparation for war. It consisted of a whole set of economic and institutional measures; though deficit spending was its most important component with regard to the liquidation of unemployment, it was not the only one. There were significant policy changes in agriculture and foreign trade and a network of controls on wages, prices, and investment;

25. Gerhard Meinck, *Hitler und die deutsche Aufrüstung, 1933–1937* (Wiesbaden, 1959), pp. 86ff.
26. Kroll, *Weltwirtschaftskrise*, p. 474; Willy Prion, *Das deutsche Finanzwunder: Die Geldbeschaffung für den deutschen Wirtschaftsaufschwung* (Berlin, 1938), pp. 9f.; H. Schacht, *Account Settled* (London, 1949), p. 362.
27. G. Schulz in K.D. Bracher, W. Sauer and G. Schulz, *Die nationalsozialistische Machtergreifung: Studien zur Errichtung des totalitären Herrschaftssystems in Deutschland 1933/34* (Cologne and Opladen, 1960).

joined together, they produced an *economic system* of nationalist etatism that was unique at the time. Ideologically this system proclaimed the rejection of liberalism, that is, free competition and regulation of the economy by market mechanisms; these were to be replaced by the dictum of state supremacy and the state's duty to intervene in all spheres of life, including the economy. This conception also granted the state absolute freedom "to create money" according to its needs, as determined by the political leadership. Under conditions of unemployment, the additional money supply generated immediate increases in employment and production before large-scale rearmament projects could be realized; it would have achieved the same results if these resources had been allocated to civil instead of military consumption. It was, therefore, *the manner of financing* government orders and work projects, not their specific allocation of resources to rearmament, that contributed to the liquidation of unemployment in Germany.

The question that provides the subject for the present discourse thus regains its proper place: did a Nazi economic system indeed exist and, if so, on what kind of ideological foundation was it based and where should one look for its historical roots? By its nature this question involves a definition of the Nazi regime's inherent character and an evaluation of social and political forces operating within its framework. Or in other, somewhat blunter words: by whom and how were economic policies in the Third Reich determined, who carried them out, and who "benefited" in the process?

Orthodox Marxist research, in particular the East German and Soviet brands, has an absolute and unequivocal answer: policy is motivated by economic interests. The state is the means by which the ruling class governs society as a whole. German National Socialism, which represents merely one among various forms of fascism, is defined (while staying close to the Dimitroff definition of 1935, mentioned above) as an obedient agent of "monopolistic finance capital," which established it as a dam to hold off Socialist revolution and as a means of protecting profit and realizing capital's imperialistic expansionist plans. "Fascism is the rule of finance capital itself," which aims continuously and consistently at a war of expansion in order to seize the markets and raw materials of Europe. "It was therefore not 'Hitler's way' that led to the outbreak of war in 1939, but the way of German 'big business.'"[28]

28. Eberhard Czichon, "Der Primat der Industrie im Kartell der nationalsozialistischen Macht," *Das Argument* 10, no. 47 (1968): 185.

Drawing on Lenin's theory of imperialism, this kind of argument explains the changes in economic methods and the structure of the economy under Nazi rule as a new and supreme stage in the development of monopolistic capitalism, namely, "political-monopolistic capitalism." At this stage the state becomes the direct and exclusive representative of monopolistic interests that subject all other economic and social interests to their ends through undisguised dictatorship. The political mass movement and its ideology play at best a secondary or even dispensable role when it comes to defining a form of government as fascism – which in principle is "the undisguised terror of a monopolist bourgeoisie."[29] In order to validate this thesis, a number of studies describe the relations between various captains of industry and the Nazi party before and after its seizure of power. Other Western studies also dealt with these relations, and East German research has added important details. Nevertheless, the facts the East Germans discovered do not justify their far-flung interpretation that the Nazi takeover was almost exclusively the result of manipulations by the captains of industry, who "hoisted Hitler into power" to ward off the threat of a Communist revolution. By now it has been established with certainty that until the electoral victory of 1930 only Thyssen, Kirdorf, and a few of their associates supported Hitler and his party, while most industrialists viewed the Nazis with a measure of suspicion. Even after 1930 financial and political support lent by large-scale industry was rather limited. Only from mid-1932, when the Nazi party had already become the most powerful political mass movement, is there evidence of considerable support from major industries.[30]

The description of Nazi rule after 1933 also suffers in Marxist literature from one-sidedness: after the Nazis had crushed the trade unions and political organizations of the working class, fulfilling the role assigned to them by big business, the representatives of the latter, or of segments within it, wielded absolute power over all sectors of the economy.[31] Conflicts and differing approaches to

---

29. K. Gossweiler, "Über Wesen und Funktion des Faschismus," in K. Gossweiler, R. Kühnl, and R. Opitz, *Faschismus – Entstehung und Verhinderung*, Antifaschistische Arbeitshefte, No. 4 (Frankfurt a.M., 1972), p. 33.

30. See, for example, G.W. Hallgarten, *Hitler, Reichswehr und Industrie* (Frankfurt a.M., 1955); H.A. Turner, Jr., *Faschismus und Kapitalismus in Deutschland: Studien zum Verhältnis zwischen Nationalsozialismus und Wirtschaft* (Göttingen, 1972); R. Neebe, *Großindustrie*. See also Abraham, *Collapse*.

31. E. Czichon, *Wer verhalf Hitler zur Macht? Zum Anteil der deutschen Indus-*

economic policies are explained as a struggle between various groups in big business, as each one sought to secure a larger slice of available profits for itself. Jürgen Kuczynski, the doyen among East German economists, divides these groups into two rival camps within the Nazi regime. On the one hand were the owners of the coal, steel, and iron industries, described as highly reactionary and conservative, who had supported Hitler and his party from the very beginning. The chemical and electrical industries, on the other hand, had maintained more democratic attitudes and switched their support to Hitler only toward the end of the Weimar Republic. The struggle between these two groups went on with varying intensity, until finally the demands of war and the necessity to produce fuel and rubber substitutes caused the economically dominant position to be ceded to chemistry and electricity.[32] Another German writer, Kurt Gossweiler, adds finance capital to this picture. In his view the latter consisted mainly of two dominant and opposed groups: the "pan-German" and the "American" group, which supported the coal-iron and electrochemical groups, respectively. Yet in contrast to Kuczynski, Gossweiler sees no substantial difference in the support both groups lent to the Nazis; each sought to harness them to its own interests by contributing to their funds and securing party membership for its own people. The documentary basis for this proposition is rather questionable, and the evidence is sometimes stretched almost to the breaking point: Schacht is described as the major representative of American interests, on the strength of personal ties and frequent trips to the United States. Gregor Strasser, the chief of the Nazi party organization, is said to represent the chemical industry for professional reasons – he was a pharmacist prior to his rise in the Nazi hierarchy and secured a job in one of the chemical enterprises after his resignation in 1932.[33] Czichon, who like Kuczynski adopts the division into interest groups, adds a component of individual opinion with regard to desirable economic policies. One pre-1933 group, defined as Nazi

trie an der Zerstörung der Weimarer Republik (Cologne, 1967).

32. J. Kuczynski, *Klassen und Klassenkämpfe im imperialistischen Deutschland und in der BRD* (Frankfurt a.M., 1972).

33. K. Gossweiler, "Die Rolle des Monopolkapitals bei der Herbeiführung der Röhm-Affäre" (dissertation, Berlin, 1963), pp. 287f., quoted by H.A. Turner, Jr., "Das Verhältnis des Großunternehmertums zur NSDAP," in H. Mommsen, D. Petzina, and B. Weisbrod, eds., *Industrielles System und politische Entwicklung in der Weimarer Republik: Verhandlungen des Internationalen Symposiums in Bochum vom 12–17. Juni 1973* (Düsseldorf, 1974), pp. 923f.

industrialists supporting rearmament and autarchy, was headed by the coal and iron industries but included others as well. The other group, whom he calls Keynesian, advocated the adoption of export-oriented, expansionist employment policies by the state. The political events preceding the establishment of Hitler's government are described as the struggle between these two groups; the Keynesian camp split into a left wing that supported General Kurt von Schleicher and was inclined to cooperate with the trade unions and a right wing that supported the Nazis and was ultimately responsible for Hitler's ascent to power.[34] In a general way Czichon identifies the Keynesian group with the electrochemical and export industries; however, at a second glance one discovers among the names belonging to members of this group important representatives of heavy industry like Krupp, Flick, and others. The division thus becomes inconsistent, and the decision to join one camp or the other appears to have been as much a matter of personal opinion as of economic interests.

Specific and empirical research into the relations between various interest groups and the Nazi regime is certainly useful per se. There is also no doubt that, as the Nazi regime developed and the importance of certain economic sectors for the preparation of war increased, those sectors received priority in raw-material and manpower allocation and assumed a special position among the powers that be. However, the weakness of orthodox Marxist research lies in its failure to accord any kind of independent role to the Nazi party itself, its leaders, or its ideological goals. In this school of thought, the "fact" that the Nazis ruled Germany in the name and for the benefit of big business interests and that the latter dictated their policies is a foregone and self-evident conclusion. It is a misstatement when Gossweiler declares that the Communists had never adopted "the dim-witted view that the leadership of this state could act only under the orders or direct instructions of big business."[35] This is precisely what the Communists did and do claim. Moreover, he himself returns to the original thesis a few pages further on: "The Fascist leadership not only had to pave the way for profit-seeking monopoly capital; it also had to create a calm hinterland for the robber wars of German imperialism."[36]

The weak link in this whole argument is the lack of any signifi-

34. Czichon, *Wer verhalf Hitler*, p. 13.
35. Gossweiler, "Über Wesen und Funktion des Faschismus," p. 13.
36. Ibid., p. 17.

cant evidence for the direct influence that industrial magnates are said to have had on decisions made by Hitler or the political leadership. One can collect an abundance of utterances made by important industrialists in support of imperialist expansion policies and the conquest of markets and natural resources – but by the same token one can also find a similar number of contradictory utterances. No decisive evidence is offered that these positions were ever brought to the attention of the authorities and that they determined the latter's political decisions. Such evidence is either simply not to be found or it is considered redundant because in this pattern of thought the basic assumption of "government by the dictatorship of monopoly capital" is self-evident. Less dogmatic Marxist scholars in the West have come to more balanced conclusions with regard to the relation between economics and politics under Nazi rule.[37] To a large extent they take up the argument where August Thalheimer, one of the German "deviationist" Communists, left off. As early as the twenties he called attention to a singular characteristic of fascism, the phenomenon of the state apparatus's gaining independence (*Verselbstständigung*), even in relation to parts of the bourgeoisie, and the separation of political government from its class base.[38] Orthodox Eastern Marxism rejects this position, considering Thalheimer's thesis "a sophisticated acquittal of monopoly capital."[39] On the other hand an English scholar, Tim Mason, attacked the Communist thesis in the name of Marxist historiography. He says that the primacy of politics in the Third Reich was indeed a unique phenomenon in the annals of bourgeois society since the Industrial Revolution, but was nevertheless an unassailable fact per se. He believes that the crises of the thirties and the specific character of the Nazi party under Hitler's leadership created a constellation in which the business community, at least from 1936 onward, had no influence on policy-making, economic policy included. Primacy of politics, a proclaimed Nazi goal, in the first place meant the primacy of foreign policy and war preparations; industrial and business magnates took part in the implementation of this policy and benefited from it, even though they had no influence whatsoever on the decision making. Mason also believes that one of

37. Reinhard Kühnl, *Formen bürgerlicher Herrschaft: Liberalismus und Faschismus* (Hamburg, 1971).
38. August Thalheimer, "Über den Faschismus," in W. Abendroth, ed., *Faschismus und Kapitalismus* (Frankfurt a.M., 1967), pp. 19–38.
39. Gossweiler, "Über Wesen und Funktion des Faschismus," p. 12.

the reasons for this situation is to be found in conflicting interests that split the coherent power block of German industry in relation to the Nazi authorities; each group strove to gain a maximum of economic benefits, so that in consequence "they marched separately, but fell together."[40] In his argument with Czichon, Mason also emphasizes the lack of evidence for any direct influence on policy-making that the economic leadership could have exerted; this weakness cannot be explained away by endless repetition of the same propositions.[41]

Mason consistently emphasizes the decisions taken by Hitler alone and does not discuss the influence of Nazi ideology. In this manner primacy of politics presents itself as arbitrary rule by a single individual, largely cut off from its ideological context and the political movement created and personified by Hitler himself. The claim that this primacy of policy applies only from 1936 onward is also not adequately documented. According to Mason, who in this respect draws on the work of Arthur Schweitzer, until 1936 the business community enjoyed a measure of independence within the limits of economic and social policy. From then on full employment and the scarcity of foreign currency generated competition, thus splitting its united front. Mason believes that this put an end to its independence in the sphere of economic policy, which had mainly been guaranteed by Schacht's dominant position as minister of economics and president of the central bank; from this juncture primacy of politics, meaning unlimited authority exercised by Hitler himself, became the hallmark of the period.

In a number of articles and in his main work, published in 1964, Schweitzer developed the thesis of two separate periods in the structure of Nazi government.[42] This is painstaking and well-documented research illuminating numerous aspects of the development of economic policy and the balance of forces within the Nazi regime, which no subsequent research can afford to ignore. Schweitzer comes to the conclusion that, in the era of "organized capitalism" (or, borrowing a concept from Max Weber, "political capitalism"), conflicting economic interests join to form united

40. T.W. Mason, "Der Primat der Politik," *Das Argument*, no. 41 (1966): 484.
41. T.W. Mason, *Das Argument*, no. 47, 200.
42. Arthur Schweitzer, *Big Business in the Third Reich* (Bloomington, 1964); idem, "Organisierter Kapitalismus und Parteidiktatur, 1933–1936," *Schmollers Jahrbuch* 79 (1959); idem, "Der organisierte Kapitalismus: Die Wirtschaftsordnung in der ersten Periode der nationalsozialistischen Herrschaft," *Hamburger Jahrbuch für Wirtschafts- und Gesellschaftspolitik* 7 (1962).

power groups: "This change enabled big business to determine the economic policy of the National Socialist government."[43] Schweitzer does not claim that economic interests determined *all policies* of the Nazi regime, but he believes that they exerted a decisive influence upon economic policy until 1936 and, to a certain extent, up to 1938. He defines this period as one of partial fascism, when rule was by a coalition of the Nazi party, big business, and the army, which he describes as a "bilateral power-structure in which organized capitalism and the party dictatorship acted as equals, each enjoying an almost exclusive sphere of domination."[44] In contrast to Marxist scholars, Schweitzer does not ignore the existence and influence of Nazi ideology. However, his definition of Nazi views as "middle-class socialism" is too narrow and in one sense at least incorrect: the Nazis never wanted to abolish private ownership of the means of production. Defining the regime until 1936 as partial fascism is also a rather doubtful procedure – particularly since he blames the transition to full fascism on the political blindness and organizational inefficiency of the leading protagonists: "It is for their ideological blindness and political ineptitude that the generals and the leaders of big business inescapably bear their share of the responsibility for the shift from partial to full fascism. If they had seen the danger and prepared for it, the Nazis' sneak attack would not have occurred or would have been defeated."[45] This is not just a remark Schweitzer makes in passing but a central thesis, leading consistently to a highly significant conclusion: "There is little doubt that partial fascism and organized capitalism in Germany could have continued to operate for a considerable period. . . . Partial fascism and organized capitalism do not necessarily constitute a transitional phase to full fascism, which in turn need not necessarily become the victim of a war of its own making."[46]

There is no question that, compared to other strata, the industrial community enjoyed a preeminent and protected position under Nazi rule and was less exposed to pressures of terror. It is also true that the Nazis allowed that community a considerable measure of self-management as long as it kept to the straight and narrow and painstakingly strove to achieve the prescribed objectives. However, to describe this state of affairs as a "coalition of equal partners" is a

43. Schweitzer, "Organisierter Kapitalismus," 73.
44. Schweitzer, *Big Business*, pp. 288f.
45. Ibid., pp. 554f.
46. Ibid., pp. 555f.

16

gross exaggeration. Schweitzer himself admits that freedom of
action in economic affairs (which, I believe, was of much smaller
scope than he assumes) was consciously and willingly bought at the
expense of ceding any influence whatsoever on domestic and foreign
policy.[47] To the extent that an alliance or partnership between
business magnates and the Nazis existed at all, the manner in which
David Schoenbaum formulates it seems to be much more to the
point: "The status of business in the Third Reich was at best the
product of a social contract between unequal partners, in which
submission was the condition for success. . . . Business recovered,
in effect, as an accomplice of the Third Reich and by the grace of it.
But the initiative was the State's and economic recovery a means,
not an end."[48]

In substance, this means that the captains of industry in the Third
Reich occupied the position of "sleeping partners," enjoying generous profits but having no say in the "management of the firm." All
groups in large-scale industry accumulated vast profits; they benefited from economic recovery and shared in the gains of plunder
without compunction – beginning with Jewish property confiscated
during the process of Aryanization and going on to the spoils of
war. However, the business community had no real say with regard
to far-reaching objectives of economic policy; at best they had a
partial and limited influence on the manner in which this policy was
implemented. I believe that this was the prevailing state of affairs
not just from 1936 onward, but right from the beginning of the
Nazi regime.

As I will attempt to show, Nazi economic policy was to a great
extent dictated by a system of ideological norms and objectives, and
preparation for war and the war itself were integral parts of this
coherent whole. It may be of interest that a similar conclusion is
sometimes reached – on the strength of evidence to be found in the
field of their research – by historians who investigate specific
economic sectors without committing themselves to an integrative
model (or, at least, without proclaiming such a commitment). In a
1947 study of private investment in the Third Reich, Samuel Lurie
concluded that Nazi investment policies were comprehensible only
in the context of an attempt to create a new economic system that
would be immune to crises; war preparations constituted but one of

47. Ibid., p. 504.
48. Schoenbaum, *Hitler's Social Revolution*, pp. 122f.

the more immediate goals within this framework. There were, according to Lurie, some points of similarity between the German economy in those years and a war economy, but "the significance of this similarity should not be overrated. Clearly the case of the German economy between 1933–1939 was more than that of a military economy operating in peace time. The set-up of controls was not a temporary expedient designed to cope with a wartime emergency, but was part of an integrated system whose long-run goals went beyond the military phase."[49]

In his 1970 book on the the "New Order" in France, Alan Milward also described German policy in the occupied territories as a consistent realization of the Nazis' economic conception as well as their political aspirations: "Fascism . . . can not be ultimately comprehended on a merely political level. Its form of economic expression and its form of political expression can not be meaningfully separated, the final end of both was the New Order."[50] Milward believes too that the Nazi party's economic objectives went beyond the extension of *Lebensraum*; they constituted a comprehensive system whose principal characteristic was the rejection of liberalism:

> At home and abroad the National-Socialist New Order can only be properly understood as an attempt to achieve an antiliberalist solution to the economic problems of the interwar period. . . . National-Socialism was an uneasy compromise between capitalism and anti-capitalism . . . a distinctive response to Germany's own economic and political development. Neither capitalist nor socialist, Germany found a different solution and one appropriate to her own history: fascism.[51]

Milward hints here at another aspect of the Nazis' economic conception, its ideological and historical roots in Germany's past. I too have come to the conclusion that the widely accepted assumption, according to which the Nazis had nothing to offer with regard to economic principles and theory, is inadmissible. In chapter 1 I will try to show how, over the years preceding the Nazis' seizure of power, these economic principles emerged as part of their general ideology; how the Nazis chose the most suitable theory from

49. Samuel Lurie, *Private Investment in a Controlled Economy (Germany, 1933–1939)*, (New York, 1947), p. 214.
50. Alan S. Milward, *The New Order and the French Economy* (Oxford, 1970), p. v.
51. Ibid., p. 28.

among existing trends in economic reassessment available at the time. The question of to what extent these ideas were original is secondary from our point of view. On the contrary, the reason they became respectable and legitimate in Germany was that they could draw on a long tradition of state-directed economic development and on a unique trend in economic thought, accepted in theory and practice also by many outside the Nazi camp. Chapter 2 will discuss the roots that the Nazis' economic views had in the German past and consciousness. I do not regard this development, which belongs to the history of ideas and thought, as the crucial or even major component of an explanation for the economic principles and subsequent policies to which the Nazis adhered. I do, however, believe that it aided them and was instrumental in their rapidly gaining widespread support among the business community, the ministerial bureaucracy, and the German public at large.

The Nazi regime was neither a historical accident, nor was it merely the fruit of political conspiracy among big business, agrarian magnates, and the German army. It is true that the Nazi party was initially founded by defeated soldiers and officers, who rode the wave of economic crisis and middle-class frustration. But it was also a distinct ideological movement; it had a comprehensive worldview (*Weltanschauung*) in which the economy occupied a well defined and significant place. The vision of a Nazi "Thousand-Year Reich" incorporated ideological norms and goals intended to shape this future society and the economy within it – and the Nazis tried to realize at least some of these at once. No one denies that they did so at least in one economic sector – agriculture; in this respect, I believe that it was not the only sector. I by no means claim that these ideological themes were the sole or even the major motive for Nazi policy in all sectors of the economy. But they should certainly be counted among the multiple motives of varying importance for different sectors at different times, and in chapters 3 and 4 I will try to prove that its importance cannot be belittled.

A considerable number of these initial ideological goals were only partially realized, or not realized at all, because they turned out to be incompatible with the demands of rearmament and the social and economic structure of existing industrial society.[52] In this respect the year 1936 was indeed a turning point; from then on full employment demanded a choice between contradictory ideological

---

52. Schoenbaum, *Hitler's Social Revolution*, pp. 245ff.

and political objectives. The order of priority Hitler and his hench-
men decided upon put rearmament and war preparations first; in
consequence, from about this time the German economy entered
upon an accelerated course designed to turn it into a war economy.
Thus short-term goals superseded ideological objectives, which
were postponed to another day. However, the Nazis themselves
regarded the shelving of some of their ideological aspirations as a
temporary measure dictated by immediate necessities. At heart they
hoped to retrieve them – after victory on the battlefield had provided the territorial basis and created secure political and military
conditions for their ultimate realization. They were finally buried
only by the rubble heaps of a long and bloody war.

Chapter 1

Nazi Economic Principles and Projects before 1933

Hitler, Feder, and the "Slavery of Interest"

Hitler's speeches and writings do not offer clear-cut attitudes to economic issues. In *Mein Kampf*, which elaborates his overall platform, he hardly mentions them. Clearly defined positions in this sphere are conspicuously absent also in later years. The tactics Hitler employed throughout those years to disguise his true ideas and goals may have been brought to bear more heavily on economic questions than on other subjects. The connections in influential circles whose support he sought made him tread lightly in sensitive areas; thus, he formulated his economic plans and goals in a general and rather vague manner. Moreover, his political ideology permitted economics only a secondary role anyway: being subject to the primacy of politics, it was to serve political objectives determined, altogether unconditionally, by the leadership of the state. Hitler tended to ignore the claim that economic processes evolved according to an inherent and independent regularity of their own. All that was necessary, in his view, was to provide economic leaders with the appropriate orders and see to it that "experts" supplied them with the necessary paraphernalia to execute those orders. For the same reasons he was later prepared to leave these affairs to lower-echelon government and party executives, paying little attention to details as long as developments tallied with his wishes.

The two permanent and unchanging elements in Hitler's weltanschauung were racial anti-Semitism and the imperialism of *Lebensraum*.[1] Both were derived from a view of history that fed on a

1. K.D. Bracher, *Die deutsche Diktatur* (Cologne and Berlin, 1965), p. 270; see also Eberhard Jäckel, *Hitlers Weltanschauung* (Tübingen, 1969); H.A. Turner, Jr., "Hitlers Einstellung zu Wirtschaft und Gesellschaft," *Geschichte und Gesellschaft* 2 (1976): 89–117; also my reply to Turner, A. Barkai, "Sozialdarwinismus und

vulgarized application of Darwinism to social life: the right of the
strong victor in the never-ending struggle for survival among races
and peoples is the only valid right. *Volk* and race are the basic point
of departure: "Foreign and economic policy are merely instrumental for the self-assertion and preservation of the entity of our
people; the factors that determine them are rooted in and shaped by
the inherent values of this entity."[2] In a confidential memorandum
of 1927 for industrialists, Hitler explicitly emphasized the serving
status of economics in relation to politics. In Hitler's words, the
Nazi movement considered the economy "merely a necessary servant in the life of our people and our nationhood. [The movement]
feels an independent national economy to be necessary, but it does
not consider it a primary factor that creates a strong state; on the
contrary: only the strong nationalist state can protect such an
economy and grant it freedom of existence and development."[3]

Hitler's concept of *Lebensraum* went beyond mere objectives of
foreign policy. It included the vision of a national economy that
would enable the German *Volk* to live on the bounty of its land,
that would be immune to crises, owing to its autarky and independence from the world economy. A strong and independent economy, firmly rooted in the soil, would cure the German people of the
ills of unbridled and harmful industrialization;[4] besides feeding its
population, it would provide them with a healthy way of life, sound
and close to nature: "Germany turns its back on all experiments in
world industry and worldwide trade policies and instead concen-
trates all its strength in order to show its people a way of life for the
next hundred years, by granting them sufficient living space."[5]
Whatever Hitler had to say on economic issues throughout this
period was to be found in his view of the economy as serving the
primacy of politics, as well as in his economic and social vision for
the future – the latter implied rather than spelled out in his concept

Antiliberalismus in Hitlers Wirtschaftskonzept: Zu Henry A. Turner, Jr., Hitler's
Einstellung zu Wirtschaft und Gesellschaft vor 1933," *Geschichte und Gesellschaft* 3
(1977): 406–17; A. Kuhn, *Hitlers außenpolitisches Programm* (Stuttgart, 1970).
    2. Entwurf eines offenen Briefes an Reichskanzler v. Papen, als Antwort auf
dessen Rede vor dem Bayerischen Industriellenverband in München, 12.10.1932,
NA, Kanzlei Adolf Hitler, microcopy T–81, roll 1, fr. no. 11448.
    3. Henry A. Turner, Jr., "Hitler's Secret Pamphlet for Industrialists," *Journal of
Modern History* 40 (1968): 362.
    4. Adolf Hitler, *Mein Kampf* (Munich, 1933), p. 255.
    5. Gerhard L. Weinberg, ed., *Hitlers zweites Buch: Ein Dokument aus dem Jahre
1928* (Stuttgart, 1961), p. 163.

anti-finance capital
along anti-semite lines

of *Lebensraum*. He repeated these ideas time and again with mono-
tonous consistency, adapting his manner of presentation to the
respective audience he was addressing in each case.

In Hitler's social views and in his concept of the state, the
economy occupied an inferior position and was subject to political
imperatives. He did not bother to hide his indifference to the whole
issue. His enthusiasm for the economic theories of Gottfried Feder
(which will be discussed further on) was generated not by a recognition of their objective value but by the political expediency they
offered: "After listening to Feder's first lecture, I knew at once that
I had found the way to establish a new party."[6] Feder's distinction
between creative capital and capital that merely rakes in interest
(*schaffendes und raffendes Kapital*) was indeed almost a stroke of
genius; it permitted the Nazi party to assume an anticapitalist stance
without frightening that part of the business world whose financial
and political support it sought. "The separation of stock-exchange
capital from the national economy made it possible to reject inter-
nationalization of the German economy without endangering independent national existence by a struggle against capital in general."[7]
All that was needed from this point onward was a minor gimmick –
equate finance capital with international Jewish capital, and the
social unrest simmering among large sections of the public would
naturally turn to anti-Semitism. Feder was the publisher of official
Nazi publications in which he elaborated his economic views quite
extensively, thereby influencing the Nazi party's economic concepts considerably throughout its initial years. It is reasonable to
assume that Feder also formulated the twenty-five point party
program (*25 Punkte Parteiprogramm*) accepted in 1920 as the
official party platform, which remained unchanged until the end of
the Third Reich. Ten out of these twenty-five points addressed
economic issues from a sharply contemporary point of view, reflecting the state of Germany's postwar economy. Point 12 demanded expropriation of war profits; point 8 emphasized the state's
primary obligation to protect its citizens' livelihood – leading to the
demand to expel all foreigners. Point 18 demanded capital punish-
ment for profiteers and moneylenders. Other points concerning the
nationalization of land for public purposes (point 14), the nationalization of large-scale combines (point 13), and participation in
big enterprises (point 14) were included as a concession to the

6. Hitler, *Mein Kampf*, pp. 209f.
7. Ibid., p. 212.

revolutionary spirit of the times. Over the years these points were subjected to suitable interpretations – notwithstanding the 1926 declaration that the whole platform was "sacred" and "could not be altered." Additional points expressed typical middle-class demands – for example, opposition to department stores and the demand to give preference to small enterprises in the placing of public orders (point 16). The latter reflected the social origins of the party's founders and the majority of its members during this period.[8]

The connection between these doctrinal demands and actual economic policy under the Nazi regime was rather loose. This is frequently used in support of the view that Nazi ideology did not really influence economic policy under Nazi rule. However, this argument ignores the principally political character of the twenty-five point program – which can be understood only in the context of the specific political situation that generated it. One should also remember that at the time the platform was formulated, the Nazi party's emerging economic principles were still in their initial stages. "What we consider the very essence of Nazi economics, that is, subjection of the economy to the state, is not proclaimed in this program at all. Nevertheless, it was kept alive and became a decisive element in the shaping of Germany's future."[9]

The core of Gottfried Feder's views was the demand "to break the slavery of interest." It appears that Feder borrowed the idea to abolish all payments of interest[10] from Silvio Gesell, a German-Swiss economist who developed a theory of free money and even founded a special association for the dissemination of this theory. The fact that the Nazis neither widely preached the abolition of interest before they assumed power nor actually abolished it afterward is used by numerous scholars as evidence that they abandoned *all* their previous economic concepts and proposals and that there was no linkage whatsoever between those concepts and the Nazis' subsequent performance. The truth is somewhat different: the Nazis indeed retained the slogan of "breaking the slavery of interest" until later in their history, but over the years its content changed from the demand to abolish all interest to the demand to lower it and thus establish a "just rate." In 1931 Gustav Stolper, editor of *Der*

8. See the Nazi party's platform in Walter Hofer, ed., *Der Nationalsozialismus: Dokumente, 1933–1945* (Frankfurt, a.M., 1959).
9. Gustav Stolper, *Deutsche Wirtschaft, 1870–1940* (Stuttgart, 1950), p. 144, n. 9.
10. Gottfried Feder, *Das Manifest zur Brechung der Zinsknechtschaft des Geldes* (Munich, 1919), and idem, *Der deutsche Staat auf nationaler und sozialer Grundlage* (Munich, 1923).

Deutsche Volkswirt, discussed the issue in his magazine: "The National Socialists naturally support the lowering of interest rates by decree. . . . One may well say that they invented the notion of 'breaking the slavery of interest.' It is therefore a measure of wise moderation if they now merely demand the lowering of interest rates."[11] The emphasis shifted to another demand, also formulated by Feder, which acquired definite significance in future developments: "sovereignty of the state with regard to currency and finance" ("Währungs- und Finanzhoheit des Staates"), as Feder called it, represented the assumption that the state could determine the amount of money circulating within the economy to an unlimited degree, according to the needs of the economy. In the early thirties he still considered "breaking the slavery of interest" and liberation from "the tyranny of credit capital" as "the greatest and most meaningful task in economic policy that the National Socialist state has to fulfill." However, it is significant that he did not define the substance of these demands "because they are well known and will be realized only in the distant future." In contrast he instead emphasized short-term demands: "During the interim period, the National Socialist state will use its right to create money wisely in order to finance large public works and the construction of housing, in the spirit of my well-known proposals (a bank for construction and economic activities, etc.)."[12]

In light of subsequent events, the proposals Feder mentions are of interest: in 1924 he presented the parliaments of Mecklenburg and Thuringia with bills for the establishment of special banks for construction and economic activity. Their purpose was to reactivate dormant production factors, especially in the construction trade, by means of moneylike promissory notes, in order to relieve the acute shortage in housing.[13] He repeated similar ideas in additional articles – for example, the financing of public investment by promissory notes, backed solely by the state's sovereignty. Feder did not see any reason why "the state should not produce the money . . . which, after all, is guaranteed by the labor force of the entire people."[14] It is true that these proposals sound somewhat amateurish (Feder was an engineer by profession, not an economist), but to the modern observer they do not appear confused at all. Once again

11. *Der Deutsche Volkswirt* 6, no. 8 (Nov. 20, 1931): 239.
12. G. Feder, *Kampf gegen die Hochfinanz*, 5th ed. (Munich, 1934), p. 305.
13. Ibid., p. 155.
14. Ibid., pp. 90, 44.

it was Stolper who claimed that, notwithstanding Feder's disappearance from the public arena soon after the Nazis assumed power, "Schacht did almost nothing but adapt Feder's ideas to the strictures of the existing currency system."[15]

Actually Feder's influence had already declined just a few years after the foundation of the party. The praise Hitler accorded him in *Mein Kampf*, which subsequently became the bible of the Nazi party, tended to inflate his importance among contemporaries. There is some evidence that Feder himself abandoned many of the economic proposals that failed to gain him support in the party.[16] In a letter of June 1930 to Hitler, he begged to be nominated Gauleiter because he was not being treated with the respect due to him: "Some Gauleiters address me with the greatest impertinence."[17] His theories regarding interest still occupied a prominent place in party publications (many of which Feder himself edited or even wrote), but neither Hitler nor other prominent leaders mentioned them in speeches or other utterances. The party bore with his "economic recipes" only until 1930; no other ideas emerged to replace them, except in the area at acute political controversy concerning war reparations. The obvious conclusion is that before 1933 the Nazi party defined its economic concepts only in a general way, without committing itself to any substantive proposals.

One should not conclude that the party had no economic principles at all; instead, they underwent a process of crystallization and became more sophisticated. At least from 1926 on, when Hitler finally became the one and only leader, the Nazis' view of the economy was purged of any anticapitalist suspicions. In order to make this point absolutely clear, an official declaration by Hitler was added to the party program – "which was unalterable" – in 1928: the party unequivocally supported private property, "in contrast to false interpretations by our rivals." But the Nazis left no doubt that this recognition of private property absolutely and aggressively rejected any notions of economic liberalism; they had no use for a laissez-faire free market. In an off-the-record talk with a newspaper editor in 1931, Hitler defined the basic principle of his economic project: "What matters is to emphasize the fundamental idea in my party's economic program clearly – the idea of authority.

15. Stolper, *Deutsche Wirtschaft*, p. 149, n. 15.
16. Interrogation of Wilhelm Keppler by U.S. State Dept. Special Interrogation Mission, Sept.–Oct. 1945, IfZ, MA 1300/2.
17. NA, T–175, roll 194, fr. no. 733734–40.

I want the authority; I want everyone to keep the property he has acquired for himself according to the principle: benefit to the community precedes benefit to the individual ["Gemeinnutz geht vor Eigennutz"]. But the state should retain supervision and each property owner should consider himself appointed by the state. It is his duty not to use his property against the interests of others among his people. This is the crucial matter. The Third Reich will always retain its right to control the owners of property."[18] Here we have all the basic assumptions that later determined the Nazis' economic plans and their actual policy: virulent antiliberalism, subjection of the economy to the primacy of political and social goals as defined by the national leadership, and state control over all economic activities.

It is true that these ideas were not original; they were part and parcel of what has been defined as "a variety of conservative state ideologies of the period." The revolutionary conservatives in particular also advocated the direction of the economy (dirigism) by an authoritarian state. "Also later on, in the National Socialist version of this policy, the fact that it was borrowed was discernible."[19] However, this merely confirms the process of rapprochement between the Nazis' economic principles and those of other groups in the rightist camp that took place toward the end of the Weimar Republic. This rapprochement was a result of contemporary realities, but it also grew out of the common ideological and spiritual soil that nourished the rightist revolution.[20] After the Nazis assumed power, it came to the fore in the willingness of numerous young conservative journalists and writers to serve their new masters gladly. But in the present context it makes no difference whether the Nazis' views were borrowed or were their own, independent invention. The crucial factor is that all subsequent preparatory work on economic issues as well as economic policy after their takeover was firmly grounded in these ideological foundations.

---

18. Eduard Calic, *Ohne Maske: Hitler – Breiting Geheimgespräche, 1931* (Frankfurt a.M., 1968), pp. 37f.

19. Schulz, in Bracher, Sauer, and Schulz, *Machtergreifung*, p. 362.

20. See Hermann Lebovics, *Social Conservatism and the Middle Class in Germany, 1914–1933* (Princeton, 1969); Klemens von Klemperer, *Konservative Bewegungen zwischen Kaiserreich und Nationalsozialismus* (Munich, 1962); Kurt Sontheimer, *Antidemokratisches Denken in der Weimarer Republik: Die politischen Ideen des deutschen Nationalismus zwischen 1918 und 1933* (Munich, 1962).

Preparatory Work by the Department for
Economic Policy, 1931–1932

The Nazis gained an impressive victory in the general elections of
1930: their share of votes rose from 2.6 to 18.3 percent. From this
date on Hitler prepared his party for the seizure of power. At the
party's headquarters in Munich (Organisationsabteilung II), he
founded a special Organizational Department headed by Konstantin Hierl, a former army officer. Within this division a Wirtschaftspolitische Abteilung (Department for Economic Policy, WPA) was
established, also headed by a former officer, Otto Wagener. Wagener's department was to redefine the party's economic objectives
and to prepare blueprints for their realization. Wagener, like Wilhelm Keppler, Hitler's advisor on economic questions, and Walter
Darré, an agrarian ideologue and agricultural expert, was one of the
"new men" recruited by Hitler at about this time, from outside the
party, who were to take care of economic issues. From notes made
by Wagener and other sources,[21] it seems that already by the very
early thirties Hitler considered Feder's knowledge and talents inadequate for the blueprinting of feasible economic policies. It is
possible that Hitler's well-known tactic of promoting rivalry between multiple institutions and authorities in order to strengthen
his own position as final arbiter also played a part. The scorn and
ridicule with which Feder's proposals were met in business and
professional circles served as the last straw. Be that as it may, during
the period 1931 to 1933 the party established at least three supreme
institutions – all authorized to determine its positions and propaganda on economic issues. The Economic Council of the National
Socialist Workers' Party's (NSDAP) National Leadership (Wirt-
schaftsrat der Reichsleitung der NSDAP), headed by Feder, was a
body that appears to have existed mainly on letterheads and was
rarely called upon to meet. Nevertheless, besides Feder the council
included members who later assumed important positions in the
economy – like Walter Funk, who replaced Schacht in 1937 as
minister of economics, or Fritz Reinhardt, subsequently secretary
of state at the Ministry of Finance. Feder also headed a subordinate
section at Wagener's department that dealt with technology and the
professions. Another "supreme" institution, independent of
Wagener's department, was the Administrative Bureau for Agrarian
Policy (Agrarpolitischer Apparat) headed by Darré, which was

21. IfZ, Aufzeichnungen Otto Wagener, ED 60; Walter Darré, ED 110.

initially accountable to Hierl but from December 1932 on to Hitler himself. In addition, from the spring of 1932 Wilhelm Keppler served as personal economic adviser to the Führer,[22] constituting a kind of independent economic advisory service. His assignment was to gain access to business circles, and his main achievement was the establishment of a permanent group of representatives from business and industry, the Keppler circle. Members of this circle supported the Nazi party financially and had an important share in the political intrigues of January 1933. Keppler maintained close relations with Himmler right from the beginning of his activity in the Nazi party. Darré relates in his notes that in 1930 Himmler had already informed him in confidence that Keppler was going to be "the coming man in foreign policy and among Hitler's economic leadership." When Keppler moved to Munich, Himmler added, again in a talk with Darré: "Hitler is fed up with the twaddle of the party's economists. From now on they can prattle to their hearts' desire; Hitler, in fact, wishes to work only with Keppler."[23]

There is no doubt that during the two years following its establishment Wagener's WPA was the most important and most active of all these bodies. Consultations on economic issues with Hitler and Gregor Strasser, then head of the Organizational Department, took place almost daily. They tried to prepare practical "work plans" for the time when the Nazi party would not only have to disseminate effective propaganda but would also have to govern. The department had a team of ten salaried "experts," including people who also continued to occupy important positions after 1933, and academically trained economists like Wagener himself, Adrian von Renteln, Oskar Lorenz, and others. Wagener sought to staff his department with people who came "from the economy itself," without making membership in the Nazi party a condition for their acceptance. The industrial section was headed by Dr. von Lucke, who had previously worked for the Flick combine. The trade section was managed by Hermann Cordemann, a former officer whose wife was the granddaughter of Werner von Siemens, one of Germany's leading industrialists. Prior to his appointment to a full-time job at Wagener's department, Cordemann had worked for Siemens branches abroad. Alongside the permanent staff Wagener established research circles on various subjects; according to his own evidence, he succeeded in attracting some notable

22. IfZ, MA 1300/2; Darré, ED 110.
23. IfZ, Darré, ED 110.

scientists and businessmen to these circles. Professor Jens Jessen of Kiel University took part in the circles for social-economic questions and for problems of international economics; the latter also included von Stauss from the Deutsche Bank management and Dr. Ernst Fischer, who was connected to I.G. Farben.[24] In time the department's activities expanded to embrace additional areas. In 1932 a shipping section was established, headed by Werner Daitz, who was responsible for North Germany on behalf of the WPA, as was a scientific department under Dietrich Klagges, Nazi prime minister of the state of Braunschweig from 1933.[25]

The WPA was an extended and well-organized body. Eleven plenipotentiaries operated on its behalf in various regions of Germany. Its instructions, whose implementation was obligatory, were passed on to forty-four regional economic experts (*Gauwirtschafts-referenten*) holding full- or part-time appointments, as well as to all Gauleiters throughout the country. Already in 1930 Wagener had founded an economic press agency, the Wirtschaftspolitischer Pressedienst, whose pamphlets were mailed twice a week to the entire party press and to all Gauleiters. An explicit ruling by Hitler stated that these pamphlets were the sole authorized source for the publication of party positions on economic issues. The editor of this pamphlet was Bernhard Köhler, no doubt an important figure now somewhat forgotten; he was the owner and the first editor of the party newspaper, *Völkischer Beobachter*. (The same Köhler headed a section for labor and employment at the WPA; after the Nazi takeover he replaced Wagener as head of the department.) In September 1930 Wagener bought the *Essener Nationalzeitung*, a daily paper, for the party with the intention of turning it into its major economic newspaper. The appointment of editor went to Otto Dietrich, later chief of the press (*Reichspressechef*) in the Third Reich.[26] As mentioned above, the principal role of the economic department was to prepare plans for the future – but it also saw to current matters, whether propaganda or practical issues. It formulated the party's positions on economic questions and maintained relations with business circles that demonstrated interest in the party's proposals and attitudes. It seems that these matters were assigned mainly to Wagener's deputy, von Renteln.[27] In a circular of

24. IfZ, Aufzeichnungen Otto Wagener, pp. 1016–34.
25. BA, NS 22/11.
26. IfZ, Aufzeichnungen Otto Wagener, Heft 4.
27. BDC, Akte REMA, and BA, Nachlaß Silverberg, no. 232, pp. 194/98.

September 1931 signed by Wagener, we find instructions to party officials on how to infiltrate existing economic bodies, with the aim of gaining influence and undermining their leadership: "The time has come to assault the structure of industrial associations. . . . They have begun to talk and to argue about the goals of the National Socialist movement." At present the main influence is still held by "the camp that considers the liberalist and capitalist economic order to be the right one" because the majority of leaders and legal advisers come from there. Precisely for this reason one should try, in the case of new elections, "to replace [this camp] with people of our way of thought." As a means to this end, Wagener points in the first place to enlightenment through lectures, and so forth, but also to the undermining of positions occupied by "currently leading personalities . . . by revealing certain events in the past and present . . . not only with regard to their activities but also in relation to their handling of money." This, however, has to be done with caution; thus, one should avoid "branding individuals as Jews if there is no proof that they are Jews or have Jewish blood." Attacks that could be shown to be false would yield opposite results and "be frowned upon."[28]

The Reichsleitung archives in Munich were lost, so Wagener's notes are the main source of information concerning his department's activities. Nevertheless, scanty as the documentary evidence is, it confirms that thorough consultations on economic questions, in principle and practice, were a matter of course at the department and that Hitler took part in most of these. The level of these discussions and their conclusions, like that of Wagener's own work, was very low, but this does not detract from their importance with regard to later developments. The minutes from a number of consultations at the end of November 1931[29] reveal a thorough discussion of the economic paragraphs in the official party platform of twenty-five points. This discussion is also reflected in Wagener's brochure published 1932 under the title *Das Wirtschaftsprogramm der NSDAP*.[30] The brochure is an attempt to update a platform that was unalterable and adapt it to "the facts of life." Thus, for instance, point 14, which speaks of worker participation in profits, is suitably interpreted: the idea of granting workers a share in the profits of enterprises is replaced by the statement "that low prices and fair

28. BA, NS 22/11.
29. BA, NS 22/11.
30. Otto Wagener, *Das Wirtschaftsprogramm der NSDAP* (Munich, 1932).

wages . . . are the best and most generalized form of a share in profits." In order to regulate worker and wage problems, Wagener proposes to pass a law relegating decisions on these matters to the local or regional level; in cases where no agreement can be achieved, the power of decision will pass to a single mediator. Most members of the committee rejected Wagener's proposals on social security, and it is significant that the final decision on this particular subject was therefore referred to Hitler himself. He ruled against Wagener's proposals and in favor of establishing a workers' Social Savings Fund, without employer participation. He stated that "the existing principle of social security is the right one." The ruling was added verbatim to the minutes.

Wagener's brochure is one of the very few existing records of the work done at the WPA. It reveals unmistakable indications of later decrees (which will be discussed below) – like the national labor law, price and wage controls, and the institution of labor trustees (*Treuhänder der Arbeit*). Other consultations, reported in detail in Wagener's notes, dealt with almost every aspect of the economy. It was Wagener who initiated a discussion of the new economic order, which he called social economy (*Sozialwirtschaft*), conceiving it with the participation of Hitler, Strasser, and Adolf Wagner, the Munich Gauleiter. He claims that Hitler was very much taken with his ideas, but in reality they were never mentioned in official publications, and there is no indication of any attempt to apply them even partially in practice. The basic idea was for gradual participation of workers in the ownership of enterprises by way of a law of property transfer that would gradually transfer ownership to the workers and the state. In this manner, within a period of ten to twenty years, only people actually working at an enterprise would own its shares. Wagener's importance lies not in his own contribution to the party's economic projects but in the fact that he created an organizational framework for the preparation of these projects. From the outside, as well as in his own eyes, he appeared at the time, after Gottfried Feder, as the Nazi party's most outstanding and influential economist. In retrospect one therefore tends to identify the Nazi party's economic concepts with the ideas of these two individuals; their disappearance from the public arena shortly after the Nazi takeover is taken as evidence that the plans for economic policy designed by them were jettisoned. In reality, however, Wagener's and his department's activities were of great import: by initiating extensive discussions on economic issues among the party leadership and by establishing relations with individuals and institutions outside the party, Wagener had considerable impact on future developments. Today there can be no doubt that the activities of his department were crucial in finally shaping the Nazis' economic principles. Although these principles were couched in general terms, we will try to show that it had a decisive influence on actual policies after the Nazis attained power.

The ambitions of Wagener and his team went far beyond the attempt to compose useful "recipes" for the solution of pressing economic problems. What they aspired to was no more and no less than to lay the foundations for new economic methods aimed at the creation of a "new economic order." To further this end, Dietrich Klagges was asked to establish a Department for the Science of Economics in order "to explore and determine the scientific foundations of National Socialist economic principles"; to establish an economic theory "with a National Socialist economic philosophy" in opposition to "the accepted liberalist-Marxist theory"; to create "a scientific basis for an organic conception and the corporate structure of the economy; for a system of economic law that must derive from the philosophic foundations of economic theory." To enable Klagges to cope with this "modest" request, all party branches and institutions were ordered to suggest suitable staff members; it was also decided to contact appropriate scientific institutes.[31] Klagges's qualifications for this appointment consisted of a few articles in which he had tried to develop "a National Socialist theory of economics." Thus, for instance, the introduction to a paper that appeared in 1927 under the title "Wealth and Social Justice" says that its aim is to contribute to a method of "social regulation of the economy in its national framework, subject to the preservation of private property."

In still-existing publications of the economic department these pretensions are only vaguely indicated. Thus, Wagener himself wrote in the *Wirtschaftsprogramm* he published that "nowadays even great leaders of the economy recognize that the current economic system is wrong and a renewal has to be brought about"; since it is "not feasible to establish a dogma for the economy," one can only "recognize the errors of the old system and mold new economic principles on the basis of a new world-view."[32] Wagener later explained this "modesty" by saying that his *Wirtschaftsprogramm*

31. BA, NS 22/11, Anordnung vom 27.5.1932.
32. Wagener, *Wirtschaftsprogramm*, p. 4.

was necessarily only "fragmentary work because he had to circumvent all issues with regard to which Hitler had ordered us to keep silent."[33] In any case, the publication of Wagener's brochure was discussed at one of the very rare meetings of the Nazi Economic Council, where Feder (who headed the council) opposed it. It is a significant indication of Feder's status at the time that, in spite of his opinion, publication of the brochure was not delayed. All Feder achieved was that the already printed pamphlet was officially stamped "for internal use only."[34]

Hitler's instruction "to keep silent" included all subjects concerning the future "economic order" discussed in his presence at the economic department. He based this instruction on the premise that the new economic system could be realized only after a new generation of young National Socialists had come of age and the political objectives of the regime had been fully achieved – a process that would take at least ten to fifteen years. Meanwhile one had to move warily "so as not to frighten the economy – let the embers glow behind locked doors."[35]

The most important and most interesting document from this period is the draft of a manifesto entitled *Wirtschaftspolitische Grundanschauungen und Ziele der NSDAP* (Basic economic principles and objectives of the NSDAP).[36] The document, which I discovered at the Berlin Document Center, is dated March 5, 1931, and is signed by the head of Organizational Department II, Konstantin Hierl. The draft fills nine typewritten pages, and its recipients were asked to present their comments in writing by March 17, that is, within a fortnight, on what was explicitly defined as "the draft for a planned manifesto by the party leadership." As far as we know, neither this manifesto nor a different one on the same subject was ever published – although its impending appearance was publicly announced and aroused great interest in certain circles. A well-known and influential internal newsletter of industrialist circles, the *Deutsche Führerbriefe*, told its readers at the beginning of February 1931 that a small committee of Nazi leaders, headed by Hitler, existed in order to clarify and determine basic concepts of

33. IfZ, Aufzeichnungen Otto Wagener, 1902/12.

34. BA, NS 22/11, Sitzung des Wirtschaftsrats vom 27.4.1932; BDC, OPG-Akte 34, Eingabe Wageners an das Parteigericht (1934).

35. IfZ, Aufzeichnungen Otto Wagener, pp. 652–61, 1773f.

36. For the full text see A. Barkai, "Wirtschaftliche Grundanshauungen und Ziele der NSDAP: Ein unveröffentlichtes Dokument aus dem Jahre 1931," *Jahrbuch des Instituts für Deutsche Geschichte* 7 (1978): 355–85.

economic policy. Although Feder was a member of this committee, he had been somewhat shunted to the sidelines. Wagener, on the other hand, was viewed by the newsletter as a serious and respected person, a high-ranking veteran officer and onetime manager of a large industrial enterprise. The newsletter mentions that the results of the committee's work were still expected, probably in the form of an economic manifesto that Hitler would publicize, perhaps at the next party convention.

After the Nazis' attained power Hierl, whose signature appears on the draft manifesto, became leader of the Labor Service – a compulsory service for every boy and girl after graduation from school and before military service. He also took part in the activities of the economic department in the same sphere – but the notion that he was the author of the draft manifesto is not reasonable at all. One receives the impression that it was a summary of discussions held at the time, orally and in writing, within the economic department and apparently also in wider party circles. A file found at the Forschungsstelle für die Geschichte des Nationalsozialismus (Research Institute for the History of National Socialism) in Hamburg contains extensive memoranda (by Klagges, von Renteln, and others) discussing the same subjects that appear in the draft manifesto. All known facts indicate that these memoranda were distributed early in 1931 as part of a written consultation conducted by Wagener's department.

The form of this document and the attempt to encompass within its pages all conceivable economic issues render it the most exhaustive and unified presentation we have of the Nazi party's economic concepts, as they are recorded a few years before the Nazis assumed power. Even though we have no hard and fast evidence that Hitler participated in its composition, it is utterly inconceivable that such an important and ideologically fundamental statement was issued from the Brown House in Munich without his explicit permission. Hence it seems worthwhile to dwell briefly on its contents. Wagener's social economy is not mentioned at all. The term *Volkswirtschaft* does not appear in the sense that it normally has in German, but is used in opposition to world economy (*Weltwirtschaft*) on the one hand and private economy (*Privatwirtschaft*) on the other. In Nazi thought the people (*Volk*) as a social, cultural, and biological entity provided the ideological basis for all spheres of life. The role accorded to the economy, "to assure the survival and the development of the people's entity [*Volkstum*] socially and culturally," was

35

therefore an appropriate point of departure for Nazi economic principles. The logical consequence of this outlook was utter rejection of a world economy which not only means that national economic interests take priority over any arguments for economic cooperation with other nations but also as a matter of principle denies the existence of universal economic laws and economic research that may be applied to any national economy.[37] As a second consequence, separate economic units were defined within the overall entity as "organic cells of the people's economy," which must not become foreign bodies within its fabric.

The Nazi concept of the state dictated its role in the economy – to fulfill the functions of the body of the people (*Volkskörper*). The state "bears the power of the people" and is responsible for the preservation of this power. It is therefore entitled as well as obliged to interfere in the economy, as in other spheres, and to restrict the freedom of decision making. The state has "supreme authority over the property of the people [*Volksvermögen*]." The section defining the nature of the national economy ends with what can be considered the key to the entire conception: "The economy of the people is therefore subject to the art of statemanship [*Staatskunst*]." Further on, the practical functions of a *völkisch* economic policy are outlined – independence with regard to the world economy through maximum self-sufficiency, that is, a preference for agriculture as "the basis for an independent *Volkswirtschaft*." Since independence can be achieved only by gaining *Lebensraum* for an expanding population, "economic necessity turns into the exigence of foreign policy."

Nowhere else do we find such a concise and succinct definition of the Nazis' economic principles at such an early date: the economy was to serve the state by providing it with the means to realize its political objectives. On the other hand, the expansion of living space would provide the necessary conditions for the future *Volkswirtschaft*. In this manner the *Lebensraum* imperialism acquired a dual political and economic meaning: it served simultaneously as an immediate "economic necessity" and as a precondition for the new economic order in the more distant future. Although realization of

37. Early in 1933 a Nazi economist attacked a book by Adolf Weber (which at the time served as a major textbook at German universities) on the grounds that no such thing as a general theory of economics existed: "We reject such a category of 'world economy' as a subject for theoretical or applied research because such a category of economics does not exist anywhere in the world" (L. Prager, *Nationalsozialismus gegen Liberalismus*, N.S. Bibliothek, Heft 49 [Munich, 1933], p. 9).

the "new order" was deferred to some unspecified date in the future, the state had the obligation to prepare for it educationally and institutionally; as "the disciplinarian of this new economic vision" it would "replace the struggle between competing interests with an all-German economic partnership [*Wirtschaftsgemein-schaft*]."

The draft emphasizes the Nazis' positive attitude to private capital and the incentive of capitalist profits; it also approves of "healthy competition." However, although the principle of private property as such is confirmed, private ownership is described, in the spirit of traditional romantic concepts, as the right to use (*usufruc-tum*) property belonging to the people as a whole, while the state is under obligation to supervise this use. State supervision concerns the "acquisition and use" of property as well as the "just" distri-bution of the income it yields. Future control of investment, prices, and wages are only hinted at, but the hint can neither be denied nor ignored. The wording reveals recognizable traces of previous in-ternal publications and draft papers demanding "fair" wages and "fair" interest rates and prices; there are even attempts to work out a method of precise calculation to guide future economic policies. Klagges took a special interest in these matters: in the paper men-tioned above and in later writings he tried to calculate fair wages, interest rates, and prices by means of the labor-value theory. His whole argument is influenced by Marxist value and surplus-value concepts.

The draft is even more explicit with regard to institutional steps to be taken in future, both on the level of the single enterprise and of the economy as a whole. In the framework of social legislation economic leaders are explicitly assured of their right to "authoritat-ive" management of their enterprises, which was later implemented by means of the leader and followers relationship (*Führer-Gefolg-schafts-Verhältnis*) in industrial enterprises. The definition of self-management and the corporate structure (*ständischer Aufbau*) of the economy prove that the Nazis were by then already far removed from middle-class and universalist concepts of corporate ideology. Although the draft speaks of "a corporate economic order" and underlines the Nazi state's intention to avoid cumbersome bureauc-racy and centralized management of the economy, the limits of economic self-management are laid down at once: "The National Socialist state will, however, reserve its right of supervision and the possibility of energetic intervention with regard to professional and trade organizations. . . . The successful conduct of the German economy is . . . possible only under the leadership of a state that has dictatorial authority and acts with determination and ruthlessness."

The significance of this document extends beyond the outline of the numerous, subsequently implemented economic policies it describes: it proves that the Nazis had a fairly articulate notion of their economic concepts already at the beginning of 1931. Deliberately general and vague though these definitions were, they nevertheless had definite significance with regard to the policies actually carried out after the Nazi takeover. It appears that in spite of the generalized wording and notwithstanding the preliminary announcement that the manifesto was about to be published, the Nazis finally shied away from making it known to all and sundry. The draft was shelved and no other manifesto was published in its stead. It is still a moot point how far this was due to the direct intervention of business circles,[38] but in the present context it does not really matter. Hitler was a sufficiently sober tactician to have had second thoughts even without actual pressure from members of the business community: during a period in which he courted them for political and financial support, it would have been unwise to arouse their suspicions. Although the draft was worded prudently and with an eye to industrial interests and wishes, it still contained hints of future economic dirigism, that is, of planned constraints and regulations, which at the time were still considered odious by business tycoons and industrial magnates. It was therefore good politics to repress the manifesto and to accept, at least until further notice, Schacht's recommendation not to publish anything on economic issues. However, one should not infer from this that Hitler had reservations about the contents of the draft he had confirmed only a short time previously. The single obvious conclusion regarding withdrawal of the manifesto is that Hitler assumed that publication at that time might do more harm than good.

In addition to the insights the draft manifesto offers through its contents, what it omits is quite illuminating, that is, a remedy for unemployment. At this date there were already over three million people unemployed in Germany, but the Nazi party, including its economic department, had nothing of value to say on the subject. A

38. See D. Stegmann, "Zum Verhältnis von Großindustrie und Nationalsozialismus, 1930–1933," *Archiv für Sozialgeschichte* 13 (1973): 416–17; H.A. Turner, Jr., "Großunternehmertum und Nationalsozialismus, 1930–1933," *Historische Zeitschrift* 221 (1975): 49f.

pamphlet published early in 1932 by the head of the WPA section for social policy suggested a settlement plan in the east and the construction of suburban housing for the unemployed as the only "remedies," to be financed through progressively graded "sacrifices" by the entire population.[39] The minutes of the economic department mentioned above dispatched the matter of unemployment with a few marginal remarks, suggesting "planned reduction of women's work . . . introduction of an obligatory labor service . . . and, anyway, unemployment will be disposed of by the economy's recovery, in particular in agriculture and commerce, which will occur by virtue of the steps we will take, deriving from our economic policy."[40] Wagener was even more optimistic in his *Wirtschaftsprogramm*; he believed that an immediate lowering of prices aimed at an increase of purchasing power could "reduce the number of unemployed by half or even two-thirds, within a couple of months."[41] Similar and equally impractical talk, given the realities of the period, was a matter of routine at the time.

The only convincing explanation for this almost complete evasion of the problem is that the Nazis simply had nothing to offer. This stands out as a fact from all that appeared in their daily papers and periodicals until May–June 1932: there was a great deal of talk about prevailing unemployment; "the system" or capitalism was blamed and "great changes" promised once they assumed power – but no concrete suggestions were presented, except for repetition of the settlement-in-the-east idea and the construction of housing, with no clearly outlined plan of how to finance these. To some extent this may have been a result of their general attitude, similar to that of the Communists, which considered unemployment an inevitable evil of the existing regime, remediable only by its abolition. In Otto Wagener's words, "When the errors of the old regime are eradicated, when National Socialist thought replaces them, unemployment will disappear and existing demand will activate the economy."[42]

It seems that the Nazis understood the weakness of this claim, especially as an economic blueprint for a party that was preparing to assume power. From the end of 1931 party publications reveal an intensive search for practical employment projects. Various mutually incompatible projects appeared, one after the other, in an

39. Ottokar Lorenz, *Die Beseitigung der Arbeitslosigkeit* (Berlin, 1932).
40. BA, NS 22/11, p. 11.
41. Wagener, *Wirtschaftsprogramm*, p. 92.
42. Ibid.

economic pamphlet edited by Fritz Reinhardt, the veteran Nazi who specialized in taxation and later became secretary of state at the Ministry of Finance. These proposals demonstrated the clash of opinions and the general confusion among competing "counselors" and "experts" within the party. This state of affairs changed in a sudden and surprising manner only at the beginning of May 1932.

The "Immediate Program" of 1932: From Economic Principles to Operative Planning

A speech delivered in the Reichstag by Gregor Strasser on May 10, 1932, aroused general astonishment: it included proposals of a detailed project for the creation of employment by means of public works, to be financed by what was defined as "productive credit expansion." Shortly afterward these proposals appeared as the official Immediate Economic Program of the party (*Wirtschaftliches Sofortprogramm der NSDAP*). Over 600,000 copies were distributed as guidelines for party speakers; the accompanying instruction by Strasser, in his capacity as chief of the Organizational Department, makes it clear that this was the sole project to which the party was committed.[43] The exact history of its appearance has not been clarified so far. Today the most reasonable assumption is that the final version was written by Adrian von Renteln, whose signature, as editor, appears on the document itself. Von Renteln was at the time deputy to Wagener as head of the economic department in Munich; he served simultaneously as a personal assistant to Strasser and as a kind of ghostwriter on economic subjects. In the latter capacity he maintained extensive contacts with important business circles.

The difference between this published program and all previous Nazi publications lies in the fact that it goes beyond the generalized and somewhat vague formulations hitherto employed; it presents detailed operational proposals that clearly anticipate a great deal of what was actually implemented after the Nazis assumed power. This fact alone already invalidates the assumption that economic policy after January 1933 was mainly due to Schacht's brilliant improvisation, with the Nazis' own contribution rated almost nil. This evaluation took root especially after the Nuremberg trials, where it figured in the indictment and was supported by some

43. *Wirtschaftliches Sofortprogramm der NSDAP* (Munich, 1932).

witnesses.[44] Throughout his own defense Schacht did nothing to dispel this impression; on the contrary, he stressed the Nazi rulers' ignorance and lack of understanding of economic affairs – thus strengthening his own claim to the "copyright" for their economic policy and the liquidation of unemployment, at least during the initial years of their regime.[45]

Actually, the Nazi program of 1932 included not a few proposals and practical suggestions implemented after January 1933. On the other hand, a paper written by Schacht in the same year shows that he explicitly rejected the reduction of unemployment by means of government-initiated public works. All Schacht had to offer toward the liquidation of unemployment was "belt-tightening," the lowering of wages and settling of the unemployed in villages or cottage holdings "where feeding and housing them would be much simpler and cheaper than by means of bureaucratic money arrangements and where their efforts promise an immediate reward."[46] Schacht mentioned the possibility of public works in this article, but only in order to reject it out of hand because such works did not yield immediate proceeds. According to him, past experience showed that "a whole series of public enterprises were established with the result that the state and its institutions not only competed with private enterprise . . . but these public ventures operated at much higher cost than [is usual in the] private economy."[47] His conclusion was that this kind of work clashes with the basic laws of economics. He also strongly rejected any notions of monetary expansion – because the major problem of the German economy in a state of crisis was the oppressive tax load and the lack of capital, as distinguished from the lack of money: "All projects that aim at issuing additional money in any form should be rejected out of hand. We are not short of circulating money in Germany, we are short of capital. But capital cannot be issued from the printing press; capital has to be gained by working and saving."[48]

In contrast to this argument, the Nazis' Immediate Economic Program begins with the denial of a shortage of capital: "Our

---

44. *Der Prozeß gegen die Hauptkriegsverbrecher vor dem Internationalen Militär Gerichtshof (International Military Tribunal), Nürnberg, 14. Nov. 1945–1. Okt. 1946* (Nuremberg, 1947–49), vol. 5, p. 138; vol. 12, p. 535.

45. Ibid., vol. 5, p. 151.

46. Hjalmar Schacht, *Grundsätze deutscher Wirtschaftspolitik* (Oldenburg i.O., 1932), pp. 56f.

47. Ibid., pp. 21f.

48. Ibid., p. 47.

economy does not suffer from a deficiency in means of production, it suffers from deficient utilization of existing means of production."[49] The problem to be tackled is therefore activation of idle production factors – with an eye to the domestic market – by means of large-scale public works. Proposed projects include drainage and soil amelioration and the construction of roads and housing, to be financed through the "creation of productive credit" by the central bank, that is, by deficit spending. According to the Nazi assessment, only 30 to 40 percent of the overall cost would have to be accounted for in this manner – since the remainder would be covered by saved unemployment benefits and increased tax revenues, following the rise in employment. The added remark that "such a small increase in the volume of credit does in no way endanger the currency" bears evidence of the caution still prevalent at this juncture; following the experience of 1922–23, the fear of inflation was deeply embedded in public consciousness and shared also by economists. The program does not specify any figure for its overall cost, but the scope of the proposed projects was extensive. Ten billion reichsmarks were to be allocated for drainage and soil amelioration alone, while the period of time in which these works were to be accomplished is not specified. The construction of 400,000 proposed housing units alone was expected to provide jobs for a million unemployed workers! One may, of course, consider these data as propaganda. Even so the program merits attention; here, for the first time and in a rather surprising manner, an official Nazi source proposed the financing of large-scale public works as a remedy for unemployment.

Additional proposals, appearing in the second part of the program under the heading "General Economic Measures," are of equal interest. The paragraph entitled "Guidelines for Trade Policy" announces the intention "to supply the needs of the German people to the largest possible extent by our own production; to acquire necessary additional raw materials preferably from friendly European states – in particular if these are prepared to order industrial products from Germany in exchange for their raw materials." What is outlined here is not only a repetition of the autarky notion, but also a forecast of the bilateral trade policies realized in September 1934 by Schacht's New Plan. The program also repeats the demand for "absolute and consistent" control of foreign currency, the

49. *Sofortprogramm*, p. 8.

proposed "law for the prevention of capital flight," and the proposal to introduce "selective devaluation" through a system of differential export premiums and import duties.

On the subject of banking and credit policy the program announces "as a preparatory measure toward the nationalization of banking . . . the right of the state to control and to intervene and the obligatory accountability of banks to the state." The Nazi government actually implemented these measures through legislation in December 1933. The need for price controls is clearly stated: "Price controls by the state are to prevent gross deviation from fair prices." There is no doubt that a number of proposals came from Walter Darré's Administrative Bureau for Agrarian Policy, and these were later on almost fully realized. The demand to impose controls on new private investment in industry in order to reduce it as far as possible was subsequently fulfilled under the regulations of the cartel law passed in July 1933.

Even if there is a measure of exaggeration in the claim brought forward by one author that Schacht implemented the ideas of the Immediate Program "to the letter,"[50] there is no doubt that the general outline of economic policies employed after the Nazis attained power is much clearer here than, for instance, in the previously quoted article by Schacht. This is even more surprising if one remembers that the life span of this program as an official party platform was very short. In October 1933 it was replaced by the Plan for Economic Reconstruction, including an announcement signed by Feder, Funk, and Gregor Strasser himself to the effect that the Immediate Program had been abolished for good. It is now clear that Hitler's order to withdraw the program after hundreds of thousands of copies had been distributed during the election campaign of 1932 was due to the intervention of business circles, whose support of the Nazis had grown in the wake of the party's impressive electoral victory: with 230 representatives instead of their previous 170, the Nazis had become the largest parliamentary group in the Reichstag.

It appears that even the relatively prudent proposal of public works and credit expansion, with mere hints at price and foreign-trade controls, aroused opposition in the business community. The heavy industry's newsletter, *Deutsche Führerbriefe*, had already received Strasser's speech with undisguised concern. This speech

50. Kroll, *Weltwirtschaftskrise*, p. 434.

had been carefully prepared, said the newsletter – it should not be dismissed as "a personal outpouring by Strasser." It presented some good ideas on social policy but on the whole its spirit was very critical of employers; it tried to link up with trade unions, in particular through its emphasis on "a broad front of anticapitalist thought among political groups. . . . Following this speech which, as mentioned before, is being backed by the Brown House, it becomes even more necessary to urge the NSDAP leadership [to make] a clear and unequivocal statement of their real economic and social platform. If Strasser's speech is in fact to be taken as an outline for National Socialist economic policy, that is, the policy to be expected from an NSDAP government, there are strong apprehensions that cannot be repressed. . . . All in all a speech that, with an eye to future developments, represents a decisive stage, a milestone for the economic consciousness of the German Right."[51] Following the publication of the Immediate Program and the electoral success of July, the *Führerbriefe* returned once again to the same subject. The editor did not need the gift of prophecy in order to state that the Nazi platform rated attention, since it was quite possible "that the National Socialists would soon have the opportunity to realize this platform, at least partly. . . . In recent years the National Socialists have learnt some lessons in economic policy. Nevertheless their economic program is still bogged down by the rudiments of economic policy; in some parts it is still so romantic and amateurish that one can only hope this plan will not be carried out. Should it be carried out consistently, one cannot but fear that German National Socialism, notwithstanding its great value for German renewal, will run aground on the rocks of its economic policy." The author aimed his anger mainly at the project for creating employment, based on deficit spending, but also at proposals to abandon the gold standard – all in the name of currency stability. It is, however, not less noteworthy that the author went straight to the core of the argument, which was not this or that detail but a comprehensive approach, an autarkist national economy based on agriculture as against industrial development aimed at export and world economy: "This is the fundamental romantic controversy that afflicts National Socialist economic theory."[52] A few weeks later the newsletter reported on a lecture by Otto Christian Fischer, a well-known banker who was close to the Nazi

51. *Deutsche Führerbriefe*, May 20, 1932.
52. Ibid., Aug. 26, 1932.

party and active in Wagener's WPA. Fischer, speaking to a select circle, tried to reassure his audience that the Immediate Program was not to be taken as a final statement of policy: "The National Socialist economic program [appears] neither as an indispensable nor as a substantial component; that is, one can think of an *entirely* different economic program under the banner of National Socialism. . . . For a political National Socialist platform a capitalist blueprint [appears] not only feasible, but actually *necessary*, and one should not permit electoral propaganda to hide this from our sight."[53] As mentioned above, Fischer was close to the Nazis and also played an important role in industry and banking after their takeover. The *Führerbriefe*, whose principal patron was Paul Silverberg, an industrialist of Jewish extraction, also maintained close connections with the Nazis – at least from the summer of 1932 on – and openly canvased for Hitler's nomination as chancellor at the head of a right-wing coalition.[54] These expressions of concern and opposition with regard to the Immediate Program no doubt influenced Hitler sufficiently to withdraw it once the 1932 election campaign was over. Schacht, in a letter of August 29 of the same year, advised Hitler to refrain altogether from the formulation of an economic master plan: "Perhaps I may, as an economist, say the following: as far as possible do not present a detailed economic plan at all. There is no plan fourteen million [voters] can agree upon. Economic policy is not a party-building factor; at best it attracts representatives of relevant interests."[55]

The timing of all these utterances and their proximity to each other lend credibility to the assumption that the withdrawal of the Immediate Program in September 1932 was due to the intervention of business circles. Schacht himself announced in a letter of September 12, 1932, that Hitler had promised to stop distribution and see to it that all remaining copies were destroyed.[56] It was replaced – also in September 1932 – by the Plan for Economic Reconstruction, which bears evidence of an effort to appease the business community. This new plan was put together jointly by Feder and Funk. Wagener had been dismissed and the department, renamed Chief

53. Ibid., Oct. 4, 1932.
54. Werner v. Alvensleben an Hitler, vom 21.9.1932, NA, T–81, fr. no. 11336; Neebe, *Großindustrie*, pp. 154f., 201.
55. Kroll, *Weltwirtschaftskrise*, p. 423.
56. Letter from Schacht to Reusch, Sept. 12, 1932, Deutsches Zentral-Archiv Potsdam, Reusch papers; quoted by Turner, "Großunternehmertum," p. 61n.

Nazi Economics

Department No. 4, divided into a desk for state economy under Feder and a desk for private economy under Funk.[57] Wagener's dismissal and the department's reorganization tally quite well with the public campaign, accompanied by confidential counseling against the Immediate Program conducted by the economic establishment. On September 8 the director general of the Reichsverband der Deutschen Industrie (RDI, Reich Association of German Industries), Dr. Jacob Herle, sent a long and detailed memorandum to von Renteln, author of the program, sharply criticizing almost all of it. The employment project based on deficit spending received the most severe treatment, but Herle also rejected long-term goals in foreign-trade policy, currency controls, and taxes. Even statements of general principles, such as every German's "right to work," were judged to be "dangerous."[58]

A mere glance at these two documents already reveals their considerable differences. In contrast to the detailed proposals of the Immediate Program, the Plan for Economic Reconstruction was merely a collection of rather vague generalities, open to a variety of interpretations – clearly an effort to circumvent controversial issues. Feder's old objective, "to throw off the slavery of interest," which was not even mentioned in the program, reappeared, though only in the rather noncommittal form of "the lowering of interest rates, while paying close attention to the special conditions of the economy." The demand for nationalization of "all finance and credit business" and for control of banking and foreign currency appeared in both plans, but the Plan for Reconstruction included a number of operative proposals explicitly contradicting those of the Immediate Program, an unmistakable concession to big-business interests. Instead of increased taxes on high incomes, previously demanded, the plan promised "to lower or to abolish taxes that hurt production." There was no trace of the detailed proposals for price and investment regulation. On the contrary, it recommended "relaxation of price controls" – a long-time demand of the business community. Although the plan stated that "agriculture is the backbone of the domestic market and the German economy," it emphasized at once that agricultural recovery was subject to the recovery of the whole economy and that giving preference to the domestic

57. "Das wirtschaftliche Aufbauprogramm der NSDAP," in Feder, *Hochfinanz*, pp. 371–82.
58. BA, Nachlaß Silverberg, no. 232. See also Stegmann, "Zum Verhältnis," pp. 452ff.

46

market "is possible only if the requirements of export, which is imperative for Germany, are taken into account." It appears that any group of businessmen, whatever the economic sector they represented, could find a paragraph that promised them some benefit. The most striking difference was that, while the Immediate Economic Program abounded in anticapitalist language like "giant capitalist combines," "the capitalist press," or "the would-be-clever capitalist economists" ("neunmalkluge kapitalistische Wirtschafts-politiker"), the terms "capitalist" and "capitalism" did not appear in the Plan for Economic Reconstruction even once. Nor did the "right to work," which had previously aroused Dr. Herle's concern.

Both blueprints were election platforms whose propaganda appealed to various strata of voters and different power groups. However, the Immediate Program, in contrast to the Plan for Reconstruction, bears evidence of careful professional preparation and consultations on matters of principle whose consequences went far beyond provisional propaganda needs. As I will demonstrate, there is a clearly recognizable affinity between its operational proposals and subsequently implemented policies. With Strasser's removal from all his party positions in December 1932 and his murder by the Nazis in June 1934, all references to the Immediate Program disappeared, of course, from party publications. As time went on it was almost forgotten by scholars outside Germany as well. Nevertheless, it is evident that the program continued to exist in the shadows by a force of its own.

It is, however, significant that the two blueprints were virtually identical with regard to the manner in which employment projects were to be financed. In view of the business community's criticism, the detailed proposals for government-initiated public works in the Immediate Program were replaced by a generalized statement about "the direct creation of employment . . . by means of new public and private investment." But the "creation of productive credit," on the other hand, appeared unchanged. Here the Plan for Reconstruction was more explicit – it specified the sum of three billion reichsmarks, to be forwarded initially by the central bank. This was probably due to the fact that Professor Ernst Wagemann, head of the official Bureau of Statistics and the Institute for Market Research (*Konjunkturforschung*), had meanwhile published a project for deficit spending using exactly the same sum, thereby generating a vigorous public debate. Specification of the same sum implied the wish to benefit from the prestige of an acknowledged authority in economic theory.

All this shows unequivocally that in the spring of 1932 the Nazis adopted an innovative blueprint for the creation of jobs and for the manner of financing this project and that in this particular sphere they withstood pressures and criticism from the business world and from influential academic economists. This was a novelty that at once aroused public interest. However, one should not interpret the project as a sharp turn in Nazi views on economic issues. With regard to the long-term proposals that appeared mainly in its second part, the Immediate Program had drawn quite extensively on preliminary work done by the economic and agrarian departments. The novelty lay principally in the plan for public works and the manner of financing it. A painstaking comparison of the Immediate Program with previous studies, in particular with the March 1931 draft manifesto, reveals the following situation: in the spring of 1932, after a prolonged period of "stumbling in the dark," the Nazis finally discovered, outside their own ranks, practical economic plans that could be integrated with their overall economic concepts. State initiative, intervention, controls, and economic dirigism certainly corresponded to their antiliberal conception of relations between the state and the economy. When Gottfried Feder appropriated the "creation of productive credit," claiming that "this is the spiritual triumph . . . of a theory I have been advocating for thirteen years,"[59] he indeed adorned himself with borrowed plumes as far as financial technique was concerned, but this statement was in principle nevertheless not far from the truth.

There remains, of course, the question of origin – the source for the ideas and proposals in Strasser's speech of May 10 and the Immediate Program of 1932. Gerhard Kroll, a writer who seems to believe that Strasser himself was the author of the Immediate Program, points to the strange fact that not even a single line on economic matters appeared in any of Strasser's speeches or writings before May 10, 1932. He therefore wonders how the same man managed "to present a persuasive and detailed blueprint without years of previous work in the same field."[60] Kroll's ready-made answer is a dramatic and somewhat mysterious story: the program was but a word-for-word copy of publications by Robert Friedländer-Prechtl, a writer of partly Jewish extraction, who un-

59. NA, T–81, roll 1, fr. no. 11510.
60. Kroll, *Weltwirtschaftskrise*, p. 435.

48

wittingly became the "theoretician of National Socialist economic policy, although his name was never mentioned in the Third Reich." According to this version, Strasser's sole merit was that he "accomplished this act of thievery adroitly and translated Friedländer-Prechtl's theses into the terms of an immediately applicable political platform."[61] Although I believe this description to be exaggerated and unnecessarily dramatic, one should not deny Kroll's book of 1958 the merit of calling attention to the person of Friedländer-Prechtl, who had hardly been mentioned in previous writings.

Friedländer-Prechtl was the son of a marriage between a wealthy Jewish merchant and a daughter of the Austrian aristocracy. He was learned in law and economics and was a partner in a combine producing and utilizing coal. In addition he was a prolific author who, besides works on literature and the arts, published a large number of writings on economics distinguished by their imaginative approach and their broad vision (I will discuss these in more detail below). He was doubtless among the first in Germany to present revolutionary proposals for finance and employment policies – proposals that influenced innovative economists in the early thirties. In this sense Friedländer-Prechtl was certainly *one* of those who supplied the Nazis with theoretical tools and practical suggestions for their economic policy. (Gregor Strasser's brother Otto confirmed this in a circumstantial way in a recorded interview with me in June 1974. He said that, although neither he nor his brother had ever met Friedländer-Prechtl, both had read and greatly appreciated his book of 1932. Otto Strasser thought that his brother Gregor "had no doubt been influenced" by Friedländer-Prechtl's ideas.) But Friedländer-Prechtl was by no means the only source for Strasser's ideas, and there is no evidence whatsoever of any contact or direct influence. Kroll's claim that Strasser was previously ignorant in economics prior to reading Friedländer-Prechtl is cancelled out by the near certainty that the Immediate Program and probably also Strasser's previous speech in the Reichstag were composed by von Renteln in the course of his work at the WPA. Von Renteln had studied economics and was no doubt familiar with the debates and arguments that were widely conducted at the time by groups of economists, businessmen, and politicians. We know for a fact that von Renteln acted as Strasser's liaison with these circles. Nor is

61. Ibid., pp. 454–55.

there any substance to Kroll's claim that "in the sphere of science there is no known publication of this period that could have provided the background for Strasser's theses." This simply does not fit the facts, some of which Kroll even presents in his book. There was lively public discussion in Germany on matters of employment at the beginning of 1932; the participants included well-known and respected economists as well as political journalists and laymen. All the proposals for public works and deficit spending, abolition of the gold standard and autarky, a network of autobahns, and a Labor Service (Arbeitsdienst) that appear in Friedländer-Prechtl's writings as well as in the Immediate Program were thrown into this debate from various quarters and were discussed in a multitude of scientific papers and articles in the popular press. The sole novelty to be found in the Immediate Program was the fact that for the first time these ideas were officially adopted by a political mass party in the form of operational proposals for economic policy.

The proposals themselves were not new. The literature of the period and later research provide a detailed and well-documented description of these discussions and the scientific and journalistic activities of the group known as the "German reformers." Here I will deal mainly with a number of outstanding individuals in this discourse who have a direct bearing on my subject and whose occupational or personal connection to the Nazi party and its economic policy can be proven. The striking feature of the whole group is that, except in one outstanding case which I will discuss below, support for proposals to expand employment by means of the government budget and frank or disguised deficit spending came principally from political bodies and individuals belonging to the extreme right. As I will demonstrate, this state of affairs was by no means accidental, and it has considerable significance for an understanding of the development of economic policy shortly before and after the Nazis attained power.

The only left-wing exception to this rule was a plan adopted in April 1932 by the Allgemeiner Deutscher Gewerkschaftsbund (ADGB, German Trade Union Federation). The outstanding figure among the authors of this plan was Wladimir Woytinsky, a Russian Jew in charge of the federation's Department for Statistics, who had made a name for himself by writing on the subject of employment as well as on economics. Besides Woytinsky, the plan was signed by Fritz Tarnow, chairman of the Woodworkers' Union and Reichstag delegate for the Social Democrats, and Fritz Baade, a well-known economist who occupied important positions in the field of economics on behalf of the Social Democrats. Named after the initials of its authors, the plan was known as the WTB Plan. At its core was the demand for immediate reemployment of one million laid-off workers at work projects initiated by government and public bodies such as the Post Office, the railways, and municipal authorities. These works were to be financed by long-term credit from the Reichsbank but also, as far as necessary, by "the issue of additional paper money" (*zusätzliche Notenschöpfung*). The WTB Plan assessed the cost of a million new jobs at about two billion reichsmarks, but also assumed that part of this sum would be covered by the reduction of unemployment benefits and an increase in tax revenues.

It is characteristic of the atmosphere of those days that the trade unions accepted the WTB Plan only after a great deal of opposition and heated debate, and then with a tiny majority. Rudolf Hilferding, onetime minister of finance (1928–29), in particular opposed the plan. Hilferding, whom the German Social Democrats rated as a top-rank authority on economic issues, wholeheartedly supported the chancellor, Heinrich Brüning's, deflationary policy; the latter regarded him as a friend and frequently consulted him.[62] As early as the twenties Hilferding had developed a theory of "organized capitalism" as a necessary and antidemocratic stage in the evolution of capitalism, which would under certain circumstances serve as a transitional stage to socialism. At the same time he held the orthodox Marxist view that economic crises were an inevitable and incurable affliction of capitalism. Endeavors such as the WTB Plan were sheer heresy from this point of view, vain efforts that in the short run endangered economic stability, and in the long run were incapable of curing the ills of the regime. Because of this attitude, supported also by the small Independent Socialist party (SAP) and the Communists, Hilferding sharply opposed the WTB Plan, even after it had been adopted by the trade unions. He argued before the Social Democratic party (SPD) leadership that the WTB Plan was "non-Marxist"! Together with Fritz Naftali (later minister of agriculture in the Israeli government) and his close friend Paul Hertz, both of whom worked with him at the Trade Union Institute for

62. Robert A. Gates, "Von der Sozialpolitik zur Wirtschaftspolitik? Das Dilemma der deutschen Sozialdemokratie in der Krise 1929–1933," in Mommsen, Petzina, and Weisbrod, eds., *Internationales Symposium*, p. 212.

Economic Research, Hilferding quietly persuaded the majority of the SPD's delegates at the Reichstag to oppose the plan.[63] Naftali had considerable authority among the German Social Democrats at the time, and in his argument against the proposals put forward by Woytinsky and his colleagues, he emphasized the "inflationary risk" they presented; since the specified sum of two billion reichsmarks was not sufficient, additional deficit spending would become necessary.[64] At discussions concerning the WTB Plan, he was firm in his opinion that the economic crisis could be defeated only on an international level and that until then autonomous employment projects could be financed only by public loans. Naftali assessed the capital reserves held by the German public to be at least one billion reichsmarks, which could be attracted by a government loan offering highly favorable terms through a variety of premiums.[65] Besides Hilferding, Naftali contributed considerably to the ultimate quiet burial of the WTB Plan: although the SPD delegates in the Reichstag had finally adopted it by a small majority, it was never presented as an official party proposal.[66] Instead, on February 27, 1932, the parliamentary SPD submitted a motion for the public premium loan proposed by Naftali.[67]

Gustav Stolper, who also criticized the WTB Plan in a trenchant article, used the occasion to attack the Wagemann project for deficit spending (see above) as well. He argued that it would be pointless to apply pump priming (*Initialzündung*) to an economy that "lacked fuel" because "priming" would not yield results. He believed that such a policy would only result in the expansion of credit and the continuation of inflationary deficit spending.[68]

There is a great deal of irony in the fact that, while Fritz Naftali sharply opposed the WTB Plan and suffered pangs of remorse in later years,[69] among the Nazis it met with undisguised sympathy. In his Reichstag speech of May 10, Strasser mentioned "the trade union plan for job creation, which is definitely worth discussing,

63. Ibid., pp. 220f.
64. Michael Schneider, "Konjunkturpolitische Vorstellungen der Gewerkschaften in den letzten Jahren der Weimarer Republik: Zur Entwicklung des Arbeitsbeschaffungsplans des ADGB," in Mommsen, Petzina, and Weisbrod, eds., *Internationales Symposium*, pp. 230ff.
65. *Gewerkschaftszeitung* 42, no. 8 (Feb. 20, 1932).
66. Gerhard Ziemer, *Inflation und Deflation zerstören die Demokratie* (Stuttgart, 1971), pp. 146f.
67. Grotkopp, *Die große Krise*, p. 130.
68. *Der Deutsche Volkswirt* 6, no. 21 (Feb. 19, 1932).
69. Fritz Naftali, *Demokratia Kalkalit – Mivkhar Ktavim* (n.p., n.d.), p. 18.

with which we would be prepared to cooperate under suitable conditions." In the same speech he also mentioned Woytinsky, "with whom I am not personally acquainted, nor do I know whether he is young or old . . . who [in contrast to the Social Democratic leadership, which is composed of Jewish intellectuals] . . . arrives at the creation of credit, that is, at ways of financing which, after all, we brought for the first time into discussion among the German people."[70] Günther Gereke, at the time a member of the national opposition and subsequently Reichskomissar for the creation of employment in the Schleicher government and during the initial months of Hitler's government, also greatly admired the WTB Plan, considering it close to his and his colleague's views.[71] The organ of the young conservatives actually congratulated the federation on its employment plan – as evidence of the affinity between National Socialist thought and trade union views.[72] As I will show further on, the applause from the right wing was not accidental: conservative nationalist ideologies and concepts of the state were much better equipped to absorb ideas of direct state intervention in the economy and "sovereign" modes of financing it than were the liberal and democratic or even the Social Democratic views of state/economy relations.

The Nazi concept of the state and the economy was close to the views of traditional German nationalists and the young conservatives who strove to initiate a right-wing revolution. The Nazis could therefore easily accept innovations proposed by the German reformers in contrast to dominant economic theories and integrate them with their concepts in economics – which until then had been formulated only in a rather vague and generalized manner. Thus the Nazi party was finally able to present an economic platform combining a theoretical basis with sufficiently convincing operational proposals that could challenge whatever its opponents and the political cum economic establishment had to offer.

In the light of these developments the exact history of this "marriage of true minds" becomes secondary: once the basic ideological concepts had been defined and the public discussion of economic issues publicly discussed, the Nazis increasingly responded to the practical proposals put forward by the "reformers,"

70. Dräger-Materialsammlung, Strasser's speech of May 10, 1932.
71. Günther Gereke, *Ich war königlich-preußischer Landrat* (Berlin [East], 1970), p. 174.
72. *Die Tat*, 1931/32, p. 1027 (Friedrich Zimmermann = F.F.).

so that the merger between the two became merely a question of time and the right kind of mediation. Today one can state that the main channel through which reformer views were passed to the Nazis, until they became part of the Immediate Program and subsequent publications, was almost certainly the Association for Finance and Credit Research (Studiengesellschaft für Geld und Kreditforschung) founded by the industrialist Heinrich Dräger of Lübeck in November 1931. Already in the summer of 1931 Dräger had initiated contacts with Professor Jens Jessen, a member of Wagener's committee at the Nazi party's WPA. (Jessen later became disillusioned and was executed at the time of the Generals' Conspiracy in July 1944.) Dräger also contacted Friedländer-Prechtl, whom he regarded as the principal influence on himself and the other reformers connected with the association. Dräger, who paid most of the association's expenses out of his own pocket, had founded it together with Wilhelm Grotkopp and Rudolf Dalberg.[73]

The aim of this research association was to disseminate ideas and practical proposals for credit expansion and government-sponsored work projects as a way out of the economic crisis. To this end it initiated public lectures and discussions, attended by renowned economists, and issued various publications. It also sent memoranda to and held meetings with government and business representatives. Two of these lectures, both given in February 1932, received special attention from the press and the radio: a lecture by the economist Werner Sombart on "The Future of Capitalism" and one by Ernst Wagemann. Following these, many people applied to the Chambers of Commerce for information about the research association. The chambers' replies did not recommend it, and a number of their internal circulars denounced the "inflationary proposals" advocated by Wagemann and the research association.[74] Schwerin von Kro-

---

73. Recorded interview with Dr. Dräger, June 1974. In general, I present facts and descriptions here that could be verified by other sources. Rudolf Dalberg (b. 1885) was a Jew. From 1919 on he served as a senior official at the Ministries of Economy and Finance; in 1923 he took an active part in the measures that ended inflation; he was a fairly well-known expert in monetary theory. His first book (1916) advocating abolition of the gold standard showed him to be a supporter of the "nominalist" school with views close to those of G.P. Knapp. Dräger approached him as the result of an article Dalberg had published in September 1932 in Friedländer-Prechtl's paper *Wirtschafts-Wende* in which he denounced Brüning's deflationist policy. Wilhelm Grotkopp, a well-known journalist who specialized in economics, was editor of the periodical *Europa-Wirtschaft*.

74. *Berliner Börsen Courier*, Feb. 2, 1932; See also BA, R 11, Deutscher Industrie- und Handelstag, no. 1371.

sigk, onetime minister of finance in the Papen, Schleicher, and Hitler governments confirmed in an interview with me in June 1974 that the research association and its proposals had been mentioned frequently in discussions at various government departments. Wilhelm Grotkopp, former secretary of the research association, described its activities in detail in his book. His assessment of its influence may be exaggerated, but there is some evidence that the association aroused attention in government and business circles when these matters were discussed. However, what is beyond doubt and convincingly documented is the association's influence on the Nazi party's economic plans and, in particular, the Immediate Program.

In the beginning of 1932 Dräger wrote a booklet entitled *Arbeitsbeschaffung durch produktive Kreditschöpfung*,[75] in which he summarized his ideas as well as the results of discussions and consultations held at the research association during the initial months of its activity. Friedländer-Prechtl, who was too seriously handicapped to travel frequently from his Munich home to Berlin, could not participate in most of the association's activities – but Dräger stated that he was in continuous touch with him and also sought his advice with regard to the booklet. When he ran into difficulties in his search for a publisher he approached Gottfried Feder, who accepted the study for publication on behalf of the National Socialist Library, which he himself edited. However, in their prefaces both Feder and Dräger stressed that the author was not a member of the Nazi party. Feder even added that this fact enhanced the paper's value because it would help to attract some people "and to dispel fears of experiments with the exchange rate."[76]

The core of Dräger's booklet was a detailed proposal for government-initiated public works. Although not all the details were identical, its similarity to the proposals in the Immediate Program stands out: settlement housing, drainage and soil amelioration, road construction, and so forth. In contrast to the Immediate Program, Dräger specified the sums to be provided, according to him, by "productive credit." Dräger had borrowed the term from an article by Professor Willi Prion and it meant roughly the following: credit expansion, geared to economic projects that promised to

75. Heinrich Dräger, *Arbeitsbeschaffung durch produktive Kreditschöpfung – Ein Beitrag zur Frage der Wirtschaftsbelebung durch das sogenannte "Federgeld,"* Nationalsozialistische Bibliothek, Heft 41 (Munich, 1932).
76. Ibid., p. 4.

yield returns within a certain period of time. Once accomplished, these projects would create "economic values" and thereby nullify the inflationary effect of the additional money in circulation that would initially accompany the process. The interesting feature in Dräger's work is his total rejection of the idea of financing such projects by means of a public loan; in his opinion this would only mean that there would be a shift of existing demand from the private to the public sector and not an increase in aggregate demand necessitated by the actual situation: "For effective job creation the only way that can and should be taken is credit expansion of adequate dimensions."[77] In practice he suggested cautious expenditure of 1.5 billion reichsmarks until the end of 1932. If it turned out that no dangerous inflationary effects had emerged (Dräger was convinced that this would, indeed, occur), the sum could be increased to five billion in 1933. The overall sum necessary for the realization of his proposals over a period of about six years was assessed at approximately thirty billion reichsmarks. Today we know that this was more or less the sum actually spent on the liquidation of unemployment up to 1936, although the projects were somewhat different from those Dräger had suggested – that is, a considerable part of the expenditure went into rearmament.

According to Dräger himself, he conducted a number of lengthy talks with the Nazis in an attempt to make the largest and most promising party adopt his proposals. To this end he met several times with Gregor Strasser and his representative, von Renteln, and also with Feder and Daitz. One cannot judge now how much weight these meetings carried, but we have unquestionable proof that Dräger's paper was in Feder's hands before Strasser's speech. Feder explicitly mentioned it as "a very interesting study, about to be published, on methods of credit creation . . . with regard to which Professor Wagemann expressed his almost complete agreement.[78] A comparison between the text and statistical figures in Dräger's study and those of the Immediate Program reveals the extensive similarity between the two documents. Nor had the term "creation of productive credit" appeared in any Nazi publication before Strasser's speech. One may therefore assume with a considerable measure of certainty that Dräger and his research association served as a link between Friedländer-Prechtl's ideas (which, as mentioned before, were not isolated at the time) and the Nazis'

77. Ibid., p. 36.
78. NA, T–81, roll 1, fr. no. 11510f.

Immediate Program. In his interview with me, Dräger himself emphasized Friedländer-Prechtl's originality and his impact on the people involved with the research association. He described his own role as that of a popularizer and follower of Friedländer-Prechtl's ideas. The fact that the Nazis published a summary of Dräger's booklet for the second time in September 1932 shortly after formulation of the Immediate Program, in a special number of their economic monthly *Die Deutsche Volkswirtschaft*, is evidence of the importance they attached to this study. It also served as a textbook at the school for party lecturers, headed by Fritz Reinhardt, a friend of Strasser's and later secretary of state at the Ministry of Finance.

The claim that Friedländer-Prechtl was the sole source for Strasser's operational proposals thus appears to be grossly exaggerated. However, he was certainly among the first in Germany to promote the idea of a government-initiated employment policy. Already in 1926[79] he had developed the thesis of a permanent structural discrepancy between the supply of labor, which had grown owing to reduction of the army and pauperization of the middle class, and the demand for labor, which had shrunk because of excessive investment in industry, a decrease in income, and a relative increase in savings. The validity of this analysis would probably not stand up under theoretical or statistical examination, but the cure Friedländer-Prechtl proposed for the "chronic labor crisis" is of interest. He firmly refused to rely on export expansion for the "absorption of surplus" labor supply: foreign trade was shrinking and the lion's share was increasingly being appropriated by the United States. "Europe has lost the war!" The trend toward autarky was recognizable all over the world. Therefore, what remained for Germany to do under these conditions was principally to pursue government-initiated investment in its infrastructure: soil amelioration and drainage works for the reagrarianization of Germany, through the settlement of at least a million new people on the land; and large-scale investment in the industrial infrastructure, which would guarantee self-sufficiency in raw materials and electricity. Friedländer-Prechtl even proposed obtaining fuel from coal as a substitute for imported fuel (he himself experimented with this process in his own plants). Private enterprise would not undertake these works because their short-term profitability was too low and the element of risk too great. As an example he cited the extraction

79. Materialsammlung-Dräger, Robert Friedländer-Prechtl, *Chronische Arbeitskrise: Ihre Ursache, ihre Bekämpfung* (Berlin, 1926).

of nitrogen from air, a process developed in wartime "without cost calculation." The execution of such projects should therefore be assigned to public and municipal authorities and be financed by a long-term loan from the Reich. How this was actually to be carried out "is a question of financial technique for which a solution will be found – because it has to be found."

The striking feature of this early study is the fact that it was published in 1926 – while the German economy was enjoying a period of relative prosperity. One cannot deny Friedländer-Prechtl's foresight and his grasp of emerging economic trends, articulated in a clear and readable style. These characteristics were even more pronounced in his 1931 study, *Wirtschafts-Wende* – the basis for Gerhard Kroll's dramatic description, in which the 1926 paper is not mentioned at all. Here Friedländer-Prechtl elaborated the theses outlined in the earlier study and linked them in more detail to current events. Surplus of labor supply was still considered the cause of the crisis, but unemployment was defined as "functional," arising out of inherent flaws in the system, or what he designated as "the spiritual factor": "We lack neither of the two necessary material factors of production: labor force and productive apparatus (*Arbeits-Apparat*). What is missing is the third factor, the spiritual one – insight, drive, will – we lack leadership. The spiritual factor is the necessary third side by means of which . . . production will grow out of production potentials and welfare out of unemployment."[80] Rightly identifying capital with means of production, Friedländer-Prechtl rejected lack of capital as the cause of the prevailing crisis. The "means" existed in abundance, standing idle. To reactivate them, the available amount of money had to be adapted to the economy's needs; in order to achieve this, one only had to get rid of the gold standard. The gold standard was fictitious because only about one-third of the currency was "covered" by gold residing in bank vaults; the rest was based on "trust" anyway. "This is indeed an excellent coverage. Why then can money not be trust money one hundred percent? That is the obvious question and there are scores of learned answers, but not a single convincing one."[81] Deflationary policy should therefore be discarded in order to overcome unemployment; instead of considering an internal or external loan, the state would obtain "a loan from everyone . . . by

80. Robert Friedländer-Prechtl, *Wirtschafts-Wende – Die Ursachen der Arbeitslosen-Krise und deren Bekämpfung* (Leipzig, 1931), pp. 65f.
81. Ibid., p. 237.

attaining authority over the stock of production and goods through the creation of additional money or credit."[82] These resources were to be utilized in public works identical to the projects we have already encountered: drainage and soil amelioration, with pronounced emphasis on reagrarianization aimed at turning Germany into "a country of peasants." Friedländer-Prechtl held to this primarily ideological tendency as late as 1948.[83] It is noteworthy that, in addition to the above, he proposed the construction of a 20,000-kilometer autobahn network, to be carried out by the state-owned railway authorities – as was indeed done after 1933. In describing the idea of a labor service, he emphasized its value as a kind of premilitary training, besides its obvious advantages for the relief of unemployment and the reduction of expenditure on infrastructure projects.[84]

Friedländer-Prechtl was unequivocal in his support of an autarky-oriented economy capable of supplying a maximum of its own demand: "The hands of the world's economic clock point to increasing autarky, to an aspiration to achieve maximum self-sufficiency within closed economic regions."[85] In the short run this trend compelled Germany to reduce its imports as far as possible and to seek maximal autarky. For the long run Friedländer-Prechtl had a different vision: "A European economic region would be able to maintain itself at an equal if not superior level to that of the four other large economic regions on earth."[86]

The excerpts I have cited as well as an examination of Friedländer-Prechtl's writings, including articles in the periodical he edited and published, lead inevitably to a single conclusion: the operational economic proposals of this half-Jewish innovator, which were incorporated into the Nazis' Immediate Program (whatever channels they passed through), arose from an ideological background and a weltanschauung not far removed from those that molded the Nazis' overall economic principles. Like them, he aspired to Germany's reagrarianization, to autarky, to self-sufficiency, to spatial economy (*Raumwirtschaft*), and to "state sovereignty" over monetary affairs. It is therefore not surprising that his operational proposals were easily absorbed into the new

---

82. Ibid.
83. Materialsammlung Dräger, "Malthus" (1948).
84. Friedländer-Prechtl, *Wirtschafts-Wende*, p. 177.
85. Ibid., p. 132.
86. Ibid., p. 134.

economic policy the Nazis and other right-wing groups tried to formulate. The similarity between some of these proposals and the measures that were subsequently implemented is indeed astonishing. He himself left no doubt with regard to the placement of his ideological and political sympathies: at the end of 1931 he had already published a highly complimentary review of the monthly *Die Tat* and its young authors in his own paper. Having praised the monthly's founder on account of "his profound attachment to the German spirit and German culture," he hailed the founder's decision to assign to the editorial board a group of youngsters who illuminated contemporary affairs "with thoroughgoing knowledge of the issues at hand, a profound common vision, spiritual mastery, and moral responsibility." According to him, they realized that their debates represented a crucial ideological reckoning: "When one talks of retaining or abandoning the gold standard, the issue at stake is a new or an old weltanschauung; different views of the world are at stake when advocates of free trade and advocates of autarky prepare for their decisive battle: the core of the matter is a comprehensive view of the world and not material or political questions."[87]

In June 1932, having received the proofs of his book from Heinrich Dräger, Friedländer-Prechtl expressed his thanks in a letter of June 30, 1932, saying among other things that "the name of the publishing house tells me that you too have turned to the Nazis. I can well understand this, since unfortunately this party is the only one active in the field of economic policy today. . . . It is therefore right that those who regard an economic reform as necessary try to influence the still rather confused Nazi party platform, with the aim of clarifying it. . . . For me this road is blocked, so that I can only be glad if my ideas find other ways to enter these circles."[88] The following day, after reading the booklet, he wrote a second letter to Dräger; he thanked him for pointing out the activities of the group attached to his periodical *Wirtschafts-Wende* and for his efforts in disseminating the paper's ideas. With regard to Gottfried Feder, he added a significant paragraph: "Feder was indeed fortunate that a political party adopted his ideas, while the social group I belong to according to my past, my upbringing, and my development, the bourgeoisie, rejected the ideas I advocated. Thus I found understanding and approval among right-wing parties, while the liberal

87. *Wirtschafts-Wende*, no. 8 (Dec. 2, 1931): 275–77.
88. Dräger-Materialsammlung.

world ignored or derided me. . . . I think highly of some people in the party, in particular Gregor Strasser."[89]

A paragraph from a letter written in early 1937 reveals how Friedländer-Prechtl assessed the manner in which the Nazis implemented their economic policy: "The ideas we used to advocate in those days have indeed been realized by a hundred percent and one can say that they have also justified themselves by a hundred percent. . . . Everything has been proven in practice and cannot be seriously denied today. It does not frequently happen that new ideas prevail and succeed so fast." It is therefore obvious that Friedländer-Prechtl was vexed by the fact that his name and writings had been consigned to oblivion: being half-Jewish, he was expelled from the Schrifttumskammer (Chamber of Letters) supervised by Goebbels's Propaganda Ministry and could not publish anything, even abroad. In spite of all this, "I can say to myself that I participated to a considerable extent in the creation and perfection of these new economic concepts."[90]

However great Friedländer-Prechtl's contribution to the Nazi's economic platform, his name was seldom mentioned in the course of professional or public debates of the period. A much more prominent position in this discourse was held by Ernst Wagemann, whose scientific and public status gained wide public response for his proposals – although, or perhaps because, they were less radical than Friedländer-Prechtl's and Dräger's projects. In a book published in 1932 Wagemann presented a plan for the liquidation of unemployment that caused great agitation in government, business, and various public circles. The core of the plan was an increase in the available amount of money through reorganization of the banking system, a change in the Reichsbank's liquidity regulations, and "partial" forsaking of the gold standard. He proposed to release notes up to a nominal value of fifty reichsmarks (labeled by him "consumer money"), derived from the requirement that they should be covered up to a level of 40 percent by gold and foreign currency reserves as laid down by Reichsbank law, and to "support" them with Reich bonds issued on a long-term basis up to a ceiling of three billion reichsmarks. It was to be spent on extensive government-initiated works projects by the government of the Reich, the individual states, and other public authorities.[91] The

89. Ibid., letter of July 1, 1932.
90. Ibid., letter of January 25, 1937.
91. Ernst Wagemann, *Geld- und Kreditreform*, Staatswissenschaftliche Zeitfragen

proposal was in fact only a call for additional expenditure in the public sector, financed by deficit spending to the tune of three billion reichsmarks or more. The plan's critics therefore denounced it on the grounds that it would endanger currency stability and conflict with Germany's international commitments. At once Gustav Stolper's newspaper began a crusade against Wagemann's "dangerously inflationary" plan under the slogan "hands off the currency."[92] It was a real windfall for Stolper's paper to be able to quote the unreserved praise Gottfried Feder had heaped on Wagemann in an argument with another economist: "Professor Wagemann, who, as is well known, was the first modern scholar and researcher to break new ground, basically in accordance with the demands concerning matters of finance that the National Socialists have been raising for twelve years." Stolper added a sarcastic question: "Will the president of the Bureau of Statistics be happy with this endorsement?"[93] Whether Wagemann was "happy" or not, he was in any case extensively quoted not only by reformers and the research association but also by the Nazi press as "supporting testimony" for their positions.[94]

Rudolf Dalberg, Dräger's Jewish cofounder of the research association, also contributed consistently to Friedländer-Prechtl's paper. Dalberg was a respected scientist in monetary theory, who in his early writings had already demanded abolition of the gold standard. In the sphere of theory he belonged to the nominalist school, which had many adherents in Germany after the publication of Georg Friedrich Knapp's work in 1905.[95] Monetary theory defines nominalism as the school that, in opposition to the "metallistic" or "commodity" concept of money, regards currency primarily as a means of payment and exchange and not as a means of preserving assets. In this role money has no material value of its own, like gold; it functions by virtue of the public's confidence in its viability, by social consensus, and/or by state legislation. In accordance with this concept, Dalberg also demanded the expansion of credit by the Reichsbank during the period under discussion in

No. 1 (Berlin, 1932), pp. 37f.

92. *Der Deutsche Volkswirt* 6, no. 19 (Feb. 5, 1932).

93. Ibid. 7, no. 10 (Dec. 9, 1932).

94. As in Arthur R. Herrmann, *Verstaatlichung des Giralgeldes: Ein Beitrag zur Frage der Währungsreform nach den Grundsätzen G. Feders* (Munich, 1932), who also thanks Wagemann for "mannigfaltige Anregungen."

95. Howard S. Ellis, *German Monetary Theory, 1905–1933* (Cambridge, Mass., 1937), pp. 19f.

order to finance government-initiated works projects; from 1931 on he strongly advocated devaluation of the reichsmark, following the devaluation of sterling.[96]

Another frequently mentioned economist was Wilhelm Lautenbach[97] (sometimes called the German Keynes) – a senior official at the Ministry of Economics; he did not publish much, but he used to give lectures and appear in internal government circles. His posthumously published writings reveal considerable erudition in economics and theoretical analysis. In 1931 he had already formulated a concept of comprehensive purchasing power (*Gesamtkaufkraftsvolumen*) very similar to the Keynesian "aggregate demand"; in a memorandum of the same period we find a well-reasoned theoretical development of the multiplier effect. In his proposals to the Brüning government, Lautenbach recommended the financing of large-scale government-initiated works projects by a foreign loan. However, he soon came to the conclusion that under given conditions of a worldwide crisis, as American capital fled Germany, this proposal was entirely unrealistic. In a newly considered opinion he suggested that these works be financed by expanded credit; he also outlined a technique of "preliminary financing" by promissory notes that was quite similar to the methods actually implemented subsequently by Schacht, in the form of the Mefo-bill procedure, and so forth. In addition, he recommended import restrictions and a tightening of foreign currency controls.[98]

An exhaustive list and detailed description of all the major and minor economists who participated in the period's controversies would be out of context here. I have mentioned those whose connection to the Nazis' economic platform of 1932 and to their policies after they attained power can be inferred or proven. From among the rest it is perhaps worthwhile to mention the Jewish banker Albert Hahn, who in a study published in 1920 had already outlined the same trends.[99] He also took an active part in the debates of the twenties and thirties.[100] Hahn did not belong to the group described here. There is no known evidence that he was

96. *Wirtschafts-Wende*, no. 9 (Dec. 9, 1931): 301–6.
97. Wilhelm Lautenbach, Oberregierungsrat i. Reichswirtschaftsministerium (1891–1948); some of his works were published posthumously by Wolfgang Stutzel, ed., *Zins, Kredit und Produktion* (Tübingen, 1952).
98. Kroll, *Weltwirtschaftskrise*, pp. 379ff.
99. L. Albert Hahn, *Volkswirtschaftliche Theorie des Bankkredits* (Tübingen, 1920).
100. Ziemer, *Inflation und Deflation*; also Grotkopp, *Die große Krise*, pp. 29f.

connected to the research association – and he also gave his name, together with the names of other conservative economists, to a public appeal against the Wagemann Plan that appeared in May 1932, bearing the signatures of thirty-two professors.[101]

The majority of German reformer economists who occupied themselves with monetary theory can be said to have adhered to the nominalist trend. But this does not imply that the whole school of thought was particularly German. Whatever the original contribution of these theoreticians, they did not find the theoretical foundation for their views only, or even primarily, in German literature. To the extent that they quoted Knapp, they also drew their references from the American Irving Fisher, from the Swedes Cassel and Wicksel, and first and foremost from John Maynard Keynes. Indeed, this means that the particular German characteristic of these concepts (which I believe exists) does not arise from their provenance but from the fact that they were accepted in Germany earlier and with a broader public consensus than anywhere else. I will elaborate on the reasons for this phenomenon toward the end of the present chapter, but it is worthwhile to preface that discussion with a few remarks concerning the possibility of Keynesian influences. Many writers (particularly the Germans among them) who in later years described the theoretical developments discussed here were eager to emphasize the similarity of their concepts to Keynesian theory, a category of "German Keynesianism prior to Keynes." Even an English scholar, C.W. Guillebaud, described the issue in a similar manner: "Since the appearance of Mr. Keynes' General Theory of Employment, Interest and Money many Germans have tried to rationalise their official policy by reference to these theories. Independently (in whole or part) of Mr. Keynes, German economic writers . . . have developed theories on somewhat similar lines. But there is no evidence to show that the original policy was influenced at all by abstract theories."[102]

To substantiate his claim, Guillebaud cited a number of later German economists, none of whom is in any way connected to the argument or to the period discussed here. On the other hand, he did not cite even one of those whom I have mentioned in the present context. It is certainly true that the authors discussed here were acquainted with Keynes's early writings and were fond of referring

101. Grotkopp, *Die große Krise*, pp. 231f.
102. C.W. Guillebaud, *The Economic Recovery of Germany* (London, 1939), pp. 215f.

to them, and although the matter is only of secondary importance for my discussion, it is appropriate to comment on it briefly. Keynes's *Treatise on Money* was translated into German in 1932,[103] and the *MacMillan Report* was widely discussed in periodicals immediately after its publication in 1931. Wilhelm Grotkopp regarded it as "the book of new discoveries concerning economic contexts, for almost all reformers."[104] It is noteworthy that Carl Krämer, translator of these Keynesian studies, was a well-known economic columnist in his own right who had a prominent share in the controversies of the period.[105] Even more interesting is the fact that the same man was head of a special bureau established by Schacht in Berlin in March 1932 and was known in the literature by the name Arbeitsstelle Schacht. The sole task of this bureau was to strengthen relations between large-scale industry and the Nazi party, as Schacht himself stated in a letter of March 18, 1932: "To establish contact with Hitler's economic bodies in order to tackle problems jointly in a manner that will enable the Nazi party to present an economic platform in which industry and commerce can participate."[106]

Wilhelm Lautenbach also referred to Keynes in a lecture at the Berlin Institute for Technology (Technische Hochschule) in 1931. He prefaced the unfolding of his proposals with the following sentence: "For your peace of mind, I wish to point out at once that this view concurs to a large extent with that of the Cambridge school in economics, in particular with Robertson and Keynes." He then explained his view of the investment/savings relation, explicitly referring to Keynes; he concluded that this relation "determined the business cycle."[107] This, however, did not prevent him from later stressing his independence in relation to Keynes. In 1937 he wrote a letter to the editor of a German periodical who had mentioned the link between his views and Keynes's theory, saying that the author "knows perfectly well that I developed all the principles that now appear in Keynes's general theory on my own and independently, while standing alone in the field here in Germany."[108]

Keynes was widely respected in Germany by virtue of his well-

103. J.M. Keynes, *Vom Gelde* (Munich and Leipzig, 1932).
104. Grotkopp, *Die große Krise*, p. 233.
105. Ibid., p. 245.
106. Letter of Schacht to Paul Reusch, Mar. 18, 1932, quoted by Stegmann, "Verhältnis," pp. 450f.
107. Lautenbach, *Zins, Kredit und Produktion*, pp. 156f.
108. Ibid., p. 194.

known position concerning the Treaty of Versailles. The Nazis and their entourage were also fond of quoting him at current economic discussions.[109] Subject to the reservations mentioned above, a paragraph in Otto Wagener's notes is also of interest; he suggested that Hitler should read Keynes's book because it was "a highly interesting study. . . . One feels that he moves in our direction without being acquainted with us or with our views." Wagener points in particular to the idea of abolishing the gold standard. Hitler replied that he was not sufficiently familiar with these matters.[110]

In the beginning of 1932 Keynes gave a lecture to the members of the Association for Foreign Trade at Hamburg. On this occasion he was contacted on behalf of the research association. According to Dräger, Keynes agreed to return and lecture under their auspices, but nothing came of it because of intervention by Reichsbank officials and the German Embassy in London; apprehensive of international repercussions following a public appearance by Keynes in Berlin, they persuaded him to cancel his trip.[111]

I am not going to pass judgment on the relation between Keynes's work and that of the German reformers, whether they learned from him or developed their concepts independently. These ideas were in the air at the time, and their initial development occurred simultaneously in various places all over the world. The crux of the matter is that there is a connection, or "convergence," of this budding new economic theory with what I have called the economic principles of the Nazis and their sympathizers. I believe that this had implications both for the formulation of their economic platform and for the policies implemented after they assumed power. With regard to the results of this convergence (which occurred in about 1931–32, although there had been earlier signs of its advent), the crucial factors were the economic principles and their ideological foundations, not the economic theory.

It is difficult to assess the impact of innovations in economic theory on actual practice and on policies anywhere and at any time. Theory is by its very nature a matter for the few who are experts in the field. Their influence on decision makers in the economy or the state depends on the predisposition of statesmen and executives to

109. Herrmann, *Giralgeldes*, p. 36; Ferdinand Fried [Friedrich Zimmermann], *Das Ende des Kapitalismus* (Jena, 1931), pp. 23, 35, passim; Werner Sombart, *Deutscher Sozialismus* (Berlin, 1934), p. 319 and passim.
110. IfZ, Aufzeichnungen Otto Wagener, p. 1650.
111. Interview with Dräger and also Dräger, *Arbeitsbeschaffung* (1956 ed.), p. 98.

be influenced, which is but a function of their social position and the interests they represent, their upbringing, their ideology, and their political opinions. If the views of the reformers carried considerable weight, it was not by virtue of their scientific or theoretical qualifications, but as a result of their propagandist activities and frequent appearances in the press. What ultimately decided the issue was the adoption of these ideas by a powerful political movement endowed with mass appeal, which was on the lookout for practical recipes in order to realize its comprehensive economic and social principles. Friedländer-Prechtl was right when he claimed (see above) that the argument for the gold standard and free trade against autarky and credit expansion was basically an argument about weltanschauung.

It would therefore be a mistake to belittle the weight and influence of these economic concepts because they were generalized and nonscientific. Their strength lay precisely in their weakness: as generalized and nonscientific concepts they were easily translated into ideological and political slogans, comprehensible and made to order for widespread public support. By virtue of their generalized nature these concepts could absorb and assimilate operational proposals worked out by theoreticians and adopted independent of the theoreticians' original intentions. Not all of those who in the twenties or thirties developed ideas of a countercyclical and "active" economic policy were Nazis or of related opinions. Many regarded the measures they proposed as a temporary necessity in time of crisis, intended as an application of pump priming to the economy in order to enable it, after this initial ignition, to return to the ways of a conventional market economy. The Nazis turned these theoretical tools into permanent features of economic dirigism serving the primacy of politics. As far as they were concerned, state intervention in the economy and a system of controls and regulations were inherent and permanent components of a new economic method whose traces were already present in their economic principles from their very beginnings.

On this level we have to seek an answer to the question of why only the extreme right of the political arena responded positively to the reformers' proposals, as Friedländer-Prechtl described so well. The first answer can be found in Germany's foreign policy: proposals to abolish the gold standard and to change Reichsbank regulations contradicted the letter and spirit of international agreements concerning the payment of war reparations. Individuals and parties who had first supported the minister for foreign affairs, Gustav Stresemann's, *Erfüllungspolitik* (that is, a policy to honor obligations) and later on Brüning's efforts to solve the problem of reparations by way of an international agreement could not support proposals liable to undermine these efforts. The Nazis and their right-wing partners in the National Opposition and the Harzburg Front had no such inhibitions. Brüning claimed later that already in 1930–31 he had instructed the relevant ministries to prepare plans for extensive public works. These were allegedly left in their files, pending the successful accomplishment of his negotiations on reparations. He also claimed that the publicity the Wagemann Plan received in 1932 made these negotiations very difficult.[112] The existence of public works plans is supported by evidence from a few sources. However, the manner of financing proposed for most of them was a public loan, which under conditions prevailing at the time was sheer fantasy, so that the argument about their allegedly temporary postponement due to foreign policy constraints is very much weakened.

The second, more substantial answer is that state intervention in the economy, controls, and direct state activity fit very well with the economic principles described above. The Nazis were not the only ones in the Weimar Republic who held such views. Similar concepts were promoted by all parts of the conservative revolution, the monarchist German Nationalist People's party (DNVP), and the Stahlhelm. The process of their ideological rapprochement with the Nazi party was clearly recognizable by the end of the twenties. The outstanding group in this camp was the circle connected with the monthly *Die Tat*, which had considerable influence among young intellectuals and is thought to have played an important role in clearing the way for the rise of Nazism.[113] The Nazis maintained close relations with this group, as one can see from an article Strasser published anonymously in the April issue in 1932.[114] The economic section of the monthly was covered mainly by Friedrich Zimmermann, who wrote under the pen name Ferdinand Fried. In his articles one finds all the elements of the Nazis' economic concepts. Zimmermann was in permanent contact with the Nazi

112. Brüning's letter to Dräger, *Arbeitsbeschaffung*, pp. 136–46.
113. Kurt Sontheimer, "Der Tat-Kreis," *Vierteljahreshefte für Zeitgeschichte*, no. 7 (1959): 229–60.
114. Albert Krebs, *Tendenzen und Gestalten der NSDAP: Erinnerungen an die Frühzeit der Partei* (Stuttgart, 1959), p. 191.

party, in particular with Himmler and his circle, from 1930 on. After the Nazi takeover he became a member of the SS and worked in Walter Darré's office.[115] He also continued to publish articles and books on economic subjects. Otto Strasser confirmed (in the interview mentioned above) that publications in *Die Tat* and, in particular, Zimmermann's articles had considerable influence also within the Nazi party. He was a friend of the Strasser brothers; in Otto Strasser's view, his book, *Das Ende des Kapitalismus*, contributed more than any other to the final shaping of the Nazi party's economic concepts. All Gauleiters read it, and according to Strasser it was the only book on economics that Hitler ever read.[116]

All these groups liked to refer to a traditional stream in German economic thought – an explicitly antiliberal trend opposed to classical economic theory. As I will show further on, the influence of this historical school reveals itself primarily in its denial of the applicability of abstract economic models. Since numerous German economists were free of any theory, they were well conditioned to absorb new approaches. But this school also fostered the particularization of national circumstances and what I call nationalist etatism in economics. In this manner it prepared the way for conceptions of national power, self-reliance, and autarky on the one hand, and for active countercyclical policies to be carried out by governments on the other hand. None other than John Maynard Keynes himself succinctly described this state of affairs in a preface to the German edition of *Economic Theory* in 1936. He defined his book as "a transition and severance from the classical English (or orthodox) tradition," which naturally aroused a great deal of protest in England. He then added: "I can imagine that all this will appear in a different light to the German reader. The orthodox tradition, which dominated England in the nineteenth century, has never had such a strong hold on German thought. There were always important economic schools in Germany which seriously questioned the applicability of classical theory to the analysis of contemporary events. . . . I may therefore perhaps expect less resistance from German than from English readers when I present a theory of employment and production as a unified entity that diverges from classical tradition in important aspects. . . . This comprehensive theory of production can be adapted to the conditions of a totalitarian state with much more ease than can the

115. BDC, Personalakte Friedrich Zimmermann.
116. Interview by the author, Munich, July 1974.

theory of production and distribution under conditions of free competition with a considerable measure of laissez-faire."[117] These words carry much significance and one is induced to add, in a paraphrase of Stolper: will latter-day Keynesians be happy with them? In any case they stimulate an interest in a brief examination of the past, whether or not elements of this conception can be found in German economic thought of previous periods, as implied here.

117. J.M. Keynes, *Allgemeine Theorie der Beschäftigung, des Zinses und des Geldes* (Berlin, 1936), pp. 8f.

Chapter 2

Nationalist Etatism in German Economic Thought

The dogmatic introduction of value judgments into economics, the process of production, the business cycle, and consumption, is something National Socialism shares with what is called the old, romantic school in German economics. . . . It also makes the further claim to pick up and retie the thread that Marxism tore apart in the forties of the last century . . . the economy is not a goal in itself. It must combine efficaciously with the living organism of the state. . . . The idea of German state economics, again and again destroyed and ultimately saved throughout longer and shorter periods of utter desolation, has not only found a romantic successor in National Socialism, but the first one to realize it to its last conclusion.[1]

As an empirical science, the new German theory made an effort to interpret economic development through methods of the historical school. . . . A direct line leads from Thünen and List through Roscher, Schmoller, and Wagner to this historical trend, whose most important representatives at that time were Sombart and Wagemann. . . . [The representatives of the new trend] were convinced that it was possible and necessary to base a new theory, as an empirical science, on the historical school and on German contributions to monetary theory during World War I.[2]

These two excerpts may be regarded as informed evidence: Hans Buchner, the author of the first, edited the economic section of the Nazi organ *Völkisher Beobachter* for many years and was therefore closely associated with its editor in chief, Alfred Rosenberg. After receiving Hitler's approval in 1929, he published his study of the basics of Nazi economic theory in five editions until 1933, through

1. Hans Buchner, *Grundriß einer nationalsozialistischen Volkswirtschaftstheorie* (Munich, 1930), p. 6.
2. Grotkopp, *Die große Krise*, p. 243.

Gottfried Feder's National Socialist Library. Grotkopp, who wrote the second quotation, was secretary of the research association; he worked in close association with "economic reformer" circles on novel employment and financing projects and the propaganda for their dissemination. In these extracts, both the Nazis and the reformers assert that their theories refer to a specifically German tradition. Such a categorical assertion of theoretical continuity rates at least a superficial examination. Even a quick review will show that the claim is not just a post-factum attempt to present an impressive pedigree. Within the body of German economic theory in the nineteenth and twentieth centuries we find a continuity of various trends whose common denominator is an authoritarian and in general organic concept of the state, applied with differing emphases to the sphere of economics.

The question of how far these ideas were original is only of secondary importance here. Seventeenth- and eighteenth- century mercantilism already interpreted the priority of national interests as the right of the state to intervene in the economy – so that the "Kameralism" of German principalities can hardly be regarded as a uniquely German phenomenon. On the other hand, from the beginning of the nineteenth century an aggressive antiliberalism emphasizing specific national characteristics in opposition to classical English or Western economic theory emerged in Germany in reaction to the French Revolution. Within the overall framework of German philosophy and political science, the spiritual and historical context that generated these economic concepts would exceed the limits of the present study – even though it may be pertinent to the matter in hand. However, before I outline the stages in the development of these concepts, a brief review of the political and economic conditions that bred them is necessary.

German liberalism had been ailing ever since 1848 and not merely because it failed to realize its political aim of a unified German state. In the sphere of economic development it had not achieved a great deal either. On the contrary, the "conservative" or "reactionary" 1850s initiated an era of economic growth with increased investment and consumption and even provided a partial solution to agrarian problems in the region to the east of the river Elbe.[3] During this decade the infrastructure for the Ruhr industries was established as a joint venture of industrial and commercial capital from

3. T.S. Hamerow, *Restoration, Revolution, Reaction, Economics, and Politics in Germany, 1815–1871* (Princeton, 1958), pp. 207f., 221f.

the western regions and Prussian Junkers[4] – heralding the notorious alliance of rye and steel that brought about Bismarck's protectionist policies in 1878–79 and left its stamp on Germany's state and society for a long time.[5] Even before the establishment of the Reich, the public and government sectors carried more weight in Germany's economy than in other countries, and the direct influence of the state was more tangible.[6]

Later, government initiatives aimed at developing the economic infrastructure and the regulation of foreign trade through customs restrictions arose from constraints imposed by retarded industrialization. All these elements did not create a suitable climate for the theory of free trade. Nor did the German state limit its intervention to protectionist customs duties in favor of the Ruhr district barons and the big landowners to the east of the Elbe – a policy that caused considerable damage to other sectors of the economy. It also nationalized the railways and engaged in a variety of direct economic activities at the governmental as well as the municipal level. Besides transport, water, gas, and power supply, these activities also spread to mining and industry.[7] Social policy too was guided by a paternalist-authoritarian view of the state which combined the "stick" of the law against Socialists with the "carrot" of a social security system that at the time was the most advanced and comprehensive in Europe.

The government quite openly favored industrial cartels, acknowledging their legal status and nominating itself mediator in their internal disputes, because it considered them forerunners of state control over the economy.[8] Gustav Stolper characterized the German economy as "an economic system very different from the so-called classical liberal system. . . . Even in its resplendent time German capitalism showed a generous admixture of state and association control of business."[9] In another paragraph he went even further, describing Germany's economy in those days as "an economic system of mixed private and public ownership. In this era

4. H. Mottek, *Studien zur Geschichte der industriellen Revolution in Deutschland* (Berlin [East], 1960), pp. 50ff.

5. A. Gerschenkron, *Bread and Democracy in Germany* (Berkeley and Los Angeles, 1943), pp. 42ff.

6. W.O. Henderson, *The State and the Industrial Revolution in Prussia* (Liverpool, 1958), pp. xxif.

7. Stolper, *German Economy*, pp. 75ff.

8. Ibid., p. 84; J.H. Clapham, *The Economic Development of France and Germany, 1815–1914* (Cambridge, 1951), p. 309.

9. Stolper, *German Economy*, p 92.

the foundations were already laid, on which later the war economy, the experiments of the republic and finally the National-Socialist system could be built."[10]

Economic initiatives and direct management by the state were facts of life in nineteenth- and twentieth- century Germany even before theoreticians and economists turned them into a normative system as well as an ideological goal. However, it would be a mistake to belittle the impact of economic and national-etatist theoreticians on university teaching, on publications in relevant periodicals, and so forth. They considered it their duty not merely to justify the establishment and current policies; they wished to influence future developments in the spirit of their convictions and in fact did so with considerable success.

The first attempt in this direction had already appeared at the beginning of the nineteenth century in a book by Johann Gottlieb Fichte, *Der geschlossene Handelsstaat* (The closed mercantile state). It outlines the vision of an autarkic society in which the state is obliged to provide all citizens with employment and a minimal income as part of their natural rights. Fichte believed that such socially revolutionary goals could be achieved only through an economy that was insulated against external influences. He therefore proposed to preserve autarky by the introduction of "domestic money." The internal exchange rate of this money would depend entirely on trust by the population and on financial control by a strong state that would adapt the supply of money to the demands of the domestic market. "World money" based on precious metals would be used only for necessary foreign trade.[11] Fichte had already implied ideas that were later advocated systematically and in detail by nationalist-etatist theoreticians.

One can summarize the basic ideological and economic principles common to all exponents of these trends in a few sentences: 1) the primary objective of any economic activity is reinforcement of the state's or the people's power and the promotion of their social and political aims and not the satisfaction of individual needs; 2) it is therefore the right and the duty of the state to direct the economy and restrict free economic initiative "for the common good," definition of which is an exclusive prerogative of the state; 3) state sovereignty includes the unlimited right to "create" money independently of the supply of precious metals or foreign-trade con-

10. Ibid., p. 77.
11. J.G. Fichte, *Der geschlossene Handelsstaat* (Leipzig, n.d. [1st ed. 1800]).

siderations; 4) the clear trend toward autarkic self-sufficiency within a continental economic region should be achieved, at least in the economic sphere, by expansion into east and southeast Europe; 5) priority status is accorded to agriculture, accompanied by a romantic idealization of rural life, in contrast to an ambivalent view of industrialization and the ensuing process of urbanization.

The Founding Fathers: Adam Müller and Friedrich List

There may be a measure of exaggeration in Wilhelm Roscher's assessment of Adam Müller (1779–1829) as "the father of the romantic school in political economics."[12] Müller's most significant writings appeared between 1808 and 1815 and were soon forgotten, to be rediscovered at the beginning of this century by adherents of the Viennese economist Othmar Spann. In 1841 Friedrich List (1789–1846) published his principal work, *Das nationale System der politischen Ökonomie* (The national system of political economics). These two scholars' "copyright" on the establishment of an original and unique German school of economics has been a subject for academic controversy ever since.

As a theoretician in economics, Müller's status has remained doubtful. He is regarded instead as a romantic philosopher occupied with constitutional matters, whose economic ideas were generalized and confused. It is difficult, however, to separate his philosophical notions from those concerning politics and economics. In 1801 he attacked Fichte's book, *Der geschlossene Handelsstaat*, from the position of an enthusiastic disciple of classical liberal economic theory.[13] Within a few years this Prussian Protestant became an Austrian Catholic and a crusading antiliberalist. Müller sharply rejected Adam Smith's classical approach "because it ignores the strength of the nation" and because it introduces the "intérêt des tous" instead of the "intérêt général."[14] Müller's conception arose from a romantic and irrational worship of the state as an eternal entity, independent and supreme in relation to all phenomena of

12. W. Roscher, "Die romantische Schule der Nationalökonomie in Deutschland," *Zeitschrift für die Gesamte Staatswissenschaft* (1870): 51–105.
13. J. Baxa, "Adam Müller und die deutsche Romantik," introduction to A. Müller, *Ausgewählte Abhandlungen* (Jena, 1921), pp. 130f.
14. A. Müller, "Elemente der Staatskunst," in *Vom Geiste der Gemeinschaft* (Leipzig, 1931 [1st ed. 1810]), p. 159.

private and public life. Müller's state was definitely authoritarian: the citizen was not only to obey its laws; he was also to acknowledge its absolute authority in all spheres of life – in everyday customs and behavior and within the family as well as in the areas of religion and science.[15] Although private property was tolerated alongside state property in this state, it was considered a fief in the spirit of German romanticism, which was inclined to idealize the Middle Ages – a kind of deposit taken out of the eternal common property, to be utilized and employed by its owners on a temporary basis for the benefit of the people.[16] Müller therefore placed state economy above any kind of private economy. The state economist (*Staatswirt*) had to protect the common interest from the destructive intervention of private interests, gaining experience and inner strength through his activity "in order to detect the antinational; to learn how to resist and reject the heartlessness and depravity of these clerical, aristocratic, or bourgeois individuals; to learn how little consideration and respect is due to such a bunch of egotists when the goal is to forge a people; to reinforce the courage necessary to conceive the eternal nature of the state, to reestablish it, and to sacrifice without compunction whatever unworthiness tries to resist it."[17] According to Müller, the economic interest was not guaranteed by maximal and "materialistic" expansion of the national product, but primarily by "harmony" and "equilibrium," or, in present-day terms, by the "crisis-immune" stability of the business cycle.[18]

The formulation of Müller's economic proposals is rather vague, but there are surprisingly modern elements in his monetary concepts. Like Fichte (whom he had sharply criticized in 1801), he distinguished between "internal" paper money, which functioned by virtue of a general consensus and faith in the government's signature, and world money based on precious metals. In contrast to Fichte, Müller did not aspire to economic autarky. As an Austrian civil servant from a country that drew a considerable part of its GNP from foreign trade, he had to acknowledge metal-based world money as a means of price equation. Nevertheless, Müller regarded paper money as more important than metal-based currency because only the former represented trust in the government, whose word

15. Ibid., p. 26.
16. Ibid., p. 246.
17. Ibid., p. 196.
18. Ibid., p. 255.

guaranteed its value. As paper money is the only "real and eternal money" and the true expression of "national strength," there is no need for additional securities.[19] According to Müller, only paper money is "live money" whose amount can be adapted to the requirements of the economy, whereas the available amount of "dead" metal money depends on accidental discovery of new deposits. In an essay of 1811 based on these concepts, Müller developed the idea of a national bank that would keep all precious metals and have unlimited authority to issue paper money and grant credit. These bank notes would be superior to any metal money and would be distinguished principally by "flexibility . . . their adaptability to the needs of the market and the business cycle. We need money that is created when required and disappears in accordance with the reduction of demand."[20]

Except for this modern monetary theory, all of Müller's economic concepts were borrowed from the Middle Ages. He idealized guilds and corporations and fought any form of unrestricted free enterprise. Although he did not advocate radical autarky, he demanded "an isolated national agriculture . . . determined by domestic and national needs." An export-oriented agriculture aimed at maximal yield and income might suit the British island kingdom, but it was out of place for a continental power: "The conserved strength of a people . . . its attachment to the soil it lives on . . . are as essential for the preservation of the state in any imaginable crisis as its military capacity."[21] Imports should be restricted in favor of local produce because the fashion of importing mainly English goods would also introduce English ways and customs: "A state that wishes to erase the influence of foreign industries will fail unless it revives the love for domestic ways of life . . . unless it arouses genuine national pride."[22]

Although Friedrich List was acquainted with Adam Müller, he violently rejected the claim that he had learned or adopted anything from this "learned obscurantist."[23] In contrast to Müller, List's concept of the state was devoid of romantic mystification and

---

19. Ibid., p. 159.
20. A. Müller, "Von den Vorteilen welche die Errichtung einer Nationalbank für die kaiserlich-österreichischen Staaten nach sich ziehen würde," in *Ausgewählte Abhandlungen*, p. 52.
21. A. Müller, "Agronomische Abhandlungen," in *Ausgewählte Abhandlungen*, pp. 73ff.
22. A. Müller, *Vom Geiste der Gemeinschaft*, p. 164.
23. F. List, *Schriften, Reden, Briefe* (Berlin, 1932–35), vol. 2, p. 463.

always remained rational. In his view the state was a contractual union of the people, created in order to achieve a maximum of personal well-being for its individual members.[24] This assertion produced the mistaken conclusion – shared by many – that List arrived at protectionist policies in foreign trade merely out of acute necessity and had in fact always remained a liberal economist. Actually his writings show that List, like Müller, rejected classical liberal economic theory, which leaves the productive forces of the nation to be developed by the competitive industry of individual entrepreneurs. List countered the basic principle of the classical school with the concept "that individuals draw the greater part of their productive force from social institutions and situations."[25] From this fundamental position List derived the necessity for state intervention in all spheres of economic activity. The state's role within the economy was "to regulate individual interests . . . in order to achieve the greatest measure of general prosperity at home and the greatest possible degree of security with regard to other nations." National security could not be achieved by the accumulation of material wealth alone; only the combination of "power and wealth," of economic assets fused with political and military power, could guarantee the security and welfare of a people.[26]

Here List showed himself to be not merely a German patriot, but also a theoretician who claimed to have established "a national system of political economics" that was universally applicable. Political dirigism, a basic element of the system, was not limited to customs protection for infant industries, nor did it end with investment in infrastructure to promote the necessary industrialization. In principle it embraced the whole economy: "I dare to insist that any industry within the state which is not guided by the state paves the way for the decline of the state itself."[27]

Unlike Müller, List did not derive a monetary theory from his economic principles, but he too favored paper money as a means to finance economically viable investment. Production, not money, creates railways and canals, said List. Money merely serves as a means to turn raw materials and labor into railways and canals. Should money be scarce, "the state would have a convenient and

(margin note: List's rational analysis of national systems of political economics)

24. Ibid., vol. 1, p. 207.
25. F. List, *Das nationale System der politischen Ökonomie* (1st ed. 1841), 5th ed. (Jena, 1928), pp. 194f.
26. F. List, *Schriften*, vol. 2, p. 105.
27. Ibid., vol. 9, p. 176.

cheap tool: it could introduce a system of paper money or increase the amount of paper money already in circulation."[28] In the present context it is of interest that List thought to evade the risk of inflation by covering the additional paper money with real economic assets. Investment companies like the railways, for instance, would pay for their orders in paper money of their own, made viable by government guarantee.[29]

Throughout this period of accelerated industrialization, List devoted most of his journalistic activity to pressing current problems of the German Customs Union, protectionist customs, and infrastructure investment. Nevertheless, he also reveals a somewhat romantic streak.[30] He looked back regretfully to economic harmony and stability in medieval Germany, when people used "to build for eternity."[31] He also demonstrated ambivalence in his attitude to free enterprise and agriculture. He viewed industrialization and the freedom of enterprise it necessitated as an unavoidable evil imposed upon Germany by the political situation and international competition. By inclination and through long-term considerations of "higher politics," he would have preferred more even and gradual economic growth based primarily on agriculture and small production units. In consequence he did not rule out the possibility of Germany's return to "sounder and more balanced ways" through renewed restriction of free enterprise, after a transition period of accelerated industrialization.[32]

In addition to the above, List was certainly one of the first to harness protectionist customs and state initiative to the imperialistic concept of a "pan-continental economy." Although theoretical definitions of nation and nationalism were rare in List's writings, his basic position was unmistakable: the introduction of protectionist customs was by no means a natural prerogative of all nations, but the exclusive privilege of continental or maritime great powers. A state might become a great power by virtue of its extended and "rounded" territory, a sufficiently large population, the possession of raw materials, highly developed agriculture, and a generally high

28. Ibid., vol. 3, p. 75.
29. Ibid., vol. 3, p. 239.
30. See G. Weippert, *Der späte List: Ein Beitrag zur Grundlegung der Wissenschaft von der Politik und zur politischen Ökonomie als Gestaltungslehre der Wirtschaft* (Erlangen, 1956), passim.
31. List, *Schriften*, vol. 1, p. 91.
32. Ibid., pp. 177f.; vol. 5, p. 424.

level of "civilization."[33] Only great powers were entitled to impose protectionist customs and to exist as independent national entities. Military power, besides adequate territory and population, was a precondition for national existence. Only strong armies and navies enabled great powers "to influence the culture of less advanced nations and to establish colonies and create nations by means of their population surplus and their spiritual and material capital." In any case, a people lacking these attributes has no chance of preserving its national independence; "only by partly sacrificing the advantages of nationality and by overexertion will it be able somehow to preserve its independence."[34]

List in support of German expansion thru regional ism

This was the guiding principle and the theoretical underpinning of the expansionist policy List advocated. As a future great power, Germany should remedy her "territorial defects" by forced annexation of small neighboring countries, thus creating a large and continuous economic region, from the river Rhine to the borders of Poland, "including Holland and Denmark. . . . The natural result will be the incorporation of these two countries into the German union, that is, German nationality. . . . These two tiny peoples belong to the German nation anyway by virtue of their origins and their character."[35]

These were the boundaries List designated in his principal work of 1841, but a few years later he extended them considerably. In accordance with his high esteem for Hungary, he added the whole Austro-Hungarian Empire and the European territories of the Ottoman Empire. As he had initially condemned the independence of Holland and Denmark as superflous, he now ignored the national aspirations of the Slavonic peoples within the Habsburg kingdom. The future belonged to great powers, among whom a large Germano-Hungarian state could successfully compete with America, France, and Russia, while cooperating with England on the basis of friendly relations. List's vision for the future was "no less than the foundation of a powerful Germano-Hungarian Eastern empire – washed by the waves of the Adriatic Sea at one end and animated by the German and Hungarian spirit."[36]

Although List did not explicitly advocate autarky, the idea was

33. List, *System*, p. 323.
34. Ibid., p. 269.
35. Ibid.
36. List, *Schriften*, vol. 5, pp. 499ff.; Weippert, *Der späte List*, pp. 39ff.; H.C. Meyer, *Mitteleuropa in German Thought and Action, 1815–1845* (The Hague, 1955), pp. 12–16.

inherent in his concept of a "metropolitan-colonial protective system." Once all expansionist aspirations were realized, economic units within the system would attain independence from imports of food and raw materials, thus securing world peace and a balance of power for a long period of time. The similarity between many of List's concepts and German romanticism has already been recognized in previous research.[37]

The Historical School and the Verein für Sozialpolitik

The historical school, which entered upon the stage in 1843 with the publication of *Grundriß zu Vorlesungen über die Staatswirtschaft nach geschichtlicher Methode* (Outline for lectures on political economy according to the historical method) by Wilhelm Roscher (1817–94), held Müller and List in high regard, though it did occasionally criticize them. Together with its younger successors, this school of thought dominated the science of economics in Germany for more than four decades and also exerted considerable influence on authoritative public opinion. Its scientific hallmarks were the preference accorded to national characteristics and the description of factual historical developments as a method of research and the rejection of universally applicable models. Younger exponents of this school were distinguished by their marked anti-liberalism and the inclination to favor state intervention in economic policies. The "veteran" historical school, which in addition to Roscher included Karl Knies (1821–91) and Bruno Hildebrand (1812–94), was more moderate in this respect than the younger generation, probably because of the difference in their contemporary circumstances. On the other hand, their emphatic historicism generated an organic concept of *Volkswirtschaft* (national economy) that was close to Adam Müller's views and formulations. Roscher was aware of this: "Adam Müller has acquired special merit with regard to the conception of state and national economy as one entity, standing above the individual and even above generations."[38]

The term *Volkswirtschaft* carried specific significance in this context, one that was different from its customarily accepted meaning in German and similar to its later use in Nazi literature. It not only

37. Weippert, *Der späte List*, p. 17; A. Sommer, "Friedrich List und Adam Müller," *Weltwirtschaftliches Archiv* 25 (1927): 376.
38. W. Roscher, *Die Grundlagen der Nationalökonomie* (Stuttgart, 1857), p. 20.

referred to the macroeconomic framework within the boundaries of combined economic interests but also suggested, in the spirit of the romantic tradition, an independent, living organism: "Like the state, the legal system, the language, the national economy embodies a substantial aspect of the nation's development: it therefore expresses the nation's character, its cultural level, and so forth; jointly they emerge, grow, flourish, and diminish again."[39] Although with Roscher and Knies antiliberalism assumed a more prudent and less aggressive form than it did with their predecessors and successors, its presence was unmistakable. It showed in Knies's assumption that the German national character and the German national economy were bound to generate a specifically German school of economics: "The influence of our national character, of our specific national traits upon the conception and the development of our political economics is also easily discernible in Germany. . . . The work of Adam Müller and Friedrich List, which grew in the light and in the shadow of German life, also had an unmistakable impact on those who clearly recognized the errors in economics made by these writers."

The special merit of German economic theory, as conceived by Knies, was its rejection of the liberalist misconception that any state intervention in the economy was wrong in principle: "Through profound comprehension of the affinity between all aspects and expressions of national life, including the economy, . . . Germany avoided a one-sided answer concerning the relation between state power and the economic activity of individuals."[40] Although the founders of the historical school did not worship the state to the extent that their successors did, Roscher also regarded the state as "the most important nonmaterial capital of a people whose existence is at least indirectly necessary for any kind of significant economic production."[41] He saw "a national peculiarity of the Germans . . . to bend the freedom of enterprise, imported from England and France, by numerous exceptions favoring state intervention."[42] The veteran historical school expressed its opposition to classical, or Western, economic theory with even greater clarity when it rejected the principle of maximal production and income.

39. Ibid., p. 3.
40. K. Knies, *Die politische Ökonomie vom geschichtlichen Standpunkte* (Braunschweig, 1883), pp. 329ff.
41. Roscher, *Grundlagen*, p. 70.
42. W. Roscher, *Geschichte der Nationalökonomie in Deutschland* (Munich, 1874), p. 1014.

[handwritten annotation: German Historical School establish the Assoc. for Social Policy just as Wisconsin School establishes the AALL during the Progressive Era]

Here again Roscher referred to Adam Müller: "One of Müller's best features is the eagerness with which he fights any exaggerated materialistic evaluation of output and benefits."[43] The same went for Knies: "The objective of the nation's organized life is more comprehensive and therefore loftier than the promise of the greatest possible production and consumption of economic assets."[44]

While the veteran historical school considered the primary goal of economic activity to be "harmony and stability in the business cycle," instead of materialistic maximal production and capital accumulation, the younger generation gave priority to reinforcement of the state's political and military power. This young historical school, whose outstanding exponents were Gustav Schmoller (1838–1917) and Georg Friedrich Knapp (1882–1926), in addition to its academic activities gained influence in government and public circles through the Verein für Sozialpolitik (Association for Social Policy) established in 1873.

By means of lectures and numerous publications, the association sought to call attention to the urgency of the "social question" and to the detailed proposals for relieving it worked out by the association's members. Because of the large number of scholars among its membership, its opponents labeled them Kathedersozialisten (lectern Socialists), at a time when the term Socialist was still a more or less dirty word.

Although the historical school stood out within the association as well as among economists, other methodological trends were also represented. Of primary importance in the present context are the ideas of Adolf Wagner (1835–1917), who expressed the demand for state intervention in the most radical manner, coining the term "state socialism." While the majority of association members supported social security arrangements and regulation of industrial relations by the state as an active "social policy," Wagner demanded comprehensive state intervention in the economy. Direct state initiative and a comprehensive system of institutionalized government controls should serve primarily to promote the economy and the power of the state, with the aim of preventing economic and social crises. Thus Wagner, more than anyone else, clearly emphasized the close relation between social and economic policy. Economic theory in the Third Reich, of course, put particular stress on

43. Ibid., p. 767.
44. Knies, *Die politische Ökonomie*, p. 70.

the fact that "economists representing the German school of economics,"[45] notwithstanding methodological differences among them, unanimously rejected "economic liberalism . . . and the principle of laissez-faire that arose from it."[46]

[margin note: similar to the U.S. AALL that Moss describes]

The influence during the Bismarck era of the Association for Social Policy and the economists within its orbit cannot be ignored. It surfaced especially with regard to social security legislation in the 1880s. Although Adolf Wagner explicitly rejected the claim that he was Bismarck's theoretician and swore that, on the contrary, he had learned a great deal from the chancellor,[47] the association's great renown certainly caused that influence to be at least mutual. Bismarck sent his personal representative to the association's founding convention at Eisenach and frequently described himself as a Kathedersozialist. He also adopted the term state socialism, using it frequently in his Reichstag speeches, in particular during debates on social security laws. According to Friedrich Meinecke, the desire of these German reformers to gain support for their ideas in government circles was characteristic of them – as opposed to the members of the Fabian Society in England, which sought to influence public opinion: "The economists of the Association for Social Policy acted in the first place as consultants to the government and as educators of its officials; their influence upon political parties and larger groups of intellectuals spread only gradually."[48]

German criticism attacked classical liberalism from two directions; accusing it on the one hand of neglecting national aspects or "the strength of the nation" and blaming it for releasing the state from its social obligations on the other.[49] Both claims always appeared jointly, but emphases changed continuously according to changing circumstances and in line with topical economic or social issues. A period of rapid industrialization, generating structural changes and political organization of the working class, initiated awareness of the social question and a call for social policy. The nationalistic euphoria after 1871, the economic crisis that began in 1873, and intensified international competition reinforced demands

45. W. Vleugels, "Die Kritik am wirtschaftlichen Liberalismus in der Entwicklung der deutschen Volkswirtschaftslehre," *Schmollers Jahrbuch* 59 (1935): 513.

46. Ibid., p. 516.

47. A. Wagner, "Finanzwissenschaft und Staatssozialismus," *Zeitschrift für die Gesamte Staatswissenschaft* 43 (1887): 679.

48. F. Meinecke, "Drei Generationen deutscher Gelehrtenpolitik," *Historische Zeitschrift* 125 (1922): 263.

49. Vleugels, "Kritik," p. 517.

for state intervention in order to prevent crises. The assumption that these are but two complementary aspects of an authoritarian state concept, as well as the interdependence of social and economic policies, is clearly demonstrated by the example of Adolf Wagner. As a young man and a pupil of Heinrich Rau, Wagner adhered to liberal, free-trade theories, but like the majority within the National Liberal party, he switched to the conservative camp in the seventies. Within the Association for Social Policy (of which he was a founder), he belonged to the right wing. Having failed to gain majority support for his proposals of state Socialism, he cooperated from 1877 on with the well-known anti-Semitic propagandist Adolf Stoecker.[50] However, in 1892 or 1893 Wagner dissociated himself from the anti-Semitism of Stoecker's party and left it.

Together with Albert Schäffle (1831–1903), Wagner was counted among the founders of the school for *Gemeinwirtschaft* (communal economy). Wagner believed that increasing state intervention in the economy was a necessary attribute of economic development. According to the principle that "the rights of society, the economy, the state stand above . . . the inferior rights of the individual," Wagner summarized his platform for state socialism in the following points: "1. Nationalization and municipalization of production enterprises for the general good; 2. the replacement of free-market prices by price controls; 3. implementation of social and just financial and taxation policies."[51]

Gustav Schmoller also advocated increased state intervention and control for the economy, though he was more moderate than Wagner. He underlined the positive experience gained in Prussia by public economic enterprises managed by well-trained and devoted officials. Thus in an article devoted to the activities of the chairman of the Allgemeine Electrizitäts-Gesellschaft (AEG, General Electric Power Company), Walter Rathenau, he comments with rather obvious though "respectable" anti-Semitic overtones that Rathenau merits praise because "his state socialism is close to that of old Prussia; his plans are great and noble." But Rathenau did not try to implement his "beautiful plans" even in his own enterprises! His basic views were certainly correct, but his proposals for their

50. See D. Lindenlaub, *Richtungskämpfe im Verein für Sozialpolitik, Wissenschaft und Sozialpolitik im Kaiserreich, vornehmlich vom Beginn des "Neuen Kurses" bis zum Ausbruch des Ersten Weltkrieges (1890–1914), Vierteljahresschrift für Sozial- und Wirtschaftsgeschichte*, Beihefte 52–53 (Wiesbaden, 1967), pp. 157ff.

51. A. Wagner, *Grundlegung der politischen Ökonomie*, vol. 2, 1894, quoted by Lindenlaub, *Richtungskämpfe*, pp. 89, 112.

application were too voluntaristic – which led Schmoller to the conclusion that "Rathenau is not sufficiently familiar with Germany's foremost asset, its officialdom, and therefore he does not value it enough. . . . He is not acquainted with the whole of our German administration and cannot know it from the inside."[52]

Georg Friedrich Knapp's and Adolf Wagner's monetary theories offer the most significant and unequivocal application of the principle of unlimited state authority over the economy. Knapp denied the need for a currency standard altogether because it too was valid only by force of a government ruling. Accordingly, the ruling or law, not the gold reserves, provided the currency with real coverage. Knapp, like Müller, stressed the inflexibility of metal-based money. In his view, only paper money was "real money" in circulation purely by force of a state law and the citizens' trust in their state, without any value of its own.[53] Knapp's qualities as a theoretician and an analyst, widely questioned (for instance, by Joseph Schumpeter), are not under discussion here. The fact is that during and after World War I he found numerous supporters in Germany. Oswald Spengler thought highly of Knapp and Gottfried Feder also quoted him frequently.[54]

Adolf Wagner similarly regarded "trust" as the true coverage for money; he also emphasized the inevitable relation between the amount of available money and the business cycle. He regarded nationalization of the credit market, or at least the introduction of strict controls and restriction of private banking initiatives, as a solution for this problem. The "money devoid of material value" issued by government-controlled banks had to continuously adapt its available quantity to the needs of the economy and guarantee price and interest-rate stability. It is therefore no surprise that a Nazi economist regarded Wagner as "the progenitor of monetary theory."[55]

A detailed description of the technical and sometimes complex aspects of these theories would exceed the limits of this brief review.

52. G. Schmoller, *Walter Rathenau und Hugo Preuß: Die Staatsmänner des neuen Deutschlands* (Munich and Leipzig, 1922), pp. 455ff.; idem, *Umrisse und Untersuchungen zur Verfassungs-, Verwaltungs- und Wirtschaftsgeschichte, besonders des preußischen Staates* (Leipzig, 1898), pp. 227ff.
53. Ch. Rist, *History of Monetary and Credit Theory from John Law to the Present Day* (London, 1940), pp. 334ff.
54. See J.A. Schumpeter, *History of Economic Analysis* (New York, 1954), p. 811; Lindenlaub, *Richtungskämpfe*, p. 156; Lebovics, *Social Conservatism*, p. 170.
55. Rist, *Monetary and Credit Theory*, p. 101; Herrmann, *Giralgeldes*, p. 41.

Their major and common aspects were the emphasis on the circulation function of money, as against its value-preserving function, and the order of priorities: the stability of domestic purchasing power and the development requirements of the national economy precede the requirements of international trade. With these objectives in mind, the gold standard or any kind of metal-based currency coverage was considered unnecessary, and a demand was made for absolute monetary authority and autonomy of the state. This authority was to be secured by an "internal exchange rate" or through additional money issued by nationalized or state-controlled banks. The point of departure for all such theories was the wish to create an autonomous money and credit system, well adapted to the economy's requirements. This explains why the same theories once again became popular during the 1929–33 crisis.

In theory one can derive various inward- or outward-oriented economic policies from the etatist conception described here. The Kathedersozialisten in Germany adhered to the idea of state initiative as a means of defusing social conflicts and the political tensions they generated and thus preempted the expansion of the Socialist workers' movement. Earlier on Friedrich List had called for the state to promote rapid industrialization and support young industries by means of protective customs. On the other hand, conservative trends motivated by exogenous, that is, noneconomic, ideological considerations sought to preserve traditional patterns in agriculture, economics, and life-style because they regarded the results of industrial urbanization as harmful from religious, social, political, and cultural points of view. These trends developed in juxtaposition to each other, though they sometimes converged at this or that focal point, according to current circumstances.

In a similar way, the varying orientations in foreign policy and their relation to the existing or desired economic establishment did not necessarily arise from an etatist view of the economy. Priority status for agriculture or the wish to achieve autarky and large *Lebensraum* were not always necessary components of such a view. During the fifties and the sixties these tendencies were even pushed out of sight. The foundation of the *kleindeutsche Reich* (the "small" Reich, excluding Austria) and years of rapid development did not provide a suitable climate for such ideas. Germany, seeking to gain a place in the sun for itself, instead aimed its aspirations at foreign trade and overseas colonies. These aspirations continued to influence the shift in emphasis until the outbreak of World War I, *regional productive system becomes Darwinist*

German

expansion

w/

WWI

but the notion of a "Central European solution" already began to gain support toward the turn of the century. Economists and politicians increasingly tended to consider Germany a deprived power in a world already parceled out, with but a single channel left open to it – the establishment of a large, territorially continuous economic region to provide eastern and southern European raw materials and domestic markets for expanding German industries. The beginning looked quite innocuous – a plan for an Austro-German customs union that would benefit all concerned. With time, however, especially after the outbreak of World War I, aspirations for conquests and expansion surfaced quite openly.

The Kathedersozialisten assumed an unequivocal position on these ideas. Even a liberal and progressive thinker like the economist Lujo Brentano published an article in 1885 that left no doubt as to the priority status Germany desired within the proposed unified economic region, although he emphasized that the process would be peaceful and for the good of all participants.[56]

Schmoller and Wagner were much more outspoken and radical than Brentano. Both were prominent members of the Navy Association founded in 1899 in support of Admiral Tirpitz's maritime rearmament plan. Schmoller, like List almost half a century earlier, regarded the economic progress of Germany's competitors as a threat "always and not just in wartime." He thought that the only way to stand up to these economic giants was to establish a customs union between Germany, Austro-Hungary, and Turkey. Such a unified block would enable Germany to pave its way to Africa, Persia, and India and to hold its own in any negotiations with other powers.[57]

The same ideas guided Schmoller's activity at the Central European Economic Association (Mitteleuropäischer Wirtschaftsverein) founded in 1904. By that time his orientation was already directed toward agriculture and a continental solution. He supported expansion of the navy not because of colonial aspirations but in order to protect Germany against a possible blockade by England: "We wish to become neither an industrial state, nor a colonial state, nor a maritime power like England, but we want to expand our trade and our industry sufficiently to live and to support a growing

56. L. Brentano, "Über die zukünftige Politik des deutschen Reiches," *Schmollers Jahrbuch* 11 (1885): 1–29, quoted by Lindenlaub, *Richtungskämpfe*, p. 60.

57. G. Schmoller, "Die Wandlungen in der Handelspolitik des 19. Jahrhunderts," *Schmollers Jahrbuch* 24 (1900): 373ff.

population."[58] Wagner also warned against interference with the balance between agriculture and industry. As an economist and an expert on finance, he ventured to prove that expansion of the navy was not only necessary to prevent a blockade and safeguard national honor, but could also be carried out as an economically viable capital investment.[59]

Fritz Fischer has described extensively how the Central European concept developed during debates on First World War objectives and what part the Kathedersozialisten played in this debate.[60] Yet in contrast to still-accepted opinion, the notion of Central Europe was not merely a "war product."[61] The idea had a past and a future in German economic thought that went beyond immediate imperialistic aspirations. It was the ultimate logical conclusion of economic principles that placed strong ideological emphasis on an extensive, territorially continuous, and autarkic region as the indispensable foundation of national power. The future direction of the Central Europe concept was outlined in an article by Friedrich Ratzel (1844–1904) published in 1901 under the heading "Lebensraum," which from that date became an accepted term and a political slogan. Following his travels on the American continent, Ratzel brought – in addition to economics and power politics – irrational and social Darwinist elements to the idea of Central Europe. These were later fully developed in Karl Haushofer's (1869–1946) theory of geopolitics. In Ratzel's view, the size and scope of the *Lebensraum* constitute the major component of national power. These are determined by a general and inclusive struggle for survival among all races – ending with the strongest and purest race in possession of the largest *Lebensraum*. Haushofer added the romantic notion of the organic growth and continental unity of the said *Lebensraum*. Haushofer's personal relations with Hitler are a known fact, and it seems that he influenced the political formulation of the *Lebensraum* concept in Hitler's *Mein Kampf*.[62] The ideas promoted by young conservative and Nazi literature during the Weimar period –

58. G. Schmoller, *Zwanzig Jahre deutscher Politik* (Munich and Leipzig, 1920), pp. 17f.

59. See A. Wagner, *Agrar- und Industriestaat* (Berlin, 1901); idem, "Die Flottenverstärkung und unsere Finanzen," in G. Schmoller, M. Sering, and A. Wagner, eds., *Handels- und Machtpolitik* (Berlin, 1900), p. 126.

60. F. Fischer, *Germany's War Aims in the First World War* (London, 1967), pp. 8f.

61. Meyer, *Mitteleuropa*, p. 140.

62. See T. Kamenetzky, *"Lebensraum": Secret Nazi Plans for Eastern Europe* (New York, 1961), passim.

whether under the heading of *Lebensraum*, or *Großraumwirtschaft* (economy of large territories), or Central Europe – were in fact but topically formulated repetitions of the Kathedersozialisten idea of Central Europe.

In scope as well as in its underlying principles, Gustav Schmoller's view of Central Europe in particular went beyond constraints that could be explained by circumstances before and during World War I. Schmoller regarded a large, unified economic region in central Europe not just as the necessary space to resettle a rapidly expanding population, but as a political power bloc that "would altogether save the superior and ancient European culture from perdition."[63] He saw a threat to this culture approaching from the direction of Russia, the United States, and perhaps China and believed England would become a natural ally in this struggle. Whatever the English might manage to save of their empire and their dominant status after the war "they will more easily keep and preserve by good future relations with Germany than against her. They will soon need our help quite urgently. Against whom it is better not yet to spell out today."[64] These thoughts are not far from Adolf Hitler's economic and geopolitical ideas or the principles of his foreign policy, as set out in *Mein Kampf* as well as in his second book, published after the war. One should not, of course, blame Schmoller as the source of Hitler's ideas; it is doubtful that Hitler ever read his articles or lectures. Nevertheless, the similarity between the two is surprising and certainly stimulates thought. The possible influence of ideas in the air upon subsequent developments should not be ignored.

By way of ending this review, it is worthwhile mentioning the activities of young Hjalmar Schacht in regard to the propaganda for Central Europe. Schacht was a pupil of Schmoller's at Berlin University and mentioned him in his memoirs as "one of the people who influenced me decisively." As a young man, Schacht had participated in a study excursion to southeast Europe and the Middle East in 1902. In 1916 we find the initiator of the 1934 New Plan among the founders of an Action Committee for Central Europe. Schacht wrote his doctoral thesis on English mercantilism, and he claimed in his memoirs that by then he had already diagnosed the weaknesses of classical economics: "The so-called classi-

63. *Schmollers Jahrbuch* 15 (1891), quoted by F. Fischer, "Weltpolitik, Weltmachtstreben und deutsche Kriegsziele," *Historische Zeitschrift* 199 (1964): 325f.
64. Schmoller, *Zwanzig Jahre*, p. 171.

cal theory of economics owes its prolonged dominance to the brilliant propaganda with which English economists muddled continental thought. Even when there was an economist who tried to protect the interests of his people against such alien theories, and [the situation] was such that, if he was German like Friedrich List, his own people ridiculed and misunderstood him."[65]

War Socialism: Walter Rathenau and Wichard von Moellendorff

The experience gained from the 1914–18 war economy reinforced existing inclinations toward state dirigism – whose operational efficacy seemed to have been proven. From the time of Alfred von Schlieffen, the field marshall whose ideas influenced military thinking before World War I, German strategic planning had been built on the assumption that for economic reasons a drawn-out war in Western Europe was no longer feasible.[66] To the surprise of many, the German state not only discovered a financial technique that enabled it to cover war expenses exceeding all forecasts but also succeeded in recruiting sufficient labor and raw materials for its war industries. Great merit in this sphere was due to Walter Rathenau, who together with Wichard von Moellendorff administered the allocation of raw materials during the war. Walter Rathenau (1867–1922) was a Jew, a son of Emil Rathenau, founder of the AEG. Rathenau had already made his reputation in business and through his literary work before the war. His writings frequently treated economic and social subjects, advocating a planned economy guided by principles of social justice and the good of the public, a kind of "state socialism from above." In 1914 he initiated the establishment of controls over vital raw materials. He was assassinated by extreme rightists in June 1922 while holding office as minister for foreign affairs. Rathenau recruited von Moellendorff from AEG. Both were able executives whose methods were based on comprehensive economic and social concepts. Rathenau presented these ideas in numerous articles years before the war – and they make worthwhile reading even today. After the war Moellendorff tried (as assistant to the Social Democratic minister of economics, Rudolf Wissel) to turn his concept of *Gemeinwirtschaft*

65. H. Schacht, *76 Jahre meines Lebens* (Bad Wörishofen, 1953), pp. 117, 101, 230, 475.
66. G. Hardach, *Der Erste Weltkrieg* (Munich, 1973), p. 64.

(communal economy), which combined etatist dirigism with conservative socialism, into the nucleus of a new economic order.

Rathenau's and Moellendorff's ideas did not gain acceptance before or after the war. Nevertheless, there is no doubt that the war experience influenced the development of new economic theories during the years of economic crisis that followed. Moellendorff's basic approach, which was colored by a romantic idealization of medieval Germany, primarily emphasized harmony and stability as desirable goals of economic activity. Freedom of private enterprise was to be rejected wholesale, not only in wartime: "The common idol was the free interplay of forces. It was worshipped as the pledge for opportunities to gain money . . . and it was forgotten . . . that older German economic patterns, like the medieval guilds with their rigid restrictions, had prospered quite considerably."[67] Moellendorff tried to promote his idea of a communal economy, which "is older than the glory of 1913 and in any case more German," by providing it with a pedigree from Frederick the Great, Fichte, List, and Bismarck.[68] State intervention and state initiative were basic principles of Moellendorff's conservative or neo-conservative economic method, which had allegedly proved its efficacy during the war and should not be jettisoned afterward: "The war was an industrial experience in the broadest sense. . . . The comprehensive economic consciousness of an omniscient state is not by chance but invariably a better repository and soil for initiative than the private enterprise of banks and stock exchanges that never represent more than a partial vision [of the whole]."[69]

Rathenau thought along similar lines: "Awareness begins to spread that all economic life is based on the state, that policy precedes profitability, and that everyone owes his possessions and his abilities to all." He summarized his views and principles in his system of economic compromise and social liberty, which contained the following guidelines: 1) allocation by the state of available production factors for consumption and investment, according to a planned and desirable rate of growth; 2) a more just and more egalitarian distribution of national income and property; 3) a ban on monopolistic mergers, which are the principal source of unjustified accumulation of wealth under modern capitalism; 4) severe restrictions on inheritance rights. These principles, combined with large-

67. W. von Moellendorff, *Deutsche Gemeinwirtschaft* (Berlin, 1916), p. 21.
68. W. von Moellendorff, *Von Einst zu Einst* (Jena, 1917), p. 26.
69. Ibid., p. 39.

scale training projects, would diminish class antagonism and guarantee long-term social mobility. They would be realized by the combined operation of direct state economic activity and comprehensive government controls on wages, profits, interest rates, and foreign trade. Rathenau regarded the public sector of the economy, enterprises managed by the government, and state investment as an effective means of influencing prices and interest rates and protecting the middle class from competition by monopolistic power groups.[70]

The persuasive social ethos in Rathenau's writings was fed by a restless and critical spirit. In social consciousness, he was close to his contemporaries, the Kathedersozialisten, even if he was frequently aware of their criticism regarding his operational plans. Although a Jewish industrialist, he harbored a strong, German national consciousness; in advocating expansion of territory and power he was not far behind the Kathedersozialisten. As early as 1898 he published an article (under an assumed name) in which he claimed that in its confrontation with the technological and economic superiority of the Western powers, Germany had "to turn to the East."[71] Rathenau, like Schmoller, was concerned about future population surplus in Germany: "Within a generation we will not be able to feed and employ a hundred million Germans on half a million square kilometers and some plot in Africa, and we do not wish to live at the mercy of the world market. We need soil on this earth." Rathenau therefore proposed to challenge the Monroe Doctrine in order to open South America for German settlement and exports. However, he was compelled to admit that the chances of success were slim and that "Germany had missed the time for great conquests." He saw the only promising way out in a central European economic and customs alliance, which would be joined "eventually and willy-nilly" by France and connected countries. This economic bloc would be able to cope effectively with Anglo-Saxon superiority as well as with the Russian threat and would secure Germany's leading status on the Continent.[72]

The inclusion of France within the projected central European economic region distinguished Rathenau's conception from that of

---

70. W. Rathenau, "Von kommenden Dingen," in *Gesammelte Schriften* (Berlin, 1929), vol. 3, pp. 96, 97, 139, 158, 159.
71. W. Rathenau, "Transatlantische Warnungssignale," *Die Zukunft*, July 30, 1898.
72. Rathenau, *Schriften*, vol. 1, p. 270; also Meyer, *Mitteleuropa*, pp. 139f.

his contemporaries or their predecessors – from England, political orientation shifted to France. He therefore lacked the nationalist and aggressive overtones of his time. [Today he appears almost as a pioneer who anticipated present-day economic cooperation in Europe.] Nevertheless, the substantial differences between these varied approaches could be bridged. Rathenau, notwithstanding his insistence on mutual benefit, was also convinced that Germany would enjoy priority status within this alliance. He therefore found no difficulty in disseminating his ideas through the Association for Central European Economy, together with Alfred Ballin, Gustav Stresemann, Friedrich Naumann, and the Kathedersozialisten, all of whom were much more radical than he.

The Weimar Period: Othmar Spann, Werner Sombart, and the Conservative Revolution

Only a handful of economists continued in the nationalist-etatist tradition under the Weimar Republic. The majority of the Kathedersozialisten had fallen away, and the historical school had already suffered a crushing defeat in a methodological controversy with Carl Menger and the Austrian school in the eighties. Liberalism and the "theory of marginal gain" dominated the universities almost without interference. Like their peers in other countries, German economists found themselves to be powerless in the face of the 1929 debacle. Economic policy was mainly determined by executives in government departments and the central bank – so much so that people were inclined to speak of a ministerial school in economic theory.[73]

The young intellectuals of the conservative revolution were instructed in the historical tradition at the hands of Werner Sombart in Berlin and Othmar Spann in Vienna. In spite of differences in their points of departure, the nationalist etatism of the state Socialists converged with Oswald Spengler and Moeller van den Bruck's Prussian or German socialism, generating a comprehensive political and social ideology that declared war on the young republic. Some of these thinkers were gifted writers who provoked widespread public controversy and successfully extended their influence, in particular among young intellectuals.[74] Some worked out detailed

73. Grotkopp, *Die große Krise*, p. 245.
74. Lebovics, *Social Conservatism*, pp. 149f.; K. Sontheimer, *Antidemokratisches*

94

proposals for economic policy based on their totalitarian concept of
the state and its role in the economy. Their ideas were very similar
to those of the reformer economists on the one hand and to those of
the Nazis on the other. The rapprochement between initially different trends and theories did not arise only from the political and
economic crisis. The common tradition of German economic
thought to which the exponents of all these trends adhered facilitated mutual recognition. Spann's universalist school emphasized its
ties with Germany's past and German economic theory, adopting
Adam Müller as its spiritual father. The corporate state and corporate economy were declared ideal forms of a new economic order –
embellished by a rather questionable historical idealization of medieval life patterns. Spann and his followers sought to establish a
corporately organized economy whose primary aims were har-
monious preservation of social equilibrium, stability, and security –
and not maximum output or a maximum rate of growth.

Werner Sombart dissociated himself from Spann and the universalist school, which he considered an unscientific theory of economics that "passed judgment."[75] Nevertheless, Sombart also
condemned the hedonism and utilitarian materialism of the "economic era." He preferred stability: "The immediate goal of any
reasonable economic policy should be to lend perseverance and
permanence to production. We forego the advantages that mark the
economic era. . . . If a slowdown of technological and economic
progress is regarded as the principal disadvantage in abolishing
capitalism, we reply that it is precisely this that we perceive as a
blessing."[76] It is true that Sombart wrote this in 1934, in a book that
is nowadays frequently belittled as a regrettable aberration by an
old scholar of great merit who wished to pacify the new rulers. Yet,
careful perusal of Sombart's previous writings does not validate this
claim: *Deutscher Sozialismus* offers a fairly consistent summary of a
spiritual and political germination whose initial signs were discernible much earlier. We will see further on that the excerpt quoted

*Denken in der Weimarer Republik: Die politischen Ideen des deutschen Nationalis-
mus zwischen 1918 und 1933* (Munich, 1962), pp. 182f.; W. Hock, *Deutscher
Antikapitalismus: Der ideologische Kampf gegen die freie Wirtschaft im Zeichen der
großen Krise* (Frankfurt. a.M., 1960), pp. 33f.; K. von Klemperer, *Germany's New
Conservatism: Its History and Dilemma in the 20th Century* (Princeton, 1968), pp.
192f.
75. W. Sombart, *Die drei Nationalökonomien: Geschichte und System der Lehre
von der Wirtschaft* (Munich and Leipzig, 1930), pp. 65ff.
76. Sombart, *Deutscher Sozialismus*, p. 318.

above was not the sole point of convergence between Sombart, Spann, and other nationalist etatists.

For the young conservative revolutionaries gathered around the periodical *Die Tat*, Sombart and Spann were respected teachers whose thinking was conceived as a foil to the sterile rationalism and detachment from real life of professional economists. They even regarded Spann as somewhat overrationalistic, but acknowledged his profound reverence for tradition: "A corporate, organic universalism is set up here against liberal-democratic and egalitarian individualism and socialism – in spiritual continuity from Thomas of Aquinas, Adam Müller, and Friedrich List." Sombart, on the other hand, merited unqualified praise and the hope that he had not yet said his last word.[77] And indeed this hope was fully realized with the publication of his book on German socialism in 1934.

However, this was not the first time Sombart had supported extensive state intervention in the economy. Already in 1903 he had pointed to increasing intervention by "the statesmanship technique" in the economy as a sign of future developmental trends leading, according to him, to a regime of "social capitalism."[78] In 1930 he called for the introduction of a "Kameralist" method appropriate to contemporary circumstances.[79] In 1932 he attracted considerable attention through a series of lectures on "The Future of Capitalism" at Heinrich Dräger's research association, in which he demanded centralized government planning for all sectors of the economy.[80] We see therefore that his German socialism was not at all an aberration, and he himself referred it back to Adam Müller, Novalis, Fichte, and others as "a genuinely German concept of the state, in conscious contrast to the individualist-rationalist concept of the state that comes from the West."[81]

Subjection of the economy to the interests and goals of the state did not in principle require centralized government planning. There were various possible models for transmission channels along which instructions or the outline of general objectives could be passed down from a supreme state authority to all levels of the economy. The corporate structure taken from medieval tradition, which Spann sought to realize, was not primarily aimed at the protection

77. P. Focks, "Die zünftigen Nationalökonomien," *Die Tat* 24 (1932): 592f.

78. W. Sombart, *Die deutsche Volkswirtschaft im 19. Jahrhundert und im Anfang des 20. Jahrhunderts* (Darmstadt, 1954 [1st ed. 1903]), p. 455.

79. Sombart, *Drei Nationalökonomien*, p. 331.

80. *Die Tat* 24 (1932): 37ff.

81. Sombart, *Deutscher Sozialismus*, p. 172.

of middle-class interests. It was the model of an institutionalized structure, leaving extensive administrative autonomy to existing interest groups, as well as to similar associations to be established in the future.[82] Sombart, on the other hand, regarded such associations as at best a means of executing government instructions, without authority or much activity of their own. He rejected the concept of a *Ständestaat* (corporate state) "if it means that the corporations [*Stände*] take part in molding the will of the state. On the contrary, the future state will always be authoritarian."[83]

As we will see below, this theoretical controversy had great significance, and the Nazi state was administered not according to Spann's model of a corporate state but in Sombart's spirit with regard to the institutional structure as well as price and wage policies, which according to Spann should have been left to the autonomous authority of corporate bodies. Followers of *Die Tat* also supported an economy directed by government instructions; associations of various economic branches were to operate as executive bodies under government leadership, instead of continuing to act as "organizations representing private interests."[84]

Government control and even administrative dictation of price and wage rates, previously advocated by some of the Kathedersozialisten, were natural components in the economic philosophy of all rightist conservative trends.[85] In addition, they regarded direct economic activity of a public sector as large as possible not only as a source of income for the state and a means for more equal distribution of national income, but also as a reliable vehicle for economic supervision. Oswald Spengler considered the Prussian state, ruled by its bureaucracy, as a first step toward Prussian socialism — the highly efficient management of its public sector providing evidence that business could flourish without the incentive of

---

82. O. Spann, *Gesellschaftslehre*, 2d ed. (Leipzig, 1923), pp. 507f.; idem, *Der wahre Staat: Vorlesungen über Abbruch und Neuaufbau der Gesellschaft*, 3d ed. (Jena, 1931), p. 189; W. Heinrich, *Das Ständewesen mit besonderer Berücksichtigung der Selbstverwaltung der Wirtschaft* (Jena, 1932), pp. 31f.

83. Sombart, *Deutscher Sozialismus*, p. 231.

84. E.W. Eschmann, "Wirtschaften auf Befehl und Übereinkunft," *Die Tat* 24 (1932): 241f.

85. See Rathenau, "Von kommenden Dingen," *Schriften*, vol. 3, pp. 96f.; Schmoller, *Zur Literaturgeschichte der Staats- und Sozialwissenschaften* (Leipzig, 1888), p. 73; Wagner, "Finanzwissenschaft," pp. 705f.; O. Spengler, *Preußentum und Sozialismus* (Munich, 1920), p. 77; F. Fried [Friedrich Zimmermann], *Die Zukunft des Außenhandels: Durch innere Marktordnung zur Außenhandelsfreiheit* (Jena, 1934), p. 45; W. Sombart, *Die Zukunft des Kapitalismus* (Berlin, 1932), p. 28.

private profit. However, this did not lead him to demand general nationalization; he merely advocated government control: "Nationalization of economic life, not by abolition of private property, but by legislation." With the economic crisis becoming increasingly worse, voices urging nationalization accordingly became louder. *Die Tat* called for the nationalization of large corporations as a minimum demand. Sombart went further than anyone else, demanding nationalization of big banks, raw-material industries, the entire transport system, and all factories producing military supplies.[86] Notwithstanding their terminology – whether it was state socialism or German or Prussian socialism – in principle all these groups remained committed to private ownership of the means of production and the incentive for private profit. They intended to restrict the freedom of business proprietors to control market prices and wages, but not the capitalistic mode of ownership per se. Sombart emphasized that "private and communal property will exist alongside each other . . . although private property will be subject to constraints . . . in any case where it concerns the means of production and land . . . property that is a fief."[87]

Sombart explicitly emphasized his consensus with Spann on this issue. He was also at one with the universalist school in the matter of agriculture and the ambivalent attitude to industrial and technological progress. The outstanding elements in Spann's way of thought included romantic idealization of rural life, as opposed to the moral deterioration of cities, and the deep-rooted earthiness of the peasant, as opposed to the "homelessness of the metropolitan proletarian, who goes through life devoid of genuine values and content." The struggle against urban life was consistently interpreted as a struggle against exaggerated industrialization; the government was required to impose "social censorship on technique." In a similar vein, Sombart had already condemned overindustrialization during World War I as the root of hedonistic "addiction to comfort . . . the enemy of all idealism and culture." As the economic crisis worsened and was widely interpreted as a sign of the end of capitalism, the idealization of agriculture deepened, although like other sectors it was grievously hit by the crisis. Sombart spoke of a "return to the land," of settling those

---

86. Schmoller, *Umrisse*, pp. 227f.; Rathenau, "Von kommenden Dingen," *Schriften*, vol. 3, p. 159; Spengler, *Preußentum*, p. 97; Eschmann, "Wirtschaften," p. 452; Sombart, *Deutscher Sozialismus*, p. 300f.
87. Sombart, *Deutscher Sozialismus*, p. 324.

with no means of livelihood in the eastern regions in numbers that would bring the ratio of agricultural employment back to between 40 and 45 percent! He did not consider this a temporary solution dictated by prevailing circumstances, but a matter of principle: "For any state . . . the rural population is of greater value and more necessary than the urban population in industry and trade."[88]

Sombart tied his demand for a return to agriculture to a call for the widest possible autarky, necessitated by internal and social as well as by military and political considerations. The fundamentals of the *Lebensraum* concept – agriculture and autarkic self-sufficiency – converge here with the vision of German socialism as the future social order, recalling Fichte's *Geschlossener Handelsstaat*: "We hold to this principle of a national economy for strategic, national, and economic reasons. However, the primary consideration is that a meaningful order of national life necessitates an economic organism whose vital activities are independent of events abroad."[89]

Robert Friedländer-Prechtl spoke in a similar vein of "preservation of the race," of the "health of the nation," and of the "soul" of German rural culture, an additional indicator of his basic ideological position. He explained the aspiration to autarky as a universally widespread trend, which he thought pointed "in the direction of increasing autarky – the wish to achieve maximal self-sufficiency within closed economic regions."[90] From this the young contributors to *Die Tat* drew their renewed call for the establishment of a *Großraumwirtschaft* over all of central Europe. Friedrich Zimmermann wrote a series of articles (under the pen name Ferdinand Fried) stressing the need for self-sufficiency not only as a consequence of the "universal trade war" but also for reasons of national specificity and life-style. Like other contributors to the periodical, he called for economic planning and government control, antiliberalism, autarky, and expansion projects into central Europe not just as a remedy for the prevailing crisis but as an integrated economic order for the future. Besides its intention to uproot free trade, the "new European order" was interpreted as reagrarianization, autarky, and the restriction of free economic activity.[91]

88. W. Heinrich, *Die soziale Frage* (Jena, 1934), quoted by M. Schneller, *Zwischen Romantik und Faschismus* (Stuttgart, 1970), pp. 66, 158; W. Sombart, *Händler und Helden: Patriotische Besinnungen* (Munich and Leipzig, 1915), p. 101; idem, *Deutscher Sozialismus*, p. 292.
89. Sombart, *Deutscher Sozialismus*, pp. 269, 284f.
90. R. Friedländer-Prechtl, *Wirtschafts-Wende*, pp. 225, 132.
91. F. Fried [Friedrich Zimmermann], "Der Übergang zur Autarkie," *Die Tat* 24

Thus the Nazis and the young conservative intellectuals found themselves in a common position – singing the same tune, so to speak, while at least some of the reformer theoreticians provided the "instrumentation." Their subsequent cooperation in economic praxis after the Nazis had assumed power was only a natural sequel to this process.

Traditional and Modern Components in Nazi Economic Policy

Other authors have preceded me in pinpointing the particular developments in German economic thought outlined here. Various terminological generalizations have emerged in the course of this process, not only as an auxiliary of scientific description but also – be it deliberate or not – as an ideological yardstick, applied by each according to his lights. Gustav Stolper, loyal to classical liberalism in economics, rejected any kind of state intervention, considering it a danger to the economy. He regarded the economic and ideological currents described here as a specifically German form of socialism and anticapitalism, including National Socialism.[92] Koppel S. Pinson, citing Stolper, also considered Spengler's and van den Bruck's Prussian or German socialism not merely a herald of Nazism but part of "the Socialist tradition in Germany, of which the German Social Democratic party was the most organized expression."[93] This view, which is widespread even today, arises from the classification of social and economic systems according to the "principle of allocation." Ignoring the mode of ownership, this approach classifies all allocation of resources and income via the free-market mechanism as capitalism and all planning and state intervention in the economy as socialism. The usefulness of such an oversimplified criterion as a tool for economic or historical analysis is rather doubtful. Notwithstanding their concern for the social question, neither Bismarck, nor von Bülow, nor Rathenau were anticapitalists, and the same goes for List, Schmoller, and Wagner.

affirmation of allocative efficiency as the basis of the critique of German social democracy

(1932): 127; idem, *Das Ende des Kapitalismus*, pp. 255, 257; G. Wirsing, "Zwangs-autarkie," *Die Tat* 23 (1931): 433; idem, "Richtung Ost-Südost," *Die Tat* 22 (1930/31), pp. 628ff.; idem, *Zwischeneuropa und die deutsche Zukunft* (Jena, 1932); E.W. Eschmann, "Nationale Planwirtschaft: Grundzüge," *Die Tat* 24 (1932): 240f.
92. Stolper, *German Economy*, p. 233.
93. K.S. Pinson, *Modern Germany: Its History and Civilization* (New York, 1954).

The anticapitalism of the conservative revolution and the Nazis was also highly questionable. All these trends and currents consistently supported private ownership of the means of production and private profit as the primary economic incentive. In terms of their specific contemporary circumstances, each represented the conservative, nationalistic, or Nazi reaction to the real or imaginary threat of a Socialist revolution – with the aim of protecting the prevailing social regime.

Wolfgang Hock defined German anticapitalism more astutely as "the economic aspect of a comprehensive ideology generally opposed to democratic liberalism . . . whose origins reach far back into German history. . . . The concepts that so strongly influenced German economic thought around 1930 can be interpreted and analyzed correctly only on the basis of this general assumption. Their importance was also crucial in determining economic policy later on."[94]

I will examine this last statement more thoroughly in the next chapter. Meanwhile, however precise the above definition, the term antiliberalism appears to be more appropriate, though it has the disadvantage of a purely negative formulation. It expresses rejection of the free enterprise system without specifying alternative objectives for the desired economic order.

The term etatism was coined by the economist Ludwig von Mises,[95] who devoted considerable (and superfluous, I believe) effort to an attempt to prove that etatism was not an original German invention. Even if the idea was initially conceived by French utopists, it was not their copyright that influenced subsequent developments. Much more to the point were the impact these theories made and the response they received at universities and among the general public as time went on. There is no doubt that these were stronger in Germany than anywhere else. The reason for this is to be found not in a particular "national character" but in economic and social developments, as well as in the ideological and political course of events in Germany in the nineteenth and twentieth centuries. In any case, the term defines the tendencies described here succinctly and scientifically, though it ignores their objectives. The present-day welfare state, which aims to supply maximum employment and provide for the needs of its citizens by government

94. Hock, *Deutscher Antikapitalismus*, pp. 33f.
95. L. von Mises, *Omnipotent Government: The Rise of the Total State and Total War* (New Haven, 1948), passim.

initiative and intervention, also bears some marks of etatism.]

In contrast, the trend in German economic thought discussed here was merely the traditional German concept of the *Obrigkeitsstaat* transcribed into economic terms. In addition, the state's political and military considerations were to receive absolute priority. Therefore I believe that, as far as a generalized term is necessary, the views and concepts of this movement are best described by the term "nationalist etatism."

What, then, do we conclude from the traditional continuity described above? It is easier to state which conclusion would be erroneous – namely, that the Nazis' economic principles and, even more, the policies that followed upon them were the only possible and inevitable result of the spiritual trends and theories that animated German tradition. The relation between any economic policy and previous or contemporary theoretical systems always elicits the question of sequence. Nevertheless, one should not belittle the influence that this tradition exerted on economic reality in the twenties and thirties. This reality was "ripe" for government intervention in the economy not only in Germany. Dirigist economic ideas that did not shy away from injuring private enterprise were also received with positive responses in other countries, in particular from the political right. However, in Germany large and influential groups were mentally prepared to accept and absorb the same ideas because it was possible to refer them to a continuum of tradition. This does not permit the historian to pass judgment upon economists or philosophers as forerunners or pathfinders of National Socialism. But neither can he ignore the fact that an influential section of university economists, senior government officials, and businessmen in Germany had been brought up and educated in a tradition that made them more receptive to these new theories than their peers in other countries.

Under the conditions prevailing in those days, the economic policy implemented by the Nazis was unfortunately the appropriate remedy. Its success not only earned them a broad political consensus but also surrounded their economic principles with the nimbus of theoretical validity. Only captive believers in historical determinism will infer from these facts that the course of events as it actually occurred was inevitable. What would have happened if previous governments, economists, or statesmen had shed the shackles of conventional economics in time to introduce countercyclical measures that are considered a matter of course today?

102

Presumably there is no satisfactory answer to the question, What would have happened if? The economic crisis and unemployment, though crucial, were after all only a few among numerous factors that ultimately enabled the Nazis to seize power. The historical truth is that the Nazis and the economists attached to their movement were almost the only figures in the pre-1933 political arena to present genuine employment projects to be financed by unconventional measures and to realize these projects successfully after assuming power.

How much of this can be attributed to successful improvisation, to comprehensive economic principles, or to previous theoretical blueprints? It is likely that each of these elements played a specific role – but it is an error to scorn the claim that the Nazis developed any "thought" in the sphere of economics. Such thought existed in their movement and in its immediate political sphere. The disaster was that they also knew how to utilize it successfully. Publications before and after 1933 show clearly that at least some Nazis were sufficiently well read to look for prior scholarly models. It remains moot how far they were actually influenced by such models, or whether they invoked well-known German economists of the past only to add weight to their own opinions post factum.

Those models were in the first place Adam Müller and Friedrich List, quoted abundantly by the Nazis and their collaborators. Friedrich Bülow, for instance, wrote a preface to the new 1932 edition of Müller's works in which he described the connection fairly well: "If a name like Adam Müller surfaces again in modern awareness and his writings are not merely reread, but are only now absorbed with full spiritual comprehension – this must arise from a profound approach to the spiritual currents of the times."[96] Among the Nazis it was Hans Buchner who made a special effort to describe their economic principles as the realization of "the traditional idea of a German state economy." In the brochure quoted at the beginning of this chapter, he listed almost all economists and philosophers mentioned here: Fichte was, according to Buchner, "the herald of a superior solidarity that, among the members of a state, goes beyond utilitarian interests." Müller's monetary theory, "which in a certain sense includes Feder's theory of a construction bank, . . . offers the best explanation of paper money . . . and is only one step removed from the rejection of free trade." List presented

96. F. Bülow, Introduction to Müller, *Vom Geiste der Gemeinschaft*, p. xv.

"the demand for a nationally oriented regional economy" in a convincing manner. Together with Fichte, Hegel, and others, he belongs among the founders of social policy, which is in a way "a grandchild of the romantic school and a child of the historical school." [Buchner regarded Bismarck's social insurance as the realization of state socialism, which is the genuine core of the Nazis' economic principles.] Altogether, "the economic ideal of National Socialism revives the best characteristics of German economic theory."[97]

Herrmann, one of the shrewder Nazi economists, tried in particular to anchor Feder's monetary proposals in traditional German ideas: "In opposition to the concept of money generated by liberalist views . . . stands the national-state conception generated by a universalist-organic view of the world . . . whose first representative certainly was Adam Müller." Particular praise went to G.F. Knapp, who "gained great merit by breaking through the fog of the money theory." Gottfried Feder's "new principles for the creation of money" were "a further-developed political theory in the spirit of Knapp." Herrmann ascribed his demand to prevent competition and free enterprise in banking to "the past master of monetary theory, Adolf Wagner."[98]

One could easily compile endless pages of excerpts from Nazi publications before and after 1933, attempting to authenticate the traditional continuity of their ideas and proposals. Otto Strasser (who left the Nazi party in 1931 and fled Germany) told me in 1974 that he had studied under Werner Sombart in Berlin and that both he and his brother Gregor had frequently met with him and been influenced by him. According to Strasser, the more intelligent Nazis were also acquainted with earlier writers besides Sombart, like Schmoller and especially Wagner. Strasser labeled all these, including Walter Rathenau, as "heralds of Fascist ideas." He especially esteemed Wichard von Moellendorff, "who had already presented a model of state socialism in his war economy."

However, it was not only the Nazis who were eager to acquire a traditional pedigree. The reformer economists, lining up closer to rightist parties in the thirties, referred their ideas to the same tradition. In 1932 Ernst Wagemann emphasized the independent development of German monetary theory in a reference to Keynes: "Keynes would drop his eyes in shame if he had the opportunity to

97. Buchner, *Grundrisse*, pp. 16, 18, 21, 22, 37, 42.
98. Herrmann, *Giralgeldes*, pp. 18f., 40, 42.

look into the important writings by Adam Müller, Adolf Wagner, and others; with Knapp's writings he seems to be acquainted at least in translation."[99] Wagemann was a friend of von Moellendorff's and counted him among those who had assisted in working out details of the Wagemann Plan. A letter in von Moellendorff's personal estate reveals his hope to be recalled, through the good offices of Wagemann, to active participation in the direction of economic policy.[100] This hope was still unfulfilled at his death in 1937.

Gustav Stolper considered state economy the true core of the Nazis' actual economic policy. He regarded the structural economic developments following the establishment of Bismarck's Reich as a continuous process, consistently and almost inevitably leading to National Socialism: "Without the preliminary work done by their predecessors, Hitler and National Socialism would not have been possible.... Hitler had only to press a button for the previously prepared mechanism to start operating. His predecessors had already done whatever was necessary for him. The inclination toward state economy, alive in German history since the establishment of the Reich under Prussia's leadership, had now reached its climax."[101] Modern research cannot confirm this statement without qualification. I will try to describe in the next chapter how National Socialist economic policy was dictated by a mixture of immediate short-term needs and long-term ideological objectives. The success of this policy also arose from the application of new theoretical achievements. Nevertheless, the tradition described below played a considerable role, not only in the design of methods and the manner of their application but also in the choice of ideological goals. However, what tradition mainly contributed was to make the measures imposed by the Nazis theoretically admissible also in respectable company, that is, among scholars in economics and among influential businessmen.

99. Wagemann, *Geld und Kreditform*, p. 85.
100. E. Wagemann, "Zum Thema Geld- und Kreditform: Mißverständnisse und Irrtümer," *Wochenbericht des Instituts für Konjunkturforschung*, Jan. 27, 1932; BA, Nachlaß Moellendorff, H. Bachem to Moellendorff, Aug. 21, 1932.
101. Stolper, *German Economy*, Aug. 21, p. xi.

Chapter 3

Ideology and the Economy
The Institutional Framework

In January 1933, when the Nazis assumed power, over six million Germans were unemployed – more than 30 percent of the country's total labor force. Four years later, by the last quarter of 1936, the German economy had achieved full employment. Additional economic indicators also pointed to a rapid recovery from the slump, unparalleled by any other industrial country (see appendix, table 1). All this was due to an active countercyclical policy of deficit spending and monetary expansion, whose scope and dimensions were until then unprecedented in peacetime economies. As far as the German people were concerned, the Nazis had kept their promise: in the course of four years they had provided *Arbeit und Brot* (work and bread) for millions of unemployed. It was largely this achievement that yielded majority support for the Nazis among the Germans and won prestige abroad.

Were these achievements the result of preliminary planning by Nazi "experts"? May one regard the policies implemented as a consistent application of the economic principles I outlined at the beginning of this study? The answers to these questions have to be sought on two levels that are not necessarily interdependent: first, the personal and institutional level – the activity and influence of party bodies and their individual representatives concerning economic decision making and the execution of the same; second, the influence of ideological norms and theoretical concepts upon various sectors of economic activity. Such influence is possible even if there is no evidence of direct intervention by the party in a given economic sector. To wit, even if it be proven – as most scholars claim to the present day (wrongly, in my opinion) – that neither the party apparatus nor its functionaries had any direct influence on the formulation of economic policy, it still remains to be demonstrated to what extent this policy was dictated by basic principles, as defined within the Nazis' economic philosophy.

106

Given the current state of research, it is impossible to conduct a full-scale examination of this matter. Notwithstanding the large body of literature dealing with Nazi economic policy that has been accumulating since the thirties, specific studies of many important sectors are still missing. Without such studies it is difficult to give a comprehensive and well-founded answer to the questions posed here. Most existing studies discuss the German economy as a whole and present theoretical generalizations intended to define the characteristics of the regime. The discussion focuses on rearmament and war preparations, while economic development during the initial years is somewhat neglected. To date no thorough research has been carried out on banking or on the system of wage and price controls in the Third Reich. We also lack research on the influence that party institutions had upon various economic sectors, upon individual enterprises, and within the regions dominated by Gauleiters. It follows that the description presented below necessarily includes numerous blank areas, and considerable parts of the argument have to rely on fragmentary evidence. My discussion should therefore be regarded as a first attempt at providing a view different from the one accepted by the majority of scholars – which will have to be completed and perhaps rectified in terms of various details through specific future research.

The Economic Party Establishment

The fact that all economic portfolios in Hitler's first coalition government (January 30, 1933) went to traditional rightists was part of the political compromise that brought about the establishment of this government. Alfred Hugenberg, leader of the DNVP, became minister of both economics and agriculture; Count Schwerin von Krosigk was appointed minister of finance; Franz Seldte, leader of the militant nationalist association Stahlhelm became minister of labor. Nazi *Staatssekretäre* (assistant ministers) were added only three to four months later: Fritz Reinhart to the Ministry of Finance, Gottfried Feder to the Ministry of Economics, and Konstantin Hierl to the Ministry of Labor. On the surface it appeared that the objective the right-wing bourgeoisie had set for itself, namely, "to confine the Nazis within appropriate boundaries," had been fully achieved, at least in the economic sphere.[1]

1. Martin Broszat, *Der Staat Hitlers* (1st ed. 1969) (Munich, 1974), pp. 83ff.

As in all other spheres, this illusion was short-lived. Hugenberg had already become aware of this fact in May 1933 and said so quite clearly in an unpublished interview with the editor in chief of the *Leipziger Neueste Nachrichten*: "We had better refrain from illusions. The National Socialists have a candidate ready for every senior position in all spheres. For the time being they still need us as window dressing, but there are ministers in line for all offices. It is no secret, indeed, that Darré is going to receive the Ministry of Agriculture, Feder the Ministry of Economics. . . . Although we were promised a free hand with regard to economic ills, we now find that our partners have ideas of their own on how to end the economic crisis and that the ideologists Feder and Darré work on projects of their own."[2]

"Projects of their own" prevailed mainly among rank-and-file party members, who were unfamiliar with the intricacies of higher politics. These members were also in a hurry to realize the paragraphs of the Nazi platform in the sphere of economics. Self-appointed SA commissioners mushroomed everywhere, conducting raids on Jewish department stores and business enterprises and generating an atmosphere of unrest and insecurity in the economy. It was presumably this state of affairs that made Hugenberg appoint Otto Wagener, jointly with an industrialist from his own party (the DNVP), as national commissioners for the economy, agriculture excepted.[3] The appointment became valid on May 3, 1933. At the same time Wagener also headed the economics department at the Coordination Headquarters of the Nazi party in Berlin. According to Wagener's own evidence, his appointment came as a surprise not only to himself – it had been made without preliminary consultation with Hitler. The Führer's consent was finally obtained only after some procrastination and with rather bad grace.[4] Wagener's evidence sounds reasonable if we recall that in September 1932 he had been dismissed from his position as head of the WPA in Munich (see above). For two months, until his dismissal from both jobs on July 12, 1933, Wagener therefore held a focal economic position, and his office in Berlin attracted droves of visitors from every sector of the economy.[5] He believed that his main task was to impose

2. Hugenberg-Breiting Interview, unpublished, by courtesy of the late Prof. Dr. Friedrich Zipfel, Berlin.
3. *Völkischer Beobachter*, May 4, 1933.
4. BDC, OPG-Akte Otto Wagener, Antrag vom 22.1.1934.
5. Interview with Dr. Dräger, May 1974.

order and to prevent unauthorized activities by party members and organizations – a move that earned him considerable esteem in business circles. Following his dismissal, the chiefs of the RDI expressed their gratitude in a special circular letter for his "valuable aid and active support during the reorganization of industrial associations and in particular for his protection of the economy from unwarranted alien interference in associations and enterprises."[6]

Wagener's dismissal from government and party offices came when Hugenberg was replaced by the new minister of economics, Kurt Schmitt (formerly general manager of the largest German insurance company, Allianz). Göring, who was the principal force behind Schmitt's appointment, provided the main initiative. The immediate pretext for Wagener's dismissal was a number of telephone calls from his Berlin office, recorded by the Gestapo. In these conversations some of his senior assistants had tried to recruit support for the appointment of Wagener as minister of economics. He himself claimed, in talks with Hitler and Göring and later before a party court, that he had been ignorant of these calls and had not aspired to this office at all. According to his plea before the same court, Wagener had a much greater aspiration: to strengthen and expand his job as commissioner for the economy, with the intention of turning it "perhaps only after many years . . . [into] a ministry embracing all sectors of the economy . . . in order to replace the system of economic liberalism with a National Socialist system."[7]

Wagener subsequently disappeared from the public arena, and some of his supporters who had been involved in those telephone calls were sent to concentration camps. However, the manner of his appointment and dismissal does not tally with the widespread interpretation that radical party members representing middle-class interests were weeded out under pressure from big business.[8] This is not to say that such a struggle did not take place, but on the individual level the Wagener case cannot serve as evidence of a struggle. Hugenberg appointed him in order to restrain party activists, and Wagener did his best to fulfill this assignment. It appears more reasonable to consider his appointment and dismissal as part of a general shift that occurred in the sphere of economics during the initial months of Nazi rule.

Hugenberg's resignation was a decisive step toward dissolution of

6. BA, R 13/1, no. 71, Rundschreiben vom 14.7.1933.
7. BDC, OPG-Akte Otto Wagener, Antrag vom 22.1.1934.
8. See, for example, Schweitzer, *Big Business*, pp. 248f.

the coalition government and the consolidation of exclusive Nazi rule. Hugenberg's forecast only partly materialized: Darré indeed inherited the Ministry of Agriculture, but the Ministry of Economics went to Schmitt and not to Feder – who became second *Staatssekretär* to Schmitt. A year later, when Schacht replaced Schmitt, he sacked Feder on the very day he assumed office. In May 1935 Schacht was appointed minister plenipotentiary for war economy, in addition to his office as temporary minister of economics and president of the central bank – a combination that for some time turned him into a kind of economic dictator with extensive authority.[9]

Besides ending Wagener's career, his dismissal designates a new stage in the organization of the party's agencies and their activity in the sphere of economics. On July 7, 1933, Hitler summoned the *Reichsstatthalter* (Reich commissioners) to his Berlin office to instruct them in his desired procedures of administration. He sharply criticized methods of boycott and violence in economic matters: "The revolution is not a permanent state of affairs. . . . The liberated current of revolution has to be guided into the safe channel of evolution. . . . We will not abolish unemployment through commissioners for economics, committees, organizations, and theories. . . . Our strongest authority will arise from the creation of jobs. . . . The Reich commissioners were to see to it and were accountable to the chancellor – that no party agencies or institutions usurped government authority in order to dismiss individuals and seize official positions . . . a task only the central government is authorized to fulfill, and with regard to the economy, the minister of economics. The party has become a state. All power is now in the hands of the Reich's government."[10]

Wagener's office in Berlin was dismantled, and party agencies dealing with economic matters were put under the authority of Wilhelm Keppler, who simultaneously held the government office of emissary of the Reichskanzler for the economy. Keppler also controlled the supreme economic party body at the Munich Brown House, the Kommission für Wirtschaftspolitik (Committee for Economic Policy) headed by Bernhard Köhler, and the *Gauwirtschaftsberater* (regional economic advisers, subject to the Gauleiter

9. Broszat, *Der Staat Hitlers*, p. 223; Schweitzer, "Organisierter Kapitalismus," pp. 43ff.

10. *Frankfurter Zeitung*, Oct. 28, 1933.

of their region).[11]

The swiftness of Schmitt's appointment during the organizational reshuffle following Wagener's dismissal can be read in various ways. Some consider it part of an agreement between Hitler and Schmitt, as the representative of big business supported by the army, according to which management of the economy was left exclusively to leading industrialists, thereby denying any party intervention in economic matters.[12] Yet no real documentary evidence has been found for the existence of such an agreement, and subsequent developments do not confirm it either. It seems much more probable that the appointment was an attempt to overcome the chaos of the initial months and impose order on the economy, as in all other spheres, by means of the state apparatus. From the organizational angle this aim was later achieved by appointing a single person – Wilhelm Keppler – to the supreme office on the governmental as well as the party level.

Such a concentration of authority at least made it possible for Keppler to assume a position of considerable weight. At the time he took part in all important consultations, sat together with Feder on the committee inquiring into the banking system, and was a permanent member of the board of the central bank.[13] He was also the final arbiter of allocations from state employment budgets for private enterprises.[14] His utterances and appearances in public received substantial press coverage, and he was frequently appealed to and consulted by members of the economic community.[15]

Yet Keppler did not ultimately achieve a position of real power, presumably because of his weak personality and rather mediocre abilities. According to von Krosigk, Keppler was "not particularly bright and was naive and limited in a rather one-sided way. He was frequently criticized in economic circles, but people in weighty positions just ignored him."[16] In his evidence after the war, Darré emphasized Keppler's great influence with Hitler, but he also stated that, owing to his character and limited talents, Keppler had not utilized "great possibilities to bring his power to bear on economic policy since he was a somewhat peculiar loner." Because of this

11. *Frankfurter Zeitung*, Sept. 1, 1933.
12. Schweitzer, *Big Business*, p. 1221.
13. *Frankfurter Zeitung*, Oct. 28, 1933.
14. BA, R 2, no. 18630.
15. Interview with Count Schwerin von Krosigk, June 1974; K.V. Krogmann diaries, HF, 11/K5, pp. 8–9.
16. Interview with Schwerin von Krosigk.

Darré thought that Keppler had largely become a puppet in the hands of others,[17] like Himmler's secretary Kranefuß, Funk, and von Ribbentrop.

It seems that Schacht also knew how to exploit Keppler in his intrigues against Schmitt and in the enhancement of his own position with Hitler, who appointed him minister of economics.[18] One should also remember that within the party Keppler was a newcomer who had not participated in the formulation of its platform or its economic projects before the Nazi takeover. His principal task was to serve as liaison officer between Hitler and industrial circles. Later on he was given executive assignments in which he apparently failed to distinguish himself. There is no evidence that identifies Keppler with a particular interest group, as some scholars, in particular East Germans, have repeatedly claimed.

Even if Keppler had been more gifted and had established himself as a bona fide decision maker, this would still not prove the continuation of the party's influence in economic matters. From the time of Keppler's appointment, the party's role was clearly defined as exclusively political, educational, and propagandist. The Munich committee headed by Köhler had no executive role. Its main task was to build up "the party's economic field troops, whose nucleus consisted of the regional economic advisers."[19] To achieve this end, Köhler, who directed the committee until his death in 1939, developed widespread propaganda activities. By means of a large apparatus consisting of about sixty employees and numerous volunteer assistants recruited from various economic sectors, he organized courses and seminars for economic functionaries in the administration, in science, and in business. These seminars, and Köhler's own public lectures in particular, were widely covered by the media, a sign that this activity by the party and the chief of its economic committee was considered important.

One wonders therefore why present-day research hardly mentions either the activity itself, or Köhler's personality, or the role he played. Nor has the influence of the regional economic advisers or the Gauleiters themselves on economic matters been subjected to serious inquiry. We will see that on a number of important issues these officials did not shy away from intervention in economic decisions, whether on the practical level, on matters of principle, or

17. IfZ, ED 110, pp. 439–45.
18. Ibid. and K.V. Krogmann diaries, HF, 11/K5, pp. 8–9.
19. BDC, PK, Personalakte Bernhard Köhler.

on issues concerning individual firms or personalities. The extent of their influence appears to have varied according to the measure of executive power each Gauleiter had achieved in his region. Köhler and the Munich committee maintained close and permanent contact with these officials and increasingly extended their activities over the years. What is documented beyond doubt is the central role the economic advisers played in the Aryanization of Jewish business enterprises. Every single "purchase" of a Jewish business had to be cleared by them, and in most cases they also determined the ridiculous price paid in these transactions, seeing to it that the juiciest bits went to party veterans.[20] From the beginning of 1936 the committee printed an internal monthly entitled *Mittelungen der Kommission für Wirtschaftspolitik der NSDAP*, which was for party members only and was accompanied by an explicit ban on further publication of excerpts from it. Köhler himself explained the ban as stemming from the bulletin's aim "to distinguish between those who are merely camp followers and those who wish to act . . . those who help within the party, its branches and associations, to carry out the work of the Committee for Economic Policy."[21]

What the bulletin published (repeated by Köhler with tedious monotony in all his lectures) was a consistent rehash of the basic principles that informed the Nazis' economic philosophy: primacy of politics; the right to work, namely, full employment as the primary objective of economic policy, to which capitalist interests had to be subjugated; and "freedom of sustenance" for the German people through the extension of their *Lebensraum*. There was also no lack of topical demands, like the lowering of interest rates[22] or thinly disguised criticism of Schacht because he asked for a return to regular international trade.[23] In one of his last speeches Köhler defined his committee's activity under the significant heading, "We Who Stand Guard!" Although the committee had as its primary task the continued indoctrination of everyone involved in any kind of economic activity, it also served as a watchdog in everyday

20. Helmut Genschel, *Die Verdrängung der Juden aus der Wirtschaft im Dritten Reich* (Göttingen, 1966), pp. 151f. and passim; Staatsarchiv Münster, Gauwirtschaftsberater, Gauleitung Westfalen-Süd, nos. 63; 682; 483; 676; 585, etc.

21. Bernhard Köhler, "Die Mitteilungen nur für Parteigenossen?" *Mitteilungen der Kommission für Wirtschaftspolitik der NSDAP München* 2, no. 1 (1937): 1–2.

22. W. Scheunemann, "NS-Programm und Wirtschaftspolitik: Brechung der Zinsknechtschaft," *Mitteilungen der Kommission für Wirtschaftspolitik der NSDAP München* 1, no. 5 (1936): 12.

23. Ibid., p. 15.

113

practice as well as in ideological matters: "We have to keep our eye on the German economy in order to report to the Führer and to those appointed by him what we see – and do so by the shortest possible route, as he has ordered us to do."[24] This speech, published after Köhler's death, was accompanied by a eulogy for the man who "had put the economy under the party flag."[25]

Given the present state of research, it is hard to determine how far this definition was accurate or simply wishful thinking. It is never-theless clear that the Nazis did not abandon the principles of their economic philosophy and that they tried systematically to plant them in the minds of their functionaries. We will see below that this activity had definite practical implications for some sectors of the economy. However, it seems that to define the economy as oper-ating under a "Gauleiter dictatorship"[26] is an unsubstantiated exag-geration. At the time, Hitler's inclination "not to frighten the economy" but to secure its voluntary cooperation was still domi-nant and even aroused some resentment and impatience among party veterans. They complained that the twenty-five point party program had not yet been fully realized, but they still expressed the hope that it would soon be time "to realize an economic and social order that fits the party platform to the largest possible extent."[27] Party publications devoted considerable effort to reinforcing this belief. The editor of the *Jahrbuch für nationalsozialistische Wirt-schaft* for 1935 admitted that not all objectives had yet been achieved, but "today the most urgent task is to provide work for all our people. . . . The burden is so great and heavy that for the time being ideas of building a National Socialist economy must wait."[28] Another contributor to the same yearbook once again presented the well-known economic demands for an emphasis on agriculture and resettlement "to replace the profit-oriented economy by one that aims to provide utilities." He explained that although the process would take time, it would ultimately be accomplished.[29]

Goebbels's newspaper was more explicit and radical. Under the

24. Europäisches Wirtschaftszentrum, *Reden und Vorträge auf dem 6. Großen Lehrgang der Kommission für Wirtschaftspolitik der NSDAP* (Munich, 1939), p. 22.
25. Ibid., p. 9.
26. See, for example, Treue and Frede, *Wirtschaft und Politik*, p. 10.
27. H. Bräutigam, *Wirtschaftssystem des Nationalsozialismus: Probleme neuzeitli-cher Wirtschaftsgestaltung*, 3d ed. (Berlin, 1936), p. iv.
28. Otto Mönckmeier, ed., *Jahrbuch für nationalsozialistische Wirtschaft*, pt. 1, *Die nationalsozialistische Wirtschaftsordnung* (Stuttgart and Berlin, 1935), pp. 4f.
29. Hans Buwert in Mönckmeier, ed., *Jahrbuch*, pt. 1, p. 35.

heading "To Overcome Capitalism," it attacked "well-known economic leaders" and "certain economic reporters" who overemphasized, according to the paper, capitalist aspects of the German economy: in conclusion, "one should stress the point that we have no complaint against capitalism as an economic technique, but we strongly reject any attempt to justify demands for leadership in economic policy by prevailing economic circumstances."[30] All these Nazi publications stressed the temporary character of existing arrangements. For the time being the urgent need to end unemployment imposed a slowdown on the realization of ideological party principles, but these had not been abandoned and their time would indeed come. Meanwhile the Nazis voiced their satisfaction at having secured control of the state and at the state's dominant position in the sphere of economics. The notorious Otto Ohlendorff, head of the Economic-Scientific Department at the Ministry of Economics (who was tried after the war and executed as a war criminal), formulated the issue in the same manner: In time the party's economic demands, even those "that were previously called middle-class policies," would be fulfilled. Until that day it was sufficient "that the economy be subjected at all to the guidelines of National Socialist policy, a conscious national policy that determines the sphere of activity for the economy and controls the manner of execution."[31]

The conclusion arising from Ohlendorff's view is that during the period under discussion the party's economic agencies had only indirect influence on economic decision making. Further on I will examine the effects of this influence, which operated through the regional economic advisers and hundreds of officials who had attended obligatory party training courses. The handing over of executive economic power to the state did in fact tally with the Nazi concept of the state's role in the economy. The party establishment was responsible for ideological indoctrination and reassurance of those members who criticized the failure to realize some economic goals in the "unchangeable" 1920 party platform. The urgency of current tasks was explained, and party members were assured that "come better times" the platform would be fully realized. There are indications that the Nazi leadership had indeed not abandoned these goals altogether.

30. "Überwindung des Kapitalismus," *Der Angriff*, Dec. 20, 1935.
31. BA, R 7, no. 1246, pp. 106ff.

Nazi Economics

The Corporate Structure: Self-Management or Transmission of Orders?

25. For the realization of all this, we demand the creation of a powerful central body of the Reich. Absolute authority of the central political parliament over the entire Reich and all its organizations. The establishment of corporate and professional chambers [*Stände und Berufskammern*] for implementation of the framework of laws, passed by the Reich, in all individual states.[32]

This paragraph from the 1920 Nazi platform generated the claim that, under the influence of an ideology widespread in particular among the middle classes, the Nazis favored a corporate structure for the economy. Othmar Spann's universal school was at the time the outstanding exponent of this ideology. During the twenties and thirties the term corporate structure (*berufsständischer Aufbau*) appeared repeatedly in Nazi publications as well as in those of other conservative groups in Germany. It designated the modeling of economic and social organization on preindustrial society, namely, in corporate professional bodies of workers and employers that would take care of conflicting interests in industrial relations, competition, prices, and the market in a more or less autonomous manner. Antiliberalist tendencies in Germany found support in the traditional corporate aspirations of the urban and rural middle classes: representatives of artisan and retail-trade interests believed that economic protectionism and restrictions on capitalist mobility of workers would shield them from industrial competition and liberalist free enterprise. The proportion of these social strata among party members and Nazi voters was relatively high from the start, and it rose from 1929 on, owing to the economic crisis and the resulting radicalization of the middle classes.[33] Since the corporate idea provided these aspirations with a comprehensive basis, it is not surprising that the Nazi platform adopted it. One should, however, note that the paragraph quoted above subordinates the call for the establishment of corporations to the demand for a strong central government of the Reich. Corporate chambers were to be created only on the level of individual states (*in einzelnen Bundesstaaten*).

32. "Das Programm der NSDAP," reprinted in Hofer, ed., *Nationalsozialismus*, pp. 28f.
33. H.A. Winkler, *Mittelstand, Demokratie und Nationalsozialismus – Die politische Entwicklung von Handwerk und Kleinhandel in der Weimarer Republik* (Cologne, 1972), passim.

This distinction is significant in terms of the following argument.

We have already seen that Othmar Spann's corporate conception strongly emphasized medieval tradition. In opposition to parliamentary democracy, this school presented the model of an authoritarian and hierarchical society based on corporate associations that conducted economic affairs with considerable scope for self-management. Within this structure the state was to occupy the position of a supreme *Stand* of its own, forming the peak of the corporate pyramid. The corporations, joined at the top in a general Corporate or Economic Chamber, were to manage the economy and thereby release the state from its economic and social obligations. Thus the state would be at liberty to act in the political sphere, over which it had absolute authority, as the supreme political "estate," free from the constraints of conflicting economic interests.[34]

Throughout the Weimar period large sections of the middle classes regarded these concepts as an answer to their prayers. The envisioned corporate associations were to be closed, hierarchical structures whose growth would be limited by severe rules of occupational training for anyone wanting to join the organization. Artisans and small traders could therefore consider them a means of protecting themselves against multiple competitors and a mechanism for regulating competition, marketing, and prices in the face of increasing encroachment from industry, department stores, and marketing networks operated by consumer cooperatives. On the other hand, conservative revolution circles as well as the Nazis utilized this ideology in their struggle against Marxism and democracy, against which Spann had declared war – the primary goal of his school – as early as 1920.[35]

The Nazis established relations with Spann and his school very early. In his official interpretation of the party platform Feder eulogized Spann and described the projected realization of Nazi plans as a triumph of "the approaching universalist social order of the True State." Feder also attended courses Spann gave to a select group of politicians and businessmen at a monastery, with the aim of disseminating his theories.[36] On account of his early ties with Spann, Feder was later censured by an internal party publication because he had tried to commit the party to an ideology that was

34. Heinrich, *Das Ständewesen*, pp. 280f.
35. Spann, *Der wahre Staat*, p. 298.
36. Schneller, *Zwischen Romantik und Faschismus*, pp. 165f.

basically alien, although it also fought Marxism and liberalism.[37]

At the end of the twenties the reciprocal relations between the Spann school and the Nazis were a well-known fact. There were some still unproven rumors of regular confidential meetings between Hitler and Spann to coordinate positions and determine party policies on economic matters.[38] A newspaper article told of Hitler appearing at a lecture Spann gave at Munich University in March 1929 on "Die Verjudung der Philosophie" (The Judaization of philosophy). Hitler was received with stormy applause and words of welcome and exchanged "handshakes and deep bows with Othmar Spann" at the end.[39] Otto Wagener also mentions relations with the universalist school in his records, which tell of a series of lectures by Walter Heinrich, one of the school's outstanding exponents, given at Hitler's special request.[40]

These connections and their severance after the Nazis attained power are often presented as evidence that the Nazi movement was basically middle class in character and that it abandoned its most loyal supporters after assuming office.[41] This claim does not stand up to examination, in the first place because Spann's concepts do not represent unequivocal middle-class interests. Artisan and small-trade associations that adopted some of these ideas did so with numerous qualifications and in the hope of recruiting support for their demands from beyond their own, narrow interest group, that is, from all divisions of the antidemocratic, conservative camp.[42] Nor did the National Socialist party ever fully identify with Spann's theory; it merely adopted some concepts and slogans that tallied with its own views, interpreting them in the spirit of the latter. Whether deliberately or not, the Nazis in this way came closer to the conservative revolution, that is, respectable opposition to democracy and liberalism, and therefore gained in prestige and legitimacy throughout the whole conservative camp.[43] Thus the corporate order (*Stände-Ordnung*) temporarily served as a broad common basis, with Spann and his followers emphasizing the

37. *Der Hoheitsträger*, Mar. 1937, pp. 17–19.
38. BA, R 11, no. 10, Prof. Kanter to Eduard Hamm, Sept. 21, 1932.
39. *Die Neue Welt*, Mar. 8, 1929, quoted by K.J. Siegfried, "Universalismus und Faschismus: Zur historischen Wirksamkeit und politischen Funktion der universalistischen Gesellschaftslehre und Ständekonzeption Othmar Spanns" (dissertation, Philipps-Universität Marburg, 1973), p. 228n.
40. IfZ, ED 60, pp. 1646ff.
41. See, for example, Hermann Lebovics, *Social Conservatism*, pp. 133ff.
42. Winkler, *Mittelstand*, pp. 152f.
43. Schulz in Bracher, Sauer, and Schulz, *Machtergreifung*, p. 400.

Stände and the Nazis stressing the dictatorial order by which the state ruled the economy.

Differences of opinion between the Nazis and the Spann school began well before January 1933. Otto Wagener stated in his postwar writings that Hitler had all along rejected Spann's theory,[44] and Hans Buchner had already described the corporate concepts of "a few theoreticians" in his 1930 study with definite reservations: "In principle National Socialism approaches the question of corporations and the manner of their theoretical or practical realization with the premise that all economic norms of activity and organization must be subject to political authority. Only from the idea of a *völkisch* state, its realization and the ensuing form of the state, does economic and social theory acquire meaning, significance, and life."[45]

Differences of opinion did not remain limited to matters of theory. In December 1931 Spann asked one of his friends, a lawyer, to sue the Großdeutscher Pressedienst newspaper, which had accused him of anti-Nazi activities: "This is truly the height of impudence . . . to accuse me of undermining the NSDAP – and with the aid of the Catholic Zentrum party no less!" An inquiry revealed that the culprit was the official bulletin of Wagener's WPA. Spann was advised to talk to the editors in order to settle the affair out of court.[46]

Besides different approaches to racial theory, the ideological controversy between Spann and his followers and the Nazis principally concerned the extent of autonomy to be granted to the self-management of economic corporations. This was the reason that well-established industrial circles and their various associations adopted corporate demands, referring to the alleged previous commitment of the Nazi party to this approach. Once the Nazis were in power, the main support for Spann and related groups came from this quarter and not from the middle class. In a confidential file on the activities of the Spann circle compiled by the Gestapo in 1936, support by large-scale industry, objections to racial theory, and attachment to the Catholic church appeared as major accusations: "Spann's corporate theory is nowadays primarily voiced by those who consider the National Socialist party and the National Socialist weltanschauung a threat to their own sphere of influence. This is

44. IfZ, ED 60, pp. 1646ff.
45. Hans Buchner, *Grundrisse*, p. 36.
46. BDC, SS-O Akte Wilhelm Höttel.

especially true with regard to big industry, which fears the shaping of the economy in the spirit of National Socialism, but it is also true of big farmers who do not want to hand over agricultural corporations to National Socialists; and the same goes for science . . . and the Church." The file goes on to say: "The only power to whom the Spann circle has always been loyal so far is large-scale industry, which provides the circle with money. The Spann circle has always represented their interests."[47]

An especially eager and active supporter of Spann was Fritz Thyssen. Owing to his early ties with Hitler and the financial support he had gained for the party, he succeeded in the spring of 1933 in obtaining Hitler's consent to establish an Institute for Corporate Research (Institut für Ständewesen) at Düsseldorf. The institute engaged in a wide range of scientific and propaganda activities until 1935, when it was closed by the Gestapo. One of the institute's directors, Joseph Klein, a veteran party member, was appointed as *Treuhänder der Arbeit* (labor trustee) for the district of Westphalia. The scientific director of the institute, Paul Karrenbrock, had been a party member from 1931; both were connected to Otto Wagener's WPA from 1930 to 1932.[48] For many years Karrenbrock was also scientific adviser to the Association of Industrialists in Rhineland-Westphalia, which represented the interests of Germany's heavy industries. In the latter capacity he sharply fought the Nazis' militant middle-class association, the Kampfbund für den Gewerblichen Mittelstand (*gewerblich*, as distinguished from the liberal professions and agriculture).[49] All this confirms that, faced with the Nazi party's demand for absolute authority, large-scale industry regarded a corporate structure as a suitable framework for the preservation of some independence – and perhaps as a means for promoting monopolistic interests as well.[50] They also hoped to find such organizations useful in protecting themselves against inroads by the National Socialist workers' organization, Deutsche Arbeitsfront (DAF, German Labor Front), which strove to gain a dominant position within industrial enterprises.

It was therefore not accidental that DAF leader Robert Ley and other party departments had already launched their attack on the

47. IfZ, Dc. 15. 15, SD-Akte der Spannkreis, 1936, pp. 3 and 10, respectively.
48. IfZ, ED 60, pp. 1646ff.
49. Siegfried, "Universalismus und Faschismus," p. 263.
50. Franz Neumann, *Behemoth: The Structure and Practice of National Socialism* (London, 1943), pp. 191f.; Schulz, p. 643.

Düsseldorf institute in the fall of 1934. An outstanding figure in this group was Max Frauendorfer, head of the party's Bureau for Corporate Structure, who claimed after the war that he had, in fact, never wielded any real influence.[51] The victor in this fray, which went on for a few months, was the party apparatus. Thyssen's appeals to Göring and Hitler were of no avail. Wilhelm Keppler voiced his explicit objection to the continued activity of the institute, and Hitler had Thyssen informed that it was to be closed down and that he altogether rejected Spann's and Heinrich's views.[52]

Controversy between the Nazis and the Spann circle became increasingly sharper in 1935 and 1936, when it focused on racial theory and anti-Semitism. It seems that Spann's followers had given up the attempt to become part of the prevailing regime by emphasizing ideological similarities. They now tried to gain support for their positions in congenial circles by stressing the difference between their views and the demands presented by the regime's ideological totalitarianism. Their magazine published a series of articles against racial theory; Karrenbrock compiled a special brochure on the subject and sent it to about three hundred prominent officials in the administration, the armed forces, and the academic community.[53] This brochure served as one of the pretexts for Karrenbrock's arrest and his expulsion from the party. The papers seized in his flat became the basis for an extensive confidential file compiled and disseminated as top secret information by the Gestapo in 1936. Spann, whose Viennese party membership card was unnumbered and dated May 1, 1933, asked in 1938, after the *Anschluß* of Austria, to be reaccepted by the party. His request was denied by a supreme party court on account of ideological incompatibility.[54] Thyssen emigrated from Germany in 1939.[55]

These events were a sequel to the 1933–34 debate on the nature of corporate structure and the extent of independence to be ceded to economic self-management bodies. The team at the Düsseldorf institute, backed by an influential group in heavy industry, aspired to more than de facto authority for autonomous management: they sought to sponsor legislative initiatives aimed at securing extensive

51. IfZ, ZS 1821.
52. BA, R 43/II, 527b.
53. Siegfried, "Universalismus und Faschismus," pp. 308ff.; IfZ, Dc. 15. 15, SD-Akte der Spannkreis, 1936, pp. 3 and 10, respectively.
54. BDC, PK, Personalakte Othmar Spann.
55. Broszat, *Der Staat Hitlers*, pp. 226f.

freedom of action for economic self-management bodies.[56] What the Nazis actually established was similar only in terminology, the substance being entirely different. Utilizing in a quite sophisticated manner the framework of industrialist and employers' associations left over from the Weimar Republic, they created, at the latest in the fall of 1934 (following a series of trials and tactical maneuvers), an institutional system whose principal task was to transmit instructions to all economic sectors, "an organization that merely received orders from the government."[57]

At the time the Nazis took power, representation of economic interests was well established on two levels. On the horizontal territorial level all industrial and commercial enterprises were obligatory members of local or regional Chambers of Commerce and Industry; as these came under public law, membership dues were collected by the government-revenue administration. At the top all Chambers of Commerce and Industry were joined in an umbrella organization, the Deutscher Industrie- und Handelstag (DIHT, Council of German Industry and Trade). On the vertical occupational level there were branch associations operating on a voluntary basis. The strongest and most influential of these was the RDI. Agriculture and crafts were organized on similar lines in territorial Chambers of Agriculture and Crafts and national associations representing branch interests, which I will discuss in greater detail below. In addition, industrialists belonged to the Deutscher Unternehmerverband (Employers' Association), which represented them in confrontations with trade unions on matters of wages and labor conditions. The largest of the trade unions was the ADGB, led in practice, though not by statute, by the SPD.

unums

The Nazis' first move was to abolish all trade unions. These, including the ADGB, tried in vain to survive by an arrangement with the new regime according to which they would accept its organizational and political authority.[58] Even the unions' appeals to the masses of German workers to attend the 1933 May Day celeb-

---

56. For example, K. Peterson in *Braune Wirtschaftspost* 3, no. 2 (1934–35): 1057f., quoted by Siegfried, "Universalismus und Faschismus," p. 283.

57. R.H. Rämisch, "Die berufsständische Verfassung in Theorie und Praxis des Nationalsozialismus" (dissertation, Freie Universität Berlin, 1957), p. 83; the same conclusion is found in Kroll, *Weltwirtschaftskrise* (Berlin, 1958), pp. 540f.; Carroll, *Design for Total War*, p. 83.

58. Dieter v. Lölhöffel, "Die Umwandlung der Gewerkschaften in eine nationalsozialistische Zwangsorganisation," in I. Esenwein-Rothe, *Die Wirtschaftsverbände von 1933 bis 1945* (Berlin, 1965), pp. 152ff.

rations (which Goebbels, in a shrewd propaganda move, renamed "The Day of National Labor") were of no avail. At ten o'clock on the following morning all trade union offices were seized. Their considerable assets were impounded and transferred to the DAF. Subsequently all smaller unions announced their "voluntary" abdication and joined the DAF.[59]

German Labor Front

However, these events still did not solve the problem of labor organizations in the National Socialist state. Abolition of the trade union network generated a struggle that went on below the surface for some months. The active core of the newly established DAF was the proletarian element among the party members and functionaries who were members of the Nationalsozialistische Betriebszellen Organisation (NSBO, National Socialist Organization of Shop Stewards). Besides receiving the assets and property of the sacked trade unions, they also aspired to fill the role the unions had played, that is, to represent the social and economic interests of the working class in the new state. The ambiguity of Hitler's attitude to organized labor left sufficient room for maneuver among conflicting interests. *Mein Kampf* allowed for trade union bargaining to regulate industrial relations and settle conflicting economic interests, as long as "no National Socialist state exists."[60] Although Gregor Strasser had been sacked, NSBO activists still adhered to his widely publicized opinion that trade unions "are as necessary and, in a certain sense, as entitled to represent the professional, economic, and class interests of wage earners as employer associations."[61] In the spring of 1933 the NSBO leader, loyal to this view, composed an organizational blueprint according to which the DAF was conceived as an umbrella organization that was to include employer associations alongside two trade unions of employees. The unions were to consist of fourteen workers' and nine office-personnel associations, on the lines of the professional organization scheme of the abolished unions. This was, in fact, a plan to preserve the existing trade union structure under NSBO leadership.[62]

It soon became clear that the Nazi leadership harbored entirely different plans. On November 27, 1933, DAF leader Robert Ley,

59. Ibid., pp. 156f.
60. Hitler, *Mein Kampf*, p. 677; H.A. Turner, Jr., "Hitlers Einstellung," pp. 105–11.
61. Strasser's speech, Nov. 15, 1931, quoted by Lölhöffel, "Die Umwandlung," p. 148.
62. H.G. Schumann, *Nationalsozialismus und Gewerkschaftsbewegung* (Hannover, 1958), pp. 285f.; Broszat, *Der Staat Hitlers*, p. 184.

Minister of Economics Kurt Schmitt, and Minister of Labor Franz Seldte published a call to "all creatively working Germans," which disposed of the blueprint once and for all. Instead, DAF membership was individual for workers and employers alike. The Front was explicitly forbidden to intervene in economic or social policy. Its role was exclusively "to educate . . . for a National Socialist state and National Socialist views." A few days later, on December 7, 1933, all branch unions were dismantled and the DAF as a whole incorporated into the NSDAP. To reinforce this arrangement the DAF leader, Robert Ley, was also appointed chief of staff of the party's Political Organization.[63]

The dismantling of all trade unions, even if under Nazi leadership, was completed by legislation. The Law for the Regulation of National Labor[64] explicitly banned all intervention by DAF or NSBO representatives in negotiations over wages or labor conditions in individual enterprises. In May 1934 Ley added an instruction of his own in the same spirit, spuriously announcing that such negotiations would be conducted by a central Action Committee for the Protection of German Labor – a body that was never to materialize.[65] In reality the Law for the Regulation of National Labor reaffirmed the unrestricted authority of state-appointed *Treuhänder der Arbeit* over wage rates and labor conditions which had been "temporarily" vested in them by the law of May 19, 1933, "until the accomplishment of new social legislation."[66] These labor trustees were accountable to the minister of labor – meaning that the state had direct control of and exclusive authority over the entire field of wage and labor conditions. All that was left for the DAF, besides its "educational" role, was some measure of control over sanitary conditions at workplaces. All its attempts to utilize this limited control to achieve some influence on labor conditions were usually of no avail.

Nevertheless, one should not disparage the psychological and propagandist impact of DAF activities. Under the slogan of the "nobility of labor," it succeeded in gaining widespread support among workers – especially by means of entertainment, excursions, and holiday arrangements offered by the mass organization Kraft

63. Siegfried, "Universalismus und Faschismus," pp. 291f.; Broszat, *Der Staat Hitlers*, p. 184; Rämisch, "Verfassung," p. 85.
64. Gesetz zur Ordnung der nationalen Arbeit (AOG) vom 20. Januar 1934, RGB1. I, p. 45.
65. *Arbeitertum*, May 15, 1933.
66. Gesetz über Treuhänder der Arbeit vom 19. Mai 1933, RGB1. I, p. 285.

durch Freude (Strength through Joy). The ensuing atmosphere at least fostered an illusion of enhanced esteem and equality – a kind of status revolution within the Third Reich: "The loss of liberté . . . was practically linked with the promotion of égalité, an equality exploited propagandistically in every Nazi-organisation and every Nazi-demonstration. . . . From our point of view it may have been slavery, but it was not necessarily slavery from the point of view of the contemporary. Or alternatively, it was a slavery which he shared with his former masters and thus a form of equality or even liberation."[67]

None of this really showed, except perhaps in joint May Day marches of workers and employers or similar celebrations. Industrial relations were determined by the "leader principle," by which employers became *Betriebsführer* (enterprise leaders) of their employees, who were subject to their undisputed authority. This principle tallied with traditional demands of German employers to be acknowledged as "masters of their house." *[margin note: er control over everything but wages]*

The sole significant restriction imposed upon these enterprise leaders concerned wage rates – determined by force of law by the labor trustees mentioned above. In this manner employers as well as workers were denied any measure of freedom in industrial bargaining. These trustees, whose appointment had to be confirmed by Hitler himself, achieved sufficient authority and power to gain positions of considerable economic influence. This explains the struggles and maneuvers – some visible, some submerged – that took place with regard to these appointments, as party representatives and individuals from various economic sectors competed for the most influential positions.

The regional distribution of trustee authority overlapped with that of the Gauleiters, who in many cases also functioned as authorized chiefs of government in their districts. Most Gauleiters demanded to share in the appointment of trustees in order to secure these positions for veteran comrades and people from their own entourage. Thus besides their wish to grant jobs and benefits to certain people, Gauleiters also viewed trustees as a means to gain influence upon wage and labor conditions, a rather sensitive issue at the time. However, when the first labor trustees were appointed in June 1933, only seven turned out to be veteran party members. Most trustees were high-ranking government officials and at least

---

67. Schoenbaum, *Hitler's Social Revolution*, p. 98.

three were attached to the business community.[68] The Gauleiters were quick to voice their disapproval. Martin Mutschmann, Gauleiter of Saxony, protested against the appointment of a trustee who had joined the party only in 1933. Silesia filed a protest with the chancellor's office in Berlin against a trustee who clearly took the employers' side. On the other hand, the trustee for the state of Thuringia was appointed on the explicit recommendation of Gauleiter Fritz Sauckel. It was characteristic that such complaints from party circles were usually heeded and the trustees they disapproved of soon replaced. In March 1934 the minister of labor compiled a list of new appointments for Hitler's approval, emphasizing that all proposed appointees were veteran party members except one, "who had gained the trust of the Labor Front and the NSBO."[69]

In this context the affair of Joseph Klein, the trustee for Westphalia, is illuminating. As mentioned above, he was head of the Düsseldorf Institute for Corporate Research, a follower of Othmar Spann, and a confidant of Fritz Thyssen.[70] After a series of clashes with local NSBO functionaries who had considerable influence in this overwhelmingly industrial region, Klein was transferred in the same capacity to another district, the switch being made at the initiative of the minister of labor. Klein's closest assistant, Hutmacher, apparently got wind of the impending transfer and tried to prevent it by writing a personal letter to Hitler. According to him, NSBO functionaries had demonstrated an "unmistakable spirit of class militancy" and he had been able to overcome this only by threatening them with the Gestapo and concentration camps. "My concept of duty, commanded and taught by Dr. Klein, has turned me, in the eyes of the DAF and the NSBO, into their best-hated functionary far beyond the borders of the Düsseldorf district."[71] Hutmacher's letter never received a reply, and Klein was transferred on the same day the letter went out.

However, beyond these details, the case of Klein and Hutmacher illuminates the state of affairs and the prevailing mood among workers on the one hand and the Nazi leadership on the other. The methods Hutmacher was proud of having used against "the spirit of class militancy" among NSBO functionaries were not considered suitable at the time. Instead, it was found preferable to appoint

68. Wolffs Telegrafisches Büro 15. Juni 1933, in BA R 43/11, 532.
69. Ibid.
70. F. Thyssen, *I Paid Hitler* (London and New York, 1941), p. 155.
71. BA, R 43/II, 532.

trustees in whom party members and Gauleiters had faith. In addition, the party made efforts to secure high salary rates for trustees, in spite of the minister of finance's objections. Once again reference was made to their merits as "veteran fighters" "who could not be asked to begin at the same rate with a junior official." When these appeals, including intervention by Rudolf Heß, the Führer's deputy, failed, the decision was passed to Hitler – who ruled in favor of the party nominees.[72]

The events just described, as well as the fact that changes in trustee appointments were in many cases carried out in spite of objections from business circles, contradict the generally accepted assumption that during the period under discussion these trustees unequivocally supported employer interests. Wage rates were determined on the basis of previous industrial agreements. In numerous cases these rates were proclaimed minimum rates in order to preempt employers' attempts to reduce wages on their own initiative.[73] It is obvious that employers were not pleased with this state of affairs. The periodical *Deutsche Führerbriefe* (whose name was subsequently changed to *Deutsche Briefe*) expressed its satisfaction with the halt that had been called to the "trend of industrial militancy" among the DAF and NSBO, but complained that NSBO activists still wielded excessive influence within enterprises. It also approved of the temporary status the law of May 1933 accorded to the office of labor trustee "until the corporate order is established and functions. . . . Wage rates will then be determined within joint corporate bodies [of workers and employers] . . . which will also watch over industrial peace [*Arbeitsfriede*]."[74] This hope never materialized, however, and labor trustees preserved their highly influential position until the end of the Third Reich.

The reorganization of employer associations turned out to be more complicated. Infighting between covert interests went on until the fall of 1934: various pressure groups and representatives of economic interests tried to bend the existing structure to their own benefit and fortify their position within the altered organizations.[75] These skirmishes surfaced both within Nazi organizations and at the top of economic bodies in the form of frequent changes of

72. BA, R2, 18590. Verified in an interview with Schwerin von Krosigk, June 1974.
73. Kroll, *Weltwirtschaftskrise*, p. 582.
74. *Deutsche Führerbriefe*, June 23, 1933.
75. Neumann, *Behemoth*, p. 192.

appointees to various positions, including many in the Ministry of Economics. The party Bureau for Corporate Structure, headed by Max Frauendorfer, still existed but had no real say in decision making. Economic top executives like Keppler and leading industrialists did not bother to consult this institution.[76] Frauendorfer had described his views on the structure of the economy in his 1932 study, referring them to Spann's theory. In this study he developed a model of worker/employer corporations, put together according to economic branches. Nevertheless at that time he already emphasized the principle of supreme state control: "The absolute primacy of the state as custodian of the entire nation, including the corporations as exclusively economic bodies, dictates the necessity for the state and its agencies to control all corporate activities."[77]

The sole genuine attempt to realize the corporate principle occurred in agriculture and will be discussed below. Although in June 1933 industrial sectors and skilled artisans were organized as Reichsstände (National Corporations), this was mainly a new name for existing bodies – and even that was later changed. Nevertheless, a few significant changes had already occurred at that time. The umbrella organization of employer associations was dismantled and previously voluntary membership in industrial branch associations became compulsory. Jews and persons the new rulers mistrusted were weeded out, and Gustav Krupp von Bohlen, head of the Krupp trust, was put in charge of the Reichsstand der Industrie (National Corporation of Industries). In spite of these changes, the leaders of industry succeeded on the whole in preserving quite a large measure of personal and organizational continuity.[78]

The appointment of Kurt Schmitt as minister of economics instead of Hugenberg in July 1933 also initiated a new stage in the attempt to reorganize the institutional structure of the economy. At that time Hitler had already put a stop to all arguments about corporate structure, claiming that its realization had to be postponed in favor of the urgent need to liquidate unemployment.[79] It is

76. Max Frauendorfer, IfZ, ZS 1821.
77. Max Frauendorfer, *Der ständische Gedanke im Nationalsozialismus* (Munich, 1932), p. 26.
78. Franz Wolf, *Umschwung: Die deutsche Wirtschaft, 1933* (Frankfurt a.M., 1934), pp. 21ff.; A.B. Krause, *Organisation von Arbeit und Wirtschaft* (Berlin, ca. 1935), p. 83; Schweitzer, *Big Business*, pp. 249f.
79. Mönckmeier, ed., *Jahrbuch*, p. 119; F. Bülow, *Der deutsche Ständestaat: Nationalsozialistische Gemeinschaftspolitik durch Wirtschaftsorganisation* (Leipzig, 1934), p. 54.

reasonable to assume that this instruction was motivated not only by the wish to impose order and stop unauthorized activities. Presumably it was also directed against attempts by party members of middle-class orientation to infiltrate the management of existing economic bodies under the corporate banner. Von Renteln succeeded in spite of Hugenberg's protest, in "being elected" head of the DIHT and the two Reichsstände für Handel und Industrie (National Corporations for Trade and Industry). In this capacity he drafted legislative proposals whose aim was to put the DIHT at the top of a new organizational structure. New Regional Economic Chambers with far-reaching authority were to be established, uniting within their framework former territorial and industrial branch associations on a regional basis. Such a structure would have been of great advantage to small and medium businessmen, who made up the majority in the regional Chambers of Industry and Commerce, as opposed to the national industrial branch associations, which were dominated by leading industrialists.[80]

However, following the appointment of Schmitt, whose plans pointed in the opposite direction, von Renteln's organizational blueprints were shelved.[81] The law on the "organic structure" (as distinguished from the corporate structure) of the economy, initiated by Schmitt, invested the minister of economics and his office with wide-ranging authority. His functionaries were entitled to dismantle and reorganize economic bodies, to control their statutes, to appoint or dismiss those who headed them. To implement the new law, Schmitt appointed the former chairman of the Association of Electrical Engineering Industries, Philipp Keßler, to the newly created office of leader of the economy. Three months later Keßler was replaced by his deputy, a veteran party member, who maintained the policy of imposing government authority on businessmen, industrialists, and their organizational agencies. He in his turn was dismissed in January 1935, and the office of leader of the economy was scrapped.

Schmitt's and Keßler's reorganization plans were intended to turn the well-functioning hierarchy of existing industrial branch associations into a major transmission channel for government instructions, thus leading the economy toward objectives to be determined by the state. They sought to establish a single and

80. Esenwein-Rothe, *Wirtschaftsverbände*, p. 39; Broszat, *Der Staat Hitlers*, pp. 210f.
81. Schulz in Bracher, Sauer, and Schulz, *Machtergreifung*, p. 651.

unified system of transmission from the top downward, unimpeded, in the name of efficiency, by parallel or competing associations. Keßler was therefore instructed to abolish the Chambers of Commerce, which customarily represented local economic interests. Cartels, to the extent that their dismantling was not feasible, were to be put under close and detailed government control.[82] Schmitt's pronounced centralism aroused opposition in business circles. The press openly criticized Keßler for his radicalism in seeking to establish a planned economy, and these differences of opinion led to his replacement.[83] Schmitt was also unsuccessful in gaining support among middle-class party members. When the army finally turned on him, following his refusal to invest substantial resources in the development of fuel and rubber-substitute industries, his position became untenable. In July 1934 he was replaced by Schacht, who was appointed minister of economics with extraordinary prerogatives.[84]

The first executive regulations concerning the Law on the Organic Structure of the Economy were published only after Schacht had assumed office, in November 1934.[85] What was realized under Schacht's leadership was a compromise incorporating, at least in part, von Renteln's previous proposals. In addition to obligatory membership and the minister's prerogative to appoint the heads of industrial branch associations and groups, a Reichswirtschaftsrat (National Economic Council) was established at the top of the whole structure. Within this council the industrial branch associations were merged with the national umbrella organization of Chambers of Commerce. The most important element in this structure was the innovation of twenty-three Bezirkswirtschaftskammern (regional Chambers of Economics), which merged local branches of industrial associations with the Chambers of Commerce and Industry. The areas over which these new chambers had authority coincided with those of the labor trustees and therefore also the Gauleiters. As time went on, these Chambers of Economics became the most important link in the chain of economic institutionalization. To the extent that government intervention increased until 1936, their importance as the principal means of

82. Esenwein-Rothe, *Wirtschaftsverbände*, p. 45.
83. F. Wolf, *Staatskonjunktur: Die deutsche Wirtschaft, 1934* (Frankfurt a.M., 1935).
84. Schweitzer, *Big Business*, p. 250; idem, "Organisierter Kapitalismus," pp. 42ff.
85. 1. Verordnung zum Gesetz zur Vorbereitung des organischen Aufbaus der Wirtschaft vom 27. November 1934, RGB1. I, p. 1194.

control and direction rose.[86] Every single factory owner, artisan, or merchant was by law subject to instructions issued by the regional chamber in authority at his place of residence. Representatives of the Reichsnährstand, that is, corporately organized agriculture and the DAF, were also attached to these Chambers of Economics – thus turning them into the center of all economic activity as well as an efficacious channel for control and direction.

At the top, the actual work was carried out within the framework of seven major industrial branch associations, now called Reichsgruppen (National Groups) rather than Reichsstände (National Corporations). For example, the new Reichsgruppe Industrie was little different, in its functions and leading personnel, from the old RDI, except that membership was now mandatory. The Berlin offices of the Reichsgruppen passed instructions to regional Chambers of Economics, which thus became focal points for the implementation of government-dictated policies. They also served as an arena for the contest between conflicting and competing interests and dominated distribution of the spoils from the Aryanization of Jewish enterprises as well as the allocation of raw materials, foreign currency, and government orders. The *Staatssekretär* at the Ministry of Economics succinctly emphasized their importance: "The Chambers of Economics are extraordinarily appropriate as a link between the government and the economy; they constitute an excellent platform for the government to reinforce comprehension of laws, decrees, and other government measures in economic circles and, on the other side, to convey particularly urgent requests from the economy to the government at any given date."[87]

The coinciding in regional distribution of the chambers' sphere of authority with that of the Gauleiters and their economic advisers presumably fomented pressures and attempts at manipulation by the party establishment, especially on this level. About half of the thirty regional economic advisers were chairmen or general managers of Chambers of Commerce and Industry – usually small businessmen, proprietors of retail shops or skilled-artisan workshops, who had achieved status and influence after the Nazis assumed power. After the war one of them described their activities: they held regular meetings, chaired by Bernhard Köhler, head of the

86. Neumann, *Behemoth*, p. 200.
87. Hans E. Posse, *Die deutsche Wirtschaft*, in H.H. Lammers and H. Pfundtner, eds., *Grundlagen, Aufbau und Wirtschaftsordnung des nationalsozialistischen Staates*, vol. 3 (Berlin, ca. 1936), p. 41.

Nazi party's Committee for Economic Policy, at which they decided "what should be fought and what should be promoted within the limits of prevailing circumstances."[88]

The institutional structure of the Third Reich's economy was to a large extent set up immediately after the appointment of Schacht, from August to November 1934. From an economic point of view one can say that whatever was realized during this period, and up to 1936, represented a measure of victory for industry and big business. Aided by Schacht, these groups successfully restrained middle-class activists as well as those who were inclined to introduce radical central planning and controls. Nevertheless, it would be an exaggeration to conclude that the Nazis sacrificed middle-class interests altogether for the benefit of big business, thus abandoning previous ideological commitments.[89] It is true that Schacht imposed considerable constraints on the influence wielded by party functionaries and on their freedom of action within skilled-artisan and retail-trade associations – positions they had rapidly seized during the initial months of Nazi rule. A number of decrees put these bodies under the control of the Ministry of Economics, whose officials cut down on their inflated administration, where a good many veteran fighters had found cushy jobs and substantial salaries.[90] However, even after the Schacht decrees, skilled-artisan and retail-trade associations were recognized as independent National Groups; in most cases they were represented at the regional Chambers of Economics by their former leaders, who knew how to safeguard their interests. Ultimately the most outstanding element in these changes was, in my opinion, the consistent realization of an organizational principle designed to neutralize any kind of competitive intervention by the party or by others in order to secure unified and exclusive control for the state, that is, the Ministry of Economics.[91]

An examination of the middle classes' economic position also fails to show that they had been abandoned in favor of big business interests. Even under Schacht, at least until 1936, they enjoyed the status of a protected sector, although their attempts to gain power over other branches of the economy had failed.[92] A special law for

88. H. Kehrl, *Krisenmanager im Dritten Reich* (Düsseldorf, 1973), pp. 40f.
89. Schweitzer, *Big Business*, p. 146.
90. Ibid., p. 142.
91. Broszat, *Der Staat Hitlers*, p. 217.
92. Winkler, *Mittelstand*, p. 181.

the protection of conventional retail trade, passed under Hugen-berg, banned the establishment of new department or chain stores.[93] Grass-roots-initiated boycott activities against department stores, accompanied by virulent anti-Semitic propaganda, had been ram-pant at the beginning of 1933, but the government subsequently restrained those activities in order not to inflate the ranks of the unemployed even more. Nevertheless, party members were forbidden to shop at department stores, and special taxes and restrictions were imposed on the latter (for instance, they were not allowed to operate snack bars or repair shops) so that they suffered consider-able losses.[94] Skilled artisans enjoyed legal and economic preference through restrictions imposed on competition and entry into their trades. Membership in their "guilds" was obligatory by decree and could be obtained only by passing rigorous examinations in "skill". All these were privileges for which artisan associations had fought for years under the Weimar regime, but they were finally achieved only under Nazi rule.[95] Some middle-class businesses benefited more than others from the general prosperity. Branches that dealt with construction work or the rising demand for electrical ap-pliances and radios prospered more than others. Traditional trades like clothing and footwear were exposed to industrial competition and therefore became more vulnerable.[96]

Even under Nazi rule the "old" middle class could not reverse the march of industrialization, which undermined its economic strong-holds. On the contrary, the demands of rearmament, which re-ceived absolute priority under the Nazis, tended to accelerate the process of industrialization. If middle-class interests were sacrificed and did not receive the preference they had been led to expect, they fell victim to the regime's political order of priorities and its war preparations. Basically this was also the reason for the position of preference accorded to industry and the special consideration awarded to branches that were directly involved in rearmament or the production of raw-material substitutes. Heavy industry retained its associations and in most cases also the positions held by individ-ual members, at the price of acquiescence to primacy of politics as the supreme guiding principle. In an article of September 1933, the

93. Gesetz zum Schutze des Einzelhandels vom 23. Juli 1934, RGBl. I, p. 262.
94. H. Uhlig, *Die Warenhäuser im Dritten Reich* (Cologne and Opladen, 1956), pp. 152, 224.
95. Winkler, *Mittelstand*, p. 185.
96. A. Gurland, O. Kirchheimer, and F. Neumann, *The Fate of Small Business in Nazi Germany*, Senate Committee print no. 14 (Washington, D.C., 1943), pp. 114f.

general manager of the RDI made it quite clear that "there is no more dualism between government policy and business," and that "the primacy of politics will be applied to associations of industrialists with the same consistency as, for instance, to cultural institutions. . . . [The] reshaping of the prevailing state of affairs . . . mostly voluntary, but partly also by intervention of government or party officials," showed itself primarily on the personal level – in the exclusion of Jewish and politically undesirable individuals, in stronger representation of small, middle-class business – but political *Gleichschaltung* was indeed the most important element.[97]

The institutional framework of the new establishment differed from what had been hailed previously as a desirable corporate structure on three important counts:

1. The newly established organizational bodies did not unite workers and employers but remained, as previously, pure employer associations. An agreement between Ley and Schacht according to which employers joined the DAF en bloc, signed in March 1935, did not alter this – a point the agreement explicitly emphasized. There is no doubt that the personal membership of employers in the DAF had implications for the internal balance of forces of the regime, within which Ley's mass organization carried considerable weight. Nevertheless, all of Ley's attempts to invest DAF agencies with genuine influence on economic decision making were successfully defeated. Although they had joined the DAF, these economic associations meticulously preserved their character as representatives of entrepreneurs.[98]

2. The whole issue of wage and labor-conditions policy was removed from the sphere of activity of economic associations on all levels. The associations were not merely forbidden (under the threat of having their organization dismantled) "to represent social and political interests of employers," but they were not even allowed to hold internal consultations or advise enterprise owners on these issues. Their sole assignment in this field was the passing on of government and labor trustees' instructions to their members, subject to the explicit qualification "that the report be made without additions intended to limit, order, or interpret its contents in the spirit of specific interests."[99]

97. Jakob Herle, "Unternehmerverbände in neuen Deutschland," *Der Deutsche Volkswirt* 7, no. 48 (Sept. 1, 1933): 1377f.
98. Lölhöffel, "Die Umwandlung," pp. 176f.
99. Krause, *Organisation*, p. 84.

3. In contrast to agriculture, where administrative bodies of the Reichsnährstand (National Sustenance Corporation) managed the whole course of processing and marketing agricultural products, industrial artisan and trade associations had no authority over market or price policies. These were exclusively handled by cartels – whether freely established or imposed by decree – which operated under tight supervision by the Ministry of Economics. Under a special law passed in July 1933, the minister had the authority to order the establishment of new cartels and/or to compel enterprises to join existing branch cartels and to restrict the inclusion of new enterprises or the expansion of existing ones.[100] This law was passed at a time of partial unemployment and was implemented in particular in branches suffering from cutthroat competition and falling prices – thus threatening to ruin enterprises and increase unemployment (for instance, in the radio retail trade and in printing shops). Known cases of compulsory cartels established under this law show that their aim was to protect small- and medium-sized enterprises in highly competitive branches. Big industrial enterprises knew how to safeguard their profits without special laws by open or covert manipulations. In any case, the establishment of cartels was by legislation taken out of the hands of all economic associations, industrial and territorial. Under the direct control of the Ministry of Economics, cartels became in principle an instrument for price regulation by the state. To what extent this instrument was used and how much freedom of action was allowed to specific interests varied, as in other spheres, according to time and circumstances.

One should remember that the major components of a principled corporate conception are price regulation, the curbing of competition, and the settlement of industrial relations. It is therefore understandable that the separation of these matters from the activity of economic associations was explained as a temporary measure, dictated by the necessity to preserve steady wage and price levels while unemployment was being liquidated, and to prevent the creation of monopolies.[101] The organizational principles applied in agriculture were still considered the model to be copied by all sectors of the economy at the appropriate time, in accordance with the original corporate concept. Nothing ever came of this, and with the increase of direct government intervention in the economy, the hints that the agricultural model would in time be applied to other

100. Gesetz über die Errichtung von Zwangskartellen, RGB1. I, p. 488.
101. Posse, *Deutsche Wirtschaft*, p. 42.

sectors just faded away. Indeed, the autonomous authority exercised by agricultural administration over marketing and price regulation was also restricted in the course of time. Ultimately, what the establishment created under the heading of a corporate structure was merely the means by which to conduct the economy in accordance with the needs of the regime. It tried to operate with a minimum of bureaucratic apparatus and direct intervention by exploiting the traditional self-management bodies of existing economic associations which were described as "a peculiar androgyne, in whom it was hard to distinguish where the self-management of various interests ended and transmission of orders by the state began."[102]

As with other institutional instruments like, for instance, price, wage, and investment controls, state economic direction could be applied to various and changing objectives according to prevailing circumstances. However, the existence of these instruments alone still does not prove that during the period under discussion the economy indeed operated mainly by means of government orders and administrative decrees. As long as the Nazi rulers were able to achieve their objectives through the willing cooperation of leading economic interests, that is, by exploiting the latter's economic motivations for their own ends, they willingly relied on the economy's self-management, keeping direct administrative intervention to a minimum. The tightly organized industrial employer associations were able to turn this state of affairs to their economic and, to a limited extent, political advantage at the expense of other interest groups. Thus leading industrialists could use their leverage to acquire the most attractive items of plundered Jewish property from the moment that the process of Aryanization was launched.[103]

However, there were limits to the freedom of these associations in decision-making; they knew very well that the established control mechanism constantly kept an eye on their activities. There was no lack of evidence that this mechanism would be used against them, if necessary; the party's propaganda machine also saw to it that this reality was not forgotten . For instance, a 1935 article by the economic editor of the party organ included the following statement: "Capitalistic arrangements that could be useful have been utilized. To shatter them would have been a costly pleasure . . . [but] all these capitalistic arrangements have received

102. Broszat, *Der Staat Hitlers*, p. 228.
103. Genschel, *Verdrängung der Juden*, pp. 211f.

new foundations. The system serves as a tool in the hands of policy. Where capitalism still considers itself untouched, it has in fact already been harnessed by policy."[104]

There is, therefore, a great deal of exaggeration in Arthur Schweitzer's assertions that the whole organizational structure established between 1934 and 1936 was adapted to serve the single objective of strengthening the position of Schacht and private capitalistic associations[105] and that economic associations were "acknowledged as representing the interests of private groups in confrontation with the state."[106] Economic associations constituted an instrument for regulation from above, ready to be activated at a moment's notice – not less and perhaps even more than being acknowledged as guardians of private interests.

The actual utilization of controls and decrees became widespread only when full employment was achieved and the objectives of accelerated rearmament could no longer be accomplished by means of purely economic motivation. During the initial years these measures were more selectively and altogether consistently less implemented, but their efficacy was already recognized: "The hierarchical structure of the whole association system and the ties of its top echelons with the state . . . make the entire economic structure transparent for the state, providing it with an unequaled tool for measures of economic policy."[107]

There is no doubt that the Nazis erected this structure with the aim of securing the power to control and regulate the economy, while utilizing established associations. They could afford to be flexible with regard to the specific manner of regulation and leave numerous functions to those who had previously performed them. Nevertheless, the state's supreme authority in economic matters was a cornerstone of the Nazi's economic principles from their very beginnings. Furthermore, one cannot deny them a measure of consistency and preliminary planning even with regard to organizational detail. The minutes of a WPA consultation at the end of 1931 summarized proposals for the corporate structuring of the economy in the following manner: "A corporate structure denotes ideal cooperation between the leadership of the state and economic

104. F. Nonnenbruch, *Die dynamische Wirtschaft*, 4th ed. (Munich, 1939), p. 42.
105. Schweitzer, "Organisierter Kapitalismus," p. 46.
106. Schweitzer, "Organisierter Kapitalismus," p. 37.
107. Alfred Müller-Armack, *Staatsidee und Wirtschaftsordnung im neuen Reich* (Berlin, 1933), pp. 149f.

self-management. Administrative bodies of the state, as the leader who is also responsible for the economy, act from above; bodies of economic self-management act from below, coming together in Corporate Chambers."[108] If one disregards terminological differences and replaces Corporate Chambers with the installed Bezirkswirtschaftskammern (regional Chambers of Economics), the distance between preliminary planning and the finished product is not large.

One should nevertheless remember that the whole institutional framework was established as an instrument of economic policy. Even if we agree that its principal aim was to create an effective transmission system for instructions on this policy, we have to investigate its nature and real objectives and its possible connection with predetermined political and ideological goals. This requires a separate examination of each sector of economic activity, as presented below.

Agriculture as a Corporate Model

In Nazi economic thought agriculture, more than any other sector, carried a load of ideological-emotive connotations. Here was a focal point for social ideas and racist mysticism that merged with political belligerence to shape concepts like *Lebensraum* and *Nahrungsfreiheit* (freedom of sustenance). It was also an important point of convergence with old and young conservative concepts as well as with the romantic tradition in German folklore and literature. From the beginning of the nineteenth century a large body of "homeland literature" (the German term *Heimatdichtung* has strong sentimental connotations) disseminated nostalgic idealizations of "sound and natural" rural life, as opposed to the immorality and vulgarity of industrial cities. The slogan of *Blut und Boden* (blood and soil) encompassed all these and invested them with an emotionally loaded mystique, an article of faith that required no rationalization.[109] In its broader sense, as conceived by Walter Darré and eagerly adopted by Himmler and the SS, the slogan contained the principal elements of racial theory: the German peasant, attached to his soil since time immemorial, stood for the race in its purity and was its source of growth and expansion. "Statistics" were called up

---

108. BA, NS 22/11, Ergebnis der Besprechungen, Nov. 26 and Dec. 1, 1931.
109. Schoenbaum, *Hitler's Social Revolution*, pp. 161f.

to prove the point: a high rate of rural population increase in contrast to the declining rate in cities resulted in the forecast that unless the process of urbanization were arrested and the birth rate rose, Germany's population would shrink to twenty million by the end of the century.[110] German peasantry was not only to safeguard the vital growth of the German people; it was also expected to provide a stream of new settlers for the expansion to the east in order to guarantee sustenance and security for the entire nation.[111]

Agriculture was the only economic sector that the Nazis began to organize according to a preconceived plan immediately after they attained power. The main elements of this plan were taken from the work of a nineteenth-century German economist, Gustav Ruhland (1860–1914).[112] In accordance with this theory, they tried to organize agriculture as a corporate structure with self-management authority in the field of labor and market regulation. In addition, a new inheritance law was to entail the agricultural economic unit, that is, make that unit stable and indivisible. A series of laws and protective measures, enacted from the earliest days of the regime, were to grant agriculture a position of preference and encouragement, easing its burden of debt and interest and promoting it in every possible manner.

Before I discuss these agricultural plans in detail, it has to be said that the efforts expended on them failed completely. Between 1933 and 1939 the rate of agricultural population fell from 20.8 to 18 percent.[113] The rate of those employed in agriculture dropped even more rapidly, from 16 percent in 1933 to 10.5 percent in 1938.[114] This means that some agricultural workers changed their occupations, even though they continued to live in their same villages. The propaganda for rural settlement and the establishment of new farms as a means of relieving unemployment, dispersing the population, and having it "strike root" in the soil failed to yield noteworthy results, even though it was continued after the Nazi takeover. Between 1933 and 1938, 20,748 new farms were estab-

---

110. J.E. Farquharson, "The NSDAP and Agriculture in Germany, 1928–1938" (dissertation, University of Kent, Canterbury, 1972), p. 163.

111. Schoenbaum, *Hitler's Social Revolution*, p. 50.

112. Darré, introduction to F. Bülow, *Gustav Ruhland – Ein deutscher Bauerndenker im Kampf gegen Liberalismus und Marxismus* (Berlin, 1936), p. 6.

113. Schoenbaum, *Hitler's Social Revolution*, p. 185.

114. R. Honigberger, "Die wirtschaftspolitische Zielsetzung des Nationalsozialismus und deren Einfluß auf die deutsche Wirtschaftsordnung, dargestellt und kritisch untersucht am Beispiel des deutschen Arbeitsmarktes von 1933 bis 1939" (dissertation, Albert Ludwig Universität, Freiburg i.Br., 1949), p. 98.

lished on 325,612 hectares, less than half of the number of new farms established under the thoroughly maligned Weimar Republic.[115] The prosperity achieved by the German economy during the period under discussion was saliently industrial: while industrial net production increased by nearly 90 percent, agricultural production rose by approximately 22 percent. These figures are significant even if we take into account that in an industrial economy cyclical fluctuations are always greater in industry than in agriculture. They prove that neither propaganda nor efforts to aid and promote agriculture could reverse the process of industrial expansion. Furthermore, whenever the trend toward "return to the soil" clashed with objectives of rearmament and war preparations, the latter were given preference. Although the Nazis were aware of these failures, they neither accepted them as final nor refuted their original concepts because of them. As in other spheres, they perceived the matter as a temporary postponement in favor of more urgent tasks. Why bother to cultivate the marshy soil of Eastern Prussia while the vast, fertile plains of the Ukraine, lying just over the horizon, were waiting for settlers of the victorious "master race"? Hitler had already expressed such sentiments in a talk with one of the big landowners in 1931: he said that he had no plans for extensive settlement in Germany, probably in order to allay fears harbored by the Junkers about the fate of their estates; real and substantial settlement would be feasible only after the expansion of Germany's *Lebensraum*.[116]

Notwithstanding its ultimate failure, Nazi policy did cause some fundamental changes in agriculture, and some of its efforts even achieved a measure of success. The Nazis treated the promotion of agriculture seriously, trying to introduce improvements immediately after they assumed power. The well-organized and subdivided Agrarian Department that since March 1930 had operated under Darré at the Brown House in Munich had rapidly penetrated rural districts all over Germany. In addition to the department's persuasive propaganda, which soon gained considerable support among the rural population, its functionaries prepared practical work plans that served as guidelines for what was actually implemented after the Nazis' attained power, in agriculture more than in any other economic sector.[117]

Within the Nazi hierarchy Darré was a newcomer who had

115. Farquharson, "Agriculture in Germany," pp. 482f.
116. Ibid., p. 470.
117. Broszat, *Der Staat Hitlers*, pp. 46f.

joined the party in 1929–30, apparently after his appointment as head of the Agrarian Department. Like many Nazi leaders, he was a German from abroad. He was born in the Argentine and served with the German embassy at Riga after World War I. His ties with conservative agrarian circles that fostered rural romanticism went back to the beginnings of his career. He was especially attached to Georg Kenstler, editor of a periodical entitled *Blut und Boden.* Toward the end of 1929 Kenstler introduced him to the Nazi party, which led to his appointment as head of the Agrarian Department.[118]

The appointment was characteristic of Hitler's inclination at the time to choose new people for various positions over the heads of veteran and deserving party members. Until the appointment of Darré, the major Nazi spokesman on agriculture had been the Reichstag delegate Werner Willikens, author of the party's 1930 Agrarian Platform. The latter was a development and extension of paragraph 17 in the party platform, emphasizing the need for self-sufficiency and economic autarky. At the same time the Nazis repeatedly denied that they intended to nationalize land, claiming that settlement was mentioned only with regard to neglected estates. This platform already included proposals for the rural inheritance law, tax and debt relief, protectionist customs for agricultural produce, reduction of marketing spread, and the price of agricultural input like fertilizers, electricity and so forth.[119]

Darré's relations with Himmler began before he joined the party. The connection was not accidental: racial theory and the agrarian conception are cast as a single entity in Nazi ideology. Nor was Himmler's attachment to agriculture merely sentimental: he declared himself a farmer with a degree in agronomics; he also headed the Association of German Agronomists for some time. His relations with Darré were very friendly. However, when in 1932 he appointed Darré as chief of the SS Rasse und Siedlungsamt (Department for Race and Settlement), this was not merely a sign of trust – it demonstrated the close relation between the Nazi concept of agriculture, the drive for territorial expansion, and their racial theory.[120]

Darré's Agrarian Department did not limit its acitivity to propaganda and the preparation of plans for future application. Through

118. Farquharson, "Agriculture in Germany," pp. 68f.
119. Ibid., pp. 62ff.
120. Ibid., p. 500; Broszat, *Der Staat Hitlers*, p. 61.

well-planned and concerted efforts, his functionaries infiltrated
voluntary agricultural associations and the Chambers for Agriculture from 1930 on. They succeeded in manning influential positions
within these bodies, thus paving the way for their complete takeover during the initial months of 1933.[121] Like industry and commerce under the Weimar Republic, agriculture was organized in
parallel systems – a network of territorial Chambers for Agriculture, joined at the top in a national Agricultural Council and two
national Agricultural Branch Associations, representing the economic and political interests of the whole sector. Big landowners
belonged to the Reichslandbund (National Agrarian Association),
which was close to President Hindenburg's entourage and wielded
considerable political influence under the republic. Small and medium farm owners established the Union of Christian Peasant
Associations. Willikens sat on the board of the Reichslandbund
from 1930; Darré's close assistant, Wilhelm Meinberg, joined the
board in March 1933. After the Nazis assumed power, the road was
clear for a merger of the two associations, and on April 4, 1933,
Darré became in fact (though not yet in title) the German
Bauernführer (peasant leader). At the end of the same month he
forced the board of the national association of agricultural cooperatives, Raiffeisen, to resign. Three of Darré's subordinates occupied
key positions on the new board. The same modus operandi was
used with regard to regional associations. Members of the DNVP
had already been systematically ousted from their positions on the
boards of the Chambers for Agriculture, while their leader, Hugenberg, still held the office of minister of agriculture. On April 5,
1933, Hitler himself addressed a plenary meeting of the Agricultural
Council. Following his speech, in which he once again presented the
principles of his policy and promised to work for "preservation of
the peasantry," the council unanimously pledged loyalty and unqualified support for the new government.[122]

All these maneuvers took only a few weeks. On May 28 Darré
united all leading positions in existing agricultural associations in his
own person, while the umbrella organization invested him with
unlimited authority and the official title of *Reichsbauernführer*
(national peasant leader). The fact that all this occurred while
Hugenberg, as minister of agriculture, took noticeable steps to aid
the peasantry, shows that previous Nazi infiltration of these bodies

121. Broszat, *Der Staat Hitlers*, p. 230.
122. Ibid., p. 231.

had already more or less ousted all possible rivals for the leadership. It also demonstrates the ideological commitment that made them secure exclusive dominance over this economic sector without delay.[123] The finishing stroke came at the end of June 1933, when Darré replaced Hugenberg as minister of agriculture, thus becoming the top authority for all of Germany's agriculture at the government level as well. It was no accident that, in addition to Goebbels's new Propaganda Ministry, agriculture alone was handed over to the head of the respective office within the party establishment, unifying in that person major positions representing sectorial interests with the top decision-making offices at the party and government levels. Now there were no institutional hurdles to impede the realization of agricultural policy, as planned and promised before the Nazi takeover.

German agriculture was severely stricken by falling agricultural prices during the depression. Grain farming, most of it in the rye-growing eastern districts, was especially hard hit. The Brüning government had tried to aid this sector by forwarding about two billion reichsmarks in relief funds, most of which went to the big landowners. However, this money did not improve the state of German agriculture. It caused public protest and some political scandals and did not gain support for the Brüning government among the Prussian Junkers, who had pocketed the money. Magnus von Braun, the conservative minister of agriculture in the von Papen government, tried in vain to introduce protective duties; industrial interests, fearing a rise in prices and therefore in production costs, were too strong. Instead, the allocation of cash relief was kept up, once again mainly to the benefit of the Junkers east of the river Elbe. The agricultural west, most of which depended on quality products, received almost no aid at all. The Schleicher government tried to break this deadlock by appeasing western farmers with the Butter Law, which compelled margarine producers to mix margarine with butter in order to utilize surplus milk. Schleicher also negotiated a compromise between the ministers of agriculture and economics, who came to an agreement on protective duties in spite of opposition from industrialists. However, this did not gain Schleicher the Junkers' loyalty: rumors about settlement plans, including land requisition, made the Reichslandbund declare war on the Schleicher government. This step was of considerable political significance in

123. Ibid., p. 236.

the campaign of intrigue and conspiracy that brought about Hitler's appointment as head of the government.[124]

As minister of both economics and agriculture, Hugenberg had almost all the authority necessary to implement vigorous agricultural relief policies and, indeed, began doing so at once with a great deal of energy. On February 14, 1933, he issued a decree protecting peasant farms and holdings from foreclosure on account of arrears. During the same months protective duties on agricultural produce were almost doubled. On February 19 a subsidy of 123 million reichsmarks was endorsed, mainly for grain production – a sop to Junker interests in East Prussia. In March farmers in the west also received subsidies to be paid by the customer: by administrative regulation, the Fat Plan reduced the production of margarine to 60 percent of current output and made the addition of butter compulsory. The price of milk and milk products rose at once by 40 to 50 percent, and so did the price of pigs, lard, and other fats. In consequence, the price index of all agricultural produce rose from 82 (1913 = 100) to 95 in December 1933. All this occurred in spite of reservations voiced by Hitler and Nazi members of the government, who were apprehensive of the psychological impact a steep rise in food prices might have.[125]

With regard to the remission of debts, Hugenberg and Darré held different opinions. Hugenberg proposed a moratorium on debts plus reduction of interest rates to 4 percent for farmers in difficult straits. Darré argued that this was a capitalist solution: such a vital issue should be determined by blood and not by economic considerations. He therefore demanded relief for all peasants, even if their farms were inefficient, by lowering interest rates to 3 percent for everyone. The minister of finance, Schwerin von Krosigk, stood by the rights of debtors and banks. As a compromise, they decided on extensive tax discounts and a conversion of debts at 4 percent, which benefited about 10 percent of peasant farms. This legislation was completed in May 1934 by a partial remission of debts, that is, by extending support to peasant farms at the expense of banks and suppliers.[126]

Following Hugenberg's replacement as minister of agriculture, the realization of preliminary planning was first launched at the

124. Petzina, *Autarkiepolitik*, pp. 49ff.
125. Ibid., pp. 52–53; Wolf, *Umschwung*, pp. 23f.
126. Farquharson, "Agriculture in Germany," pp. 155f.; Wolf, *Umschwung*, pp. 23f.; Petzina, *Autarkiepolitik*, p. 53.

institutional level through the establishment of the Reichsnährstand (RNS, National Sustenance Corporation). By the spring of 1934, with the aid of two newly passed laws,[127] a comprehensive framework had been established, that came as close as possible to the corporate model promised in early blueprints. The RNS was a giant organization, based on obligatory membership, which in addition to peasant farms and holdings also encompassed fisheries, trade in agricultural produce, and processing industries. Its administration had twenty thousand salaried employees at its disposal, plus thirteen thousand voluntary officials and "appointees." Two of Darré's senior employees, drawn from the Nazi party's Agrarian Department, were responsible for the appointment of peasant leaders for all villages, districts, and states, without even a vestige of elections. Nonparty functionaries had to become members in order to keep their jobs. Thus the RNS became a jealously guarded party domain. Although its functionaries were usually farmers, their required qualifications were neither occupational skills nor popularity among the peasants in their region, but instead their degree of loyalty to the party.[128] By force of law the RNS had extensive authority to control and intervene. It determined wholesale and retail prices and production quotas, and it controlled the quality of fresh as well as of processed products. It was entitled to impose fines of up to one hundred thousand reichsmarks or prison sentences and to close business enterprises or shops. The modus operandi of this market regulation was dictated by its aims: to detach agriculture completely from the interplay of forces within the market economy; to guarantee its preferred and stable status by fixing production quotas and prices all the way from producer to consumer.[129] This aim was largely achieved by the aid of foreign-currency and trade controls. The latter gave rise to some disguised criticism in the press: at the close of 1934 the economic editor of the *Frankfurter Zeitung* published a comparison between agricultural

127. 1) Gesetz über die Zuständigkeit des Reiches für die Regelung des ständischen Aufbaus der Landwirtschaft vom 15. Juli 1933, RGBl, I, p. 495; 2) Gesetz über den vorläufigen Aufbau des Reichsnährstandes und Maßnahmen zur Markt- und Preisregelung für landw. Erzeugnisse vom 13. September 1933, RGBl, I, p. 626.
128. R. Grunberger, *A Social History of the Third Reich* (London, 1971), p. 155: Farquharson, "Agriculture in Germany," p. 626.
129. Herrmann Reischle, "Die Entwicklung der Marktordnung des Reichsnährstandes i.d. Jahren 1935/36," in O. Mönckmeier, ed., *Jahrbuch für nationalsozialistische Wirtschaft*, pt. 2, *Das nationalsozialistische Wirtschaftsrecht* (Stuttgart and Berlin, 1937), pp. 216f.

produce prices in Germany and world market prices showing
differences of up to 300 percent and added the following comment:
"The chancellor explained immediately after the takeover that the
consumer would have to make sacrifices for the sake of the peasant
class . . . [but] within the large industrial RNS sector there is no
reason for the people as a whole to forego radical economic efficiency, as they are asked to do for the benefit of the peasants."[130]

Nevertheless, the RNS was not an entirely autonomous corporate
body. Darré himself emphasized that its independence was limited
and that it was the chancellor who determined its overall policies.[131]
In 1930 Darré still envisioned the corporate structure as "a coherent
bloc of agriculture against other interests . . . as well as in confrontation with the state leadership."[132] On the face of it, the scope
of the organization's authority had been extended by the inclusion
of occupations related to agriculture, to trade in its produce and the
processing of foodstuffs. However, this extension made the RNS
responsible for such a vast economic sector that it had to be
subjected to state authority. Such wide-ranging and vital matters
concerning the entire economy could not possibly remain under the
autonomous authority of a corporate body that by definition represented specific branch interests against all other sectors of the
economy. The fact that the leadership of the corporation and the
relevant government authority were combined in the person of
Darré also had its share in changing the nature of the corporate
structure: "Behind a pseudocorporate facade the independent life of
these associations could but stagnate; the organization devaluated
itself into an information and control mechanism for the management of the economy by the state."[133]

The attempt to honor the commitment to preserve a stable class
of small- and medium-sized peasant farms generated a second
measure, the Erbhofsgesetz, a law entailing all farms up to a specified size. Here the ideological motivation stood out more than in
any other law – so much so that besides the real interests of those
concerned it also ignored the proclaimed objectives of the regime
itself. The entailment law, intended to "root" the peasant firmly on
his land, ultimately accelerated the migration of young peasants
whose right to inherit part of their homestead had been abolished.

130. Wolf, *Staatskonjunktur*, p. 10.
131. Farquharson, "Agriculture in Germany," pp. 165f.
132. R.W. Darré, *Neuadel durch Blut und Boden* (Munich, 1930), p. 114.
133. Esenwein-Rothe, *Wirtschaftsverbände*, pp. 21, 24.

Having no option for resettlement through alternative land allocation and unwilling to become agricultural laborers in their villages, they really had no choice but to accept the well-paid jobs offered by expanding industrial production. Hugenberg's former *Staatssekretär* hit the nail on the head when he complained in a memorandum to Hitler of August 1934 that this law "was apparently dictated by peasant literature rather than by the realities of peasant life."[134] However, Hitler's ideological assertion in *Mein Kampf* (subsequently a permanent Nazi *Leitmotiv*) that "a stable peasant stock on small and medium holdings was at all times the best protection against the social ills we suffer from at present"[135] was certainly no less decisive than rural literature.

Owing to opposition from Hugenberg and other conservatives, the law was passed only in December 1933. Seven hundred thousand agricultural farms and holdings, up to 125 hectares in size, that is, about 40 percent of all cultivated land, were registered as entails.[136] The owners of these farms and holdings held the prestigious title of *Bauer* (peasant), while the owners of larger farms were merely *Landwirte* (farmers). A *Bauer* had to be a racially pure German whose farm or holding passed by inheritance to one of his heirs, with no obligation to recompense remaining sons. The peasant's sole obligation was to have his landless sons trained in some skill and to provide each of his daughters with a trousseau, but no dowry, on the occasion of her marriage. A holding was pronounced entailed by RNS authorities, who were also entitled to expropriate a peasant's land, if he was shown to be "undeserving."[137]

Although on the face of it the law granted peasants a preferred and protected status, in addition to genuine improvements in input and output prices, they were not happy with its results. They were protected against foreclosure, but their freedom of movement and economic decision-making were restricted. Had the law been accompanied by an agrarian reform plan, thus increasing the number of small and medium holdings, cutting up large estates, and joining or enlarging the tens of thousands of dwarf holdings of less than 7.5 hectares not recognized as entails, it might have stabilized the rural population. It might even have helped to realize, at least partly, the

134. Broszat, *Der Staat Hitlers*, p. 237.
135. Hitler, *Mein Kampf*, p. 151.
136. Reichserbhofsgesetz vom 29. September 1933, RGB1, I, p. 685; H. Backe, "Agrarpolitik und Vierjahresplan," in Mönckmeier, ed., *Jahrbuch*, pt. 2, p. 208.
137. Farquharson, "Agriculture in Germany," p. 357.

Nazis' proclaimed goal of reagrarianization. However, nothing occurred in this direction, not even some initial show of good intentions. The percentage of entailed holdings did not change from 1933 until the end of the war. Apparently the Nazis preferred not to tangle with grain-supplying big landowners while the future promised extensive settlement on vast tracts of fertile land in the east. Considerations of self-sufficiency and efficient cereal production on the Junker estates to the east of the Elbe received priority for the time being, even at the cost of accelerating the flight from the villages.

Not a few reports of peasant dissatisfaction with this law reached Berlin. Complaints were not limited to the restriction of ownership rights with regard to inheritance. There were difficulties in the raising of loans needed to improve cultivation methods. Since the holdings and farms could not be mortgaged, banks were certainly not eager to forward credit. The government, on the other hand, had more pressing matters to attend to than aid for inefficient peasant holdings.[138] Instead, a vast propaganda apparatus was set in motion to award peasants prestige and social status, which as it turned out yielded considerable success. Once a year thousands of peasants gathered on the Bückeberg for magnificent harvest celebrations, held in the presence of Hitler and all the major Nazi figures. The press, on Darré's explicit instruction, adorned Hitler with the title of *Bauernkanzler* and published numerous pictures showing him in the company of peasants wearing traditional rural costume and merry village children. During the initial years, while there was still considerable unemployment, youngsters were encouraged to enlist for a year of agricultural service. Propaganda romanticized rural calm and the sound "educational" ways of rustic life. Darré assigned a special functionary to the promotion of peasant culture. Fashion designers were sent to districts whose peasants had long since forgotten their traditional costume, in order to reinvent them. Goebbels's propaganda machine categorically banned jokes and caricatures ridiculing peasants and imposed an idyllic mode on all reports concerning peasants and village life. There is no doubt that these efforts boosted peasant morale by granting them social status and attention. Nevertheless, one wonders whether the peasants, at least the more sober ones, felt comfortable with being presented as medieval "museum pieces" in the midst of a bustling, modern,

138. Broszat, *Der Staat Hitlers*, pp. 236; Farquharson, "Agriculture in Germany," pp. 237f.

industrial society. The facts show that when the opportunity arose to secure easier and better-paid jobs in urban industry this fake romanticism failed to keep people in the village, where work was harder and the standard of living considerably lower than that of the average city dweller.[139]

The policy of raising agricultural output did, in fact, raise the level of income from agriculture during the early years. But by 1935–36 the relation had already changed for the worse in comparison to other economic sectors (see appendix, tables 5–6). Although low agricultural input prices still enabled peasants to accumulate some surplus income, the annual growth of income was higher in all other sectors of the economy from that year on. This state of affairs was particularly conspicuous among agricultural laborers. While their level of income was higher than it had been during the Great Depression, it lagged behind the rising income of their peers in industry. Thus the average annual wage of an agricultural laborer east of the Elbe was almost 25 percent lower than that of a semi-skilled industrial worker, while the former's workday was longer and part of his wage was paid in kind instead of cash.[140] Under these conditions, grants to young couples after five years of agricultural labor as well as financial assistance in housing failed to prevent flight from the villages. Instructions that employers were to dismiss workers who had left agriculture for other branches were of no avail either. On the contrary, in order to circumvent these instructions from the outset, parents did their best to secure industrial jobs for their offspring on the latter's graduation from school. Since young women preferred to marry in town anyway, the average age of the rural population rose visibly.[141]

Between 1935 and 1938 650,000 people left villages for towns. In spite of their ideology and proclaimed objectives, the authorities did almost nothing to stop this population shift. During the initial years, while there was still much unemployment, agrarian policy was meant to complement employment policy. The economic and administrative preference for agriculture was therefore preserved. Protectionist customs encouraged the production of import substitutes, thus improving the balance of payments and increasing rural employment. However, the closer the industrial upswing came to achieving full employment, the more this trend slowed down. The

139. Farquharson, "Agriculture in Germany," pp. 173, 407.
140. Grunberger, *Social History of the Third Reich*, p. 156.
141. Farquharson, "Agriculture in Germany," pp. 252f., 269.

exigencies of village life, the migration of youngsters deprived by law of a share in their family's land, and the increasing opportunities for work in town all combined to accelerate the flow of people from villages to towns. The authorities, who at least from 1936 on, were faced with a shortage of industrial labor, in fact accepted this state of affairs as advantageous to their aim of producing guns instead of butter. Paradoxically, the shortage in agricultural labor was temporarily solved by employing foreigners, mainly Poles, a practice previously condemned as a danger to "racial purity." While seven thousand foreign workers were employed in German agriculture in 1932, about fifty thousand permits for the employment of seasonal foreign labor were issued in 1935.[142]

However, the full consequences of this process surfaced only after 1936. Throughout the early years agriculture still enjoyed economic and administrative preference. Its large and relatively independent administrative establishment, close ties with the party apparatus, and nimbus of actively implemented Nazi ideology made the position of agriculture unique and powerful, almost as if it were a state within the state.[143] This state of affairs obviously generated friction and conflicts with local and national authorities as well as with party bodies like the DAF and the Gauleiters, who strove to reinforce their own domestic power. In most cases these controversies were settled according to the balance of power between the rival parties, but Darré and his assistants were frequently compelled to forego their corporate independence and accept unpleasant compromises imposed by the party, apparently on Hitler's own initiative.[144] Clashes between Darré's establishment and the Gauleiters were especially frequent in 1933 and 1934, when Darré was at the height of his career and the balance of power not yet settled.

The most famous quarrel occurred with Erich Koch, the Gauleiter of East Prussia, who was close to the Nazi "left" and a sworn enemy of agrarian reactionaries. Matters rose to a pitch when Koch expelled some of Darré's employees from the party and even had a few arrested and sent to concentration camps. In addition, in the summer of 1933 he organized the seizure of certain grain supplies for the benefit of the party. Darré complained to Rudolf Heß and in

142. Honigberger, "Wirtschaftspolitische Zielsetzung," pp. 76, 81; Farquharson, "Agriculture in Germany," pp. 272f.
143. Farquharson, "Agriculture in Germany," p. 295; Broszat, *Der Staat Hitlers*, p. 238.
144. Farquharson, "Agriculture in Germany," p. 500.

consequence appointed his deputy, Meinberg, as peasant leader for East Prussia, to serve as a foil to Koch. Following these events, Darré's people were released from concentration camps but lost their previous jobs. Similar quarrels, though on a lesser scale, occurred with the Gauleiter of Pomerania and the SA headquarters there, who complained that the RNS neglected resettlement.[145]. To put an end to these frictions Heß summoned Darré and his staff to a meeting with the Gauleiters in December 1934. The result was an announcement, signed by Heß and published two months later, delineating party and RNS authority in rural districts. The party was forbidden to intervene in specific agricultural matters, but Darré had to consult each Gauleiter before he appointed his representative for the Gauleiter's district. The party's women's organization, it was also decided, would replace the RNS as the office responsible for all matters concerning village women. The concluding paragraph proclaimed unquestionable supremacy of the party over all spheres of activity. It was quite clear that the announcement imposed restrictions upon RNS authority.[146]

Similar conflicts arose between Darré and Robert Ley, the DAF leader, who seems to have been supported by the Gauleiters. Besides their basic opposition to the measure of corporate autonomy the RNS enjoyed, DAF functionaries complained in particular about the sorry state of agricultural laborers. Writing to Darré in the spring of 1938, Ley blamed the RNS for the continued flight from rural districts: "The drift to industry, where wages and prices are not so harshly restricted, is no wonder when the still partially disastrous working and living conditions of agricultural laborers are considered." He argued that the DAF and the party should be responsible for the social situation of these workers, not the RNS, which represented one-sided interests. Darré responded with an angry letter, accusing Ley of exceeding DAF authority and seeking excessive power.[147]

Although Darré was not powerful enough to stand up to the combined pressure of Ley and the Gauleiters, he usually got the upper hand in his frequent clashes with Schacht and the Ministry of Economics, even in 1934 and 1935, at the height of Schacht's influence. This was at least partly due to the special ideological

---

145. Farquharson, "Agriculture in Germany," pp. 300ff.; Broszat, *Der Staat Hitlers*, p. 239.
146. Farquharson, "Agriculture in Germany," p. 308.
147. Ibid., p. 315; Broszat, *Der Staat Hitlers*, p. 240.

position held by the RNS and Darré's close relations with the SS. RNS offices systematically compiled evidence against Schacht. Especially distinguished in this activity was Friedrich Zimmermann (better known, as I mentioned earlier, by his pen name, Ferdinand Fried, used in *Die Tat*), whom Himmler had transferred to Darré's headquarters. In October 1934 Zimmermann filed a complaint stating "that Schacht demands international trust to be vested in himself, not as the Führer's emissary, but only in himself."[148]

Open clashes occurred between Schacht and Darré on the question of RNS authority over retail trade in processed food products and over food-processing industries. In the summer of 1934, following a ruling by Hitler in favor of Darré, eighty thousand companies dealing in food products were put under RNS authority.[149] The pricing of agricultural produce was also a bone of contention between Darré and the superintendent of prices, Carl Friedrich Goerdeler, who was backed by Schacht. In a speech on National Peasant Day in November 1934 Darré sharply attacked Goerdeler , an event that was widely interpreted as "a frank declaration of war against Dr. Schacht."[150] Goerdeler's resignation and the fact that for a whole year no one was appointed to replace him left the RNS as sole arbiter in the field of agricultural produce pricing. Ultimately in 1935, the government was called upon to decide the issue. Due to pressures from the party establishment and labor trustees Darré had to agree to preserve the current price levels.

In 1935 and 1936, when the state of foreign currency reserves further declined, a new conflict broke out between Schacht and Darré, who demanded additional currency allocations for the import of foodstuffs, mainly fats and livestock fodder. Schacht responded by blaming Darré for the fall in agricultural output compared to 1933, a decline that had in fact occurred – mainly in cattle, pigs, and some field crops (see appendix, tables 8–9). Once again Hitler ruled in favor of Darré, and the RNS received an additional sixty million reichsmarks in foreign currency. There is no doubt that Hitler's fear of food shortages and their impact on public opinion played a decisive role in his ruling. Be that as it may, Schacht had lost another round in his continuous battle with party functionaries, a battle that in time undermined his position and

148. BDC, PK Personalakte Friedrich Zimmermann.
149. Schweitzer, *Big Business*, p. 167.
150. HF, K.V. Krogmann diaries, 11/K5, p. 38.

hastened his dismissal.[151]

Darré's opponents in the matter of price policies were made of sterner stuff. The rise in food prices and the peasants' visibly better situation when compared to industrial workers, whose wages were frozen, caused indignation and unrest among party members. Darré's *Staatssekretär* and troubleshooter, Herbert Backe, met on August 27, 1935, with all labor trustees and the Labor Front leader, Robert Ley, to discuss foodstuff prices. The trustees argued against Backe's claim that consumer prices had not risen, citing examples of 40 to 50 percent rises. They complained that the growing discontent among workers was being exploited by Communist propaganda. By the end of this meeting, as well as at a similar meeting with the Gauleiters that took place a few days later, none of the concerned parties apparently had convinced each other.[152] Although the RNS avoided further price boosting, it did not reduce prevailing prices either. Thus even after the close of 1935 high prices for agricultural produce remained the principal source of the increase in peasant income.

I believe that the peasants were allowed to preserve this achievement in spite of opposition from Schacht as well as other influential party authorities on the basis of ideological, not economic, considerations. The claim that rising incomes in agriculture were good for the whole economy because they would boost rural demand for industrial products[153] was valid within limits only for the beginning of the period and at the latest until the end of 1934. From then on the industrial boom fed mainly on demand from the public sector; private consumption was restrained by all available means. On the other hand, rising agricultural prices increased production costs in some industries and generated pressures to raise wages. The fact that in spite of these economic considerations agricultural produce prices rose until 1936 and were kept at that high level afterward demonstrates the relative autonomy of the agricultural sector with regard to marketing and pricing. Besides the regime's ideological commitment to the preservation of a strong peasantry, proclaimed by Hitler in his Reichstag speech of March 23, 1933, as being a primary objective that took precedence even over the liquidation of

151. Farquharson, "Agriculture in Germany," pp. 189f., 221f.; Broszat, *Der Staat Hitlers*, p. 238.
152. BA, R 43II, nos. 317/18.
153. Grunberger, *Social History of the Third Reich*, p. 60.

unemployment,[154] the advantage of the agricultural sector arose also from the dominant position of the party at all levels of the agricultural establishment. Subsequently even these strongholds failed to preserve the preferred status of agriculture. The RNS gradually lost ground until Darré himself was compelled to put it under the authority of the government establishment. His own position was also gradually eroded. In 1936, when agriculture came under Göring's authority, the latter appointed Backe, not Darré, as *Ernährungskommissar* under the Four-Year Plan.[155]

We have already seen that Nazi agrarian policy failed to achieve some of its primary ideological objectives, such as resettlement and preservation of the rural population percentage. We will see below that it did not come up to expectations in self-sufficiency and autarky either, although it scored certain achievements in this field. On the other hand, the speed and ease with which the Nazis assumed control of this economic sector constituted an enormous political triumph. Powerful economic associations rapidly became exclusive Nazi dominions, while their previous leaders were completely ousted. Until the Nazis assumed power, the East Prussian Junkers had ruled this sector economically and politically without interference. Seventeen thousand estate owners, who constituted only about 0.5 percent of all farm owners but possessed one-sixth of all acreage, determined the politics of the Reichslandbund, which especially during the final years of the Weimar Republic became a powerful political tool. The Junkers made and toppled governments, playing a central role in the game of political intrigue around Hindenburg that ultimately brought Hitler to power. Even after 1933 the majority of senior officers came from this class, which had jealously guarded its elite military status as an exclusive position of political power to be wielded efficiently whenever necessary. In the light of these facts it is astonishing that this class was ousted from all of its economic positions in the course of just a few weeks, without the slightest show of resistance. A large economic sector, still encompassing 20 percent of the population and of the GNP, passed into the hands of the Nazis at one blow, without so much as a whimper! In striking contrast to their methods in industry, the Nazis did not even leave the execution of government instructions to the former lords of agriculture.

154. Quoted by B. Ries, "Die Finanzpolitik im Deutschen Reich von 1933 bis 1935," (dissertation, Freiburg i. Br., 1964), p. 22.
155. Farquharson, "Agriculture in Germany," p. 502.

Arthur Schweitzer's explanation that the surrender of agriculture was the price paid by big business "for the exclusive privilege to rule the economic sphere of urban business"[156] appears to me farfetched. In spite of the large landowners' involvement with industrial interests, they were still an independent class that knew very well how to represent their specific economic interests even against industry. This was by no means some marginal group in big business that could be easily "sold" in return for the preservation of industrial interests. It is more reasonable to assume that the Nazis owed their success with agricultural associations to early infiltration and to the support they had gained among the rural population. In addition the process was facilitated because the traditional agrarian elite perceived Nazi ideology concerning agriculture and the institutional structure of the RNS as "the realization of all corporate demands which have ever been raised by agricultural associations. . . . It looked as if Darré's organizational system would safeguard the interests of agrarian policy against all nonagricultural sectors and as if overall economic policy had also been influenced in favor of these interests."[157]

However, this is also only a partial explanation. Even if the Nazis' ideological and corporate concepts largely coincided with those of the Junker landowners (and this is true only within certain limits), it is hard to believe that this fact alone made them hand over their dominant position willingly and in good faith to Darré and his colleagues. It seems that the real reason rested with the Nazis themselves and not with those they chose to oust: ideologically committed to this economic sector more than to any other, they wished to reorganize agriculture according to their own notions at once and without interference. If one can speak at all of a "National Socialist Revolution," it occurred primarily in agriculture, which was a cornerstone of their whole economic, social, and political philosophy. In consequence, as an independent political force the Prussian Junkers had already disappeared permanently from the public arena in 1933. What happened subsequently and came to a head on July 20, 1944, was but the sound of the death rattle.

The Nazis failed to realize their sacrosanct objectives in agricultural policy not because they abjured this ideological commitment. Their failure arose from a clash between long-term ideological aspirations and the constraints of immediate political goals: rearma-

156. Schweitzer, *Big Business*, p. 200.
157. Esenwein-Rothe, *Wirtschaftsverbände*, p. 51.

ment and preparation for war. Faced with this dilemma, the Nazis chose to devote their resources to preparation for war, a choice which a priori accommodated their basic view that their socio-economic vision of the future would become viable only within the boundaries of a greater *Lebensraum*. But even if continued migration from the countryside to urban industry and neglect of resettlement could be justified as temporary compromises, the failure to achieve self-sufficiency in foodstuffs and raw materials was much harder to sustain and explain away. The effort to increase agricultural production was an intrinsic part of war preparations. In this sphere the regime achieved some success only during its initial years. In 1933–34 domestic produce provided 80 percent of total food product consumption and in 1938–39 it rose to 83 percent, compared to 68 percent in 1927–28. Full self-sufficiency was achieved only in cereals: 99 percent of domestic consumption in 1933–34 and even some surplus in 1938–39. On the other hand, the regime failed to escape dependence on imports of some vital crops. In 1934–35 Germany was still compelled to import about 90 percent of vegetable fats, 20 percent of animal fats, 85 percent of fiber crops, and 90 percent of wool.[158] In 1934 foodstuffs still made up 35.5 percent of the import total, as against 40 percent in 1933. For every year from 1933 to 1936 over three billion reichsmarks were spent on foodstuff imports, a sum that rose to five billion reichsmarks in 1938 (see appendix, tables 7–8).

The scarcity of foreign currency for imports and the lag in self-sufficiency, especially with regard to industrial crops and fats, resulted in the proclamation of an agricultural production campaign in November 1934 (the German term *Erzeugungsschlacht* was probably borrowed from Mussolini's *battaglia di grano*). The implementation of an extensive plan for the improvement of agricultural methods was proclaimed at the same time. This included cultivation and fertilizing methods, seed sorting, expansion of cultivated land by means of drainage and soil amelioration, the breeding of pedigree livestock, and so forth.[159] The project operated by means of guidance in agricultural expertise and favorable price policies. Investment grants or loans were limited on account of rearmament constraints, but the Labor Service was called upon to assist in soil amelioration works. In spite of all these efforts, real agricultural output rose only by 7 percent between 1933 and 1936. The reason

158. Hans E. Priester, *Das deutsche Wirtschaftswunder* (Amsterdam, 1936), p. 93.
159. Ibid., p. 94; Farquharson, "Agriculture in Germany," p. 212f.

for these poor results is not quite clear, as statistics show increased yields per hectare as well as an overall increase in the amount of land cultivated. It seems that the period included a few years of poor harvest caused by climatic conditions and that the scarcity of rural labor prevented optimal utilization of existing production factors[160] (see appendix, table 9). It is therefore reasonable to assume that much better results would have been achieved if the state had invested larger sums in agricultural development. It follows that because of the regime's political order of priorities even short-term economic goals were not realized. On the other hand, the failure to achieve self-sufficiency in foodstuffs until the outbreak of the war, in spite of all efforts, reinforced the wish to achieve a durable solution by imposing the "new order" on the whole of Europe. At the same time the poisonous racist-agrarian vision of the future continued to "simmer" in Himmler's and the SS's ideological cauldrons, "and Hitler also carried with him the unfulfilled vision of the *Blut und Boden* nation and projected into the utopic distance a vast agrarian *Großraum* that was to be conquered by the sword, [a vision] that could not be realized within Germany's frontiers until 1939."[161]

160. Guillebaud, *Economic Recovery*, pp. 96f.
161. Broszat, *Der Staat Hitlers*, p. 241.

Chapter 4

Ideology and the Economy
Implemented Policies, 1933–1936

Between 1933 and 1936 the German GNP increased by an average annual rate of 9.5 percent, and the annual production index for industry and crafts rose by 17.2 percent. The principal source of this growth, which propelled the German economy out of a deep depression into full employment within less than four years, was increased demand by the public sector, defined by German economists of the period as *Staatskonjunktur* (state prosperity). The average annual growth of public consumption during these four years was 18.7 percent, while private consumption rose only by 3.6 percent annually. These data alone already show that the Nazis overcame unemployment primarily through government-initiated public works and/or orders by the government and other public-sector authorities (see appendix, table 1).

Additional public consumption and investment in the period 1933 to 1936 came to over twenty-seven billion reichsmarks. Of this sum, eleven billion was forwarded by the Reichsbank; the remainder came from additional taxes, "donations," and loans raised from the public and from banks (see appendix, table 3). An overall summary for these four years shows that no less than 80 percent of all additional spending went into rearmament and expansion of the army. It is therefore true that rearmament played a major role in the liquidation of unemployment. Nevertheless, it would be erroneous to conclude that the latter was merely a fringe benefit of rearmament, successfully exploited by the propaganda machine. Full employment was an autonomous objective of Nazi policy, both as a principle and as a means of stabilizing the regime as well as recruiting public support. The availability of idle production factors combined with their open-mindedness vis-à-vis novel economic concepts enabled the Nazis to achieve this objective simultaneously with their political goal of rearmament and preparation for an

158

expansionist war. They could have achieved the same economic effect by allocating all additional resources to public works and the increase of private consumption, with no connection whatever to preparation for war. On the other hand, there is no doubt that, because of their ideological and political principles, they would have executed rearmament plans even if the state of the German economy had been different. They would not have hesitated to finance war in the traditional manner, using higher taxes and public loans at the expense of radically reduced private consumption. However, the political objectives of rearmament had economic implications besides increased employment, which will be discussed below.

The Financing of Works Projects

Statistical data support the assumption that the liquidation of unemployment was an autonomous economic objective alongside military preparations. Expenditure on nonmilitary employment projects exceeded rearmament expenses in 1933 and remained approximately equal to them within the overall summary of the first two years. In 1933, 3.1 billion reichsmarks was spent on housing and road-development projects executed by municipal authorities, as against 0.7–1.9 billion (according to varying estimates) spent on rearmament. The total for two years, until the end of 1934, was 5 billion on nonmilitary public works as against 6 billion on rearmament and the army (see appendix, table 4). The combined expenditure reduced the 1932 average of 5.6 million registered unemployed to 4.8 in 1933 and 2.7 in 1934.[1] This does not mean that the Nazis accorded priority to civil employment projects during these years and that rearmament as a political objective surfaced only later. On the contrary, the preparation for war was Hitler's primary project, and his orders were to direct allocations for job creation accordingly. This order was not carried out at once because during the first few years the army could not absorb larger sums for technical reasons and because it lacked manpower. Alert to the urgency of unemployment relief, the Nazis immediately launched public works projects, projects that had in part been planned by previous governments. Toward the end of 1934 the center of gravity finally passed to military expenditure.

This state of affairs is unequivocally confirmed by Hitler's

1. Fischer, *Deutsche Wirtschaftspolitik*, p. 108.

utterances on employment and rearmament immediately after his appointment as chancellor. As early as February 8th, at a government-level meeting in the chancellor's office, Hitler rejected a proposal (presented by the transport minister) to allocate a certain sum for the construction of a dam in Upper Silesia, arguing that for the coming five years all available money should go into rearmament: "The next five years must be devoted to the rearmament of the German people. Every public plan for the creation of jobs has to be judged from the point of view of whether it is necessary for the rearmament of the German people. This thought must remain in the foreground, always and everywhere." Hitler's position at this meeting was supported by Göring and Blomberg, minister for the armed forces. The minister of labor agreed with Hitler's argument but thought "that besides the goals of defense policy, there are other valuable economic tasks which should not be neglected." At the conclusion of the meeting it was decided to postpone construction of the dam for the time being.[2]

On the following day, February 9, 1933, at a session of the government committee for employment affairs, Hitler once again stated his point of view: "Absolute priority to be given to the interests of defense while public orders are distributed. . . . He could accept the limited resources demanded by the Armed Forces Ministry at the time only from the point of view that faster rearmament was impossible during the coming year. . . . Allocations for the Immediate Program should also be determined in this spirit. In the battle against unemployment the appropriate auxiliary remedy was public works ordered by the state. The five-hundred-million plan was the largest of its kind and especially suitable to serve rearmament interests; it allowed for the camouflage of defense projects in the best possible manner. In the near future this camouflage would be of particular value."[3] It was eminently clear that Hitler's primary goal was rearmament, to which employment projects were subordinate. He acknowledged the importance of liquidating unemployment as such, but understood that rearmament projects would also create jobs. This view was demonstrated in his talk to Rauschning in August 1932: "I can achieve just as much by rearmament as by the construction of houses and by settlement. I can also give the unemployed more money to meet

2. BA, R 43/II, 536, Ministerbesprechung vom 8. Februar 1933.
3. Ibid., Sitzung des Ausschusses der Reichsregierung für Arbeitsbeschaffung vom 9. Februar 1933.

their needs. Thus I create purchasing power and increase the circulation of money."[4]

Public works financed by deficit spending were not invented by the Nazis. As we have already seen, the theoretical foundations for such a policy were established in previous years, and the Papen and Schleicher governments had begun to prepare practical plans in this spirit. The Nazi rulers appropriated both the theoretical propositions and the ready-made plans, but they implemented them with a degree of decisiveness and to an extent that exceeded all forecasts. The Brüning government had already announced a one-billion-reichmark plan for additional public works in 1930.[5] But it was never even initiated, since the realization of the plan, like some later ones, depended on loans from abroad; no one even thought of financing public works by deficit spending through the offices of the Reichsbank. The notion of such a loan under prevailing international conditions was utterly unrealistic. Though a special company was founded to this end, nothing ever came of it. The special committee appointed for this purpose (the Brauń Committee) also made the granting of an international loan a condition for the extension of credit to government-initiated public works, which for the same reason never materialized.[6]

The first move toward deficit spending on employment projects was announced by the Papen government in September 1932 through one of its emergency decrees.[7] The Papen plan was to promote employment primarily in the private sector: initially only three hundred million out of the two billion planned for the first year was to go into public works. The bulk of the money was earmarked for the private sector in the form of tax reductions and employment premiums. A proposal was made to give employers "tax-credit notes" representing 40 to 100 percent of the taxes due, to be utilized in the payment of taxes in subsequent years – that is, as tax discounts for the future. As these "notes" were immediately discountable by the Reichsbank at a very low discount rate, they were actually liquid assets that increased the money supply. In addition employers received an annual bonus of four hundred reichsmarks (also in the form of tax-credit notes) for every new

4. H. Rauschning, *Gespräche mit Hitler, 1932–1934* (New York, 1940), p. 27.
5. K. Schiller, *Arbeitsbeschaffung und Finanzordnung in Deutschland* (Berlin, 1936), pp. 48f.
6. Ibid., p. 52.
7. Verordnung des Reichspräsidenten zur Belebung der Wirtschaft, vom 4. September 1932, RGB1. I, p. 425.

employee. As a special bonus employers who hired new workers were permitted to lower wages beneath the legal tariff, a proposal that made the trade unions reject the entire Papen Plan at once, whereas employers on the whole tended to endorse it.[8] However, the RDI opposed any projects of public works as a matter of principle, stated in a declaration they had settled upon on August 17, 1923.[9] As it turned out, under then-prevailing economic conditions these tax discounts were not a sufficiently attractive incentive for private enterprises. Employers did not utilize this opening and did not hire additional workers; the allocated sums were not spent. In consequence the head of the Reichsbank, Hans Luther, and the minister of finance Schwerin von Krosigk, agreed to add five hundred million reichsmarks to the public works allocation.[10]

The first significant move toward public works financed by the Reichsbank came with the Immediate Program launched by the Schleicher government. The plan's author, Günther Gereke, was employment commissioner in this government and remained in office for a few months in Hitler's first government. According to his plan, five hundred million reichsmarks was allocated at once to public works, to which another one hundred million was added after Hitler's takeover. The project was financed by bills drawn on fictitious companies, extendable without a deadline and at once discountable by the Reichsbank, thereby providing a basis for an immediate increase in the money supply. This was a special technique of deficit spending devised in keeping with Reichsbank statutes, which permitted the forwarding of credit to the government only in return for "ordinary commercial bills" for a period that did not exceed three months. This procedure became a precedent for preliminary financing by Mefo-bills, a technique that Schacht subsequently turned into the main instrument for deficit spending.

The Gereke Plan is of interest in the present context not only because it represents the first serious move toward deficit spending on a relatively large project of government-initiated public works but also on account of its origins. Its outline was worked out by Günther Gereke in the summer of 1932 while he was chairman of the Verband Deutscher Landgemeinden (Association of German Rural Communities), which officially adopted the plan in August 1932; Gereke was also a Reichstag delegate on behalf of the DNVP.

8. Petzina, "Hauptprobleme," p. 23.
9. BA, Nachlaß Silverberg, no. 223, pp. 184f.
10. Interview with Schwerin von Krosigk, June 1974.

His plan was composed in close cooperation with Ludwig Herpel, the editor of a right-wing periodical, and according to another source, with Werner Sombart's active participation.[11] The Gereke Plan was brought to Schleicher's attention by a veteran officer of the right-wing Stahlhelm, who tried to recruit wider support for the plan, even among trade unions and Social Democrats.[12] This once again confirms Friedländer-Prechtl's claim, mentioned above, that all plans for job creation through public works and deficit spending were supported mainly by right-wing circles. Heinrich Dräger's research association and its followers supported the Gereke Plan enthusiastically; they devoted a special issue of the periodical *Wirtschafts-Wende*, edited by Friedländer-Prechtl, to a discussion of it. On the other hand, business circles, which had received the Papen Plan favorably, sharply opposed the Gereke Plan because of its emphasis on public works and inflationary financing.[13] The Nazis admitted that among all available plans this was the best one, but attributed its merits to their own influence. Bernhard Köhler claimed that whatever was good in this plan the authors had adopted from Nazi sources: they had learned from Strasser's Reichstag speech of May 10, 1932, and Ludwig Herpel, who had once been a member of the party, was influenced by Gottfried Feder. Beyond that, according to Köhler, the plan was too modest and would at best only partially relieve unemployment.[14] After they attained power the Nazis left Gereke in his post until March 1933. In his own memoirs Gereke claimed that he was dismissed because he refused Hitler's request to join the party. According to Gereke, Hitler argued that the liquidation of unemployment had to be "our own feat" and therefore Gereke had to join the party. When he refused, he was dismissed by means of a fabricated trial in which he was accused of embezzling some of Hindenburg's election funds in 1932. In the fifties Gereke moved from West to East Germany, where he was received with high regard. There he wrote his memoirs, a task in which he was aided by the East German historian Eberhard Czichon, who "edited" his work.[15]

We see therefore that when the Nazis took power they found two

11. Czichon, *Wer verhalf Hitler*, pp. 31f.
12. Dräger-Materialsammlung.
13. Petzina, "Hauptprobleme," p. 26.
14. B. Köhler, "Wir wollen das Recht auf Arbeit," *Arbeitertum*, Jan. 15, 1933.
15. Gereke, *Ich war königlich-preußischer Landrat*, p. 158.

ready-made public works projects, plus the necessary legal arrangements for their financing. Work plans for the execution of specific projects were also available, mainly from municipalities where lack of funds had compelled postponement of numerous plans, but also from post-office and railway agencies. Their implementation could begin without delay. With regard to the Papen Plan, some changes were made at once: money allocated for activation of the private sector was redirected to government-initiated public works, to be carried out by public authorities. In April 1933 this was put into effect through modification of the respective law, which stopped the issue of tax-credit notes for the employment of additional workers and instead allocated the money to public works mainly through community agencies.[16] During the first months of 1933 the Nazis added large-scale works projects to those they had found waiting. The first Reinhardt Plan (named after Fritz Reinhardt, the first Nazi *Staatssekretär* at the Ministry of Finance) allocated one billion reichsmarks to public works. It was financed by means of treasury notes discounted by the Reichsbank, that is, by the undisguised printing of money.[17] In September the second Reinhardt Plan added another five hundred million reichsmarks, aimed principally at the construction of housing. The money was allocated for additions to and renovation of residential and commercial buildings, on condition that the owners invested matching sums from their own resources.[18] Alongside these projects for immediate creation of jobs through public works, the Nazis encouraged investment and consumption in preferred branches of the private sector, in particular by abolishing the tax on motor vehicles[19] and by tax exemption for the renewal of industrial equipment.[20] Jointly these projects came to another two billion reichsmarks, which was spent on employment projects for state-owned companies like the post office and the railways. Out of a total of 350 million reichsmarks allocated for the construction of motorways (*Reichsautobahnen*), only 166 million had been spent by the end of 1934.[21]

16. Schiller, *Arbeitsbeschaffung*, p. 57.
17. Gesetz zur Verminderung der Arbeitslosigkeit vom 1. Juni 1933, RGB1. I, p. 323.
18. Gesetz zur Verminderung der Arbeitslosigkeit vom 21. September 1933, RGB1. I, p. 651.
19. Gesetz zur Änderung des Kraftfahrzeugsteuergesetzes vom 10. April 1933, RGB1. I, p. 192.
20. Gesetz zur Verminderung der Arbeitslosigkeit vom 1. Juni 1933, Abschnitt II, Steuerfreiheit für Ersatzbeschaffungen, RGB1. I, p. 323.
21. Schiller, *Arbeitsbeschaffung*, p. 155.

The projects described here actually include almost the whole range of nonmilitary employment projects launched between 1933 and 1936. Of the twenty-eight billion reichsmarks that represented the total of additional annual state expenditures during these years as compared to 1932, only 5.5 billion were devoted to civil employment projects (see appendix, table 4). Most of this sum was spent during the first two years; beginning at the end of 1934, deficit spending went almost exclusively on rearmament. To finance rearmament, the government and the Reichsbank (under Schacht) initiated the creation of a special company with a one-million-reichsmark equity, the Metallurgische Forschungsgesellschaft m.b.H. (MEFO, Metallurgic Research Company, Ltd.) in August 1933. As owners of the company, each of the four leading enterprises in Germany's metal industry (Krupp, Siemens, Rheinmetall, and Gutehoffnungshütte) signed up for 250,000 reichsmarks' worth of share capital. Representatives of the Reichsbank and the War Ministry were members of the company's managing board. Rearmament orders were paid for, by whatever agency had issued the order, in bills for a period of three months, extendable for up to five years. The bills were endorsed by the said company, which accounts for their name, Mefo-Wechsel (Mefo-bills). The absolute secrecy of this arrangement was preserved until after the war. The fictitious character of the company is obvious from the fact that, on the basis of one million reichsmarks' share capital, the company endorsed a total of twelve billion reichsmarks until the end of 1937. The Reichsbank discounted these bills on presentation, thus immediately increasing the current money supply. Although until the war only 20 percent of the total rearmament expenditure was financed in this manner, it made up 50 percent of the total expenditure on military orders during the initial years.[22]

This system of preliminary financing by means of bills had a double purpose: first, it circumvented Reichsbank statutes, which permitted only limited financing of government expenses in the form of a loan but allowed for the inclusion of short-term commercial bills as legal coverage of the currency; second, it served to keep the scope of rearmament secret, at least until 1934, when even the publication of data concerning the national budget was stopped. As mentioned above, Schacht had already voiced his opposition to monetary experiments in 1932. Now he feared the psychological

22. Fischer, *Deutsche Wirtschaftspolitik*, pp. 86, 102.

Nazi Economics

impact that publication of the true dimensions of rearmament might have on the population. He must have realized that the economic effect of Mefo-bills was not less inflationary than any other form of money issued from the printing press, but he accorded considerable importance to possible psychological effects. At a meeting of the Supreme Economic Council on September 20, 1933, Schacht announced that he was prepared to forward any required amount but not to name figures and that it was of great importance to prevent talk about "theories and billions" in public.[23]

This economic council was appointed by Hitler at the beginning of 1933 but was convened only a few times, merely in order to listen to speeches. In the light of all this, it is rather difficult to agree with Burton Klein, who argues that Schacht was ultraconservative and that the Nazis' whole economic policy, including their shying away from more massive rearmament, suffered from exaggerated fears of inflation.[24] Schacht and his Nazi masters were not wanting in fiscal adventurism; they conducted a policy of deficit spending that was unprecedented in peacetime economies. It is nevertheless true that their fear of inflation was deeply embedded and partly determined the means by which they carried out deficit spending. Among these was the special form of preliminary financing through bills that were to be paid off (as claimed at the time) by budgetary surpluses in coming years. However, in 1939, when the first Mefo-bills came due for payment, the Third Reich was caught up in hectic rearmament efforts, and the Mefo-bills were simply exchanged for ordinary treasury notes. After the war Schacht claimed that this "violation of the agreement" was the last straw that made him resign from the Reichsbank[25] while Schwerin von Krosigk, who was minister of finance at the time, said that this arrangement had been agreed upon from the outset.[26] It really makes no difference, either in theory or in practice: Mefo-bills or any other bills issued to finance employment were merely paper money printed by the Reichsbank. Even the fact that in general only a third of Mefo-bills were presented to the Reichsbank for discount did not change their character as a principal means for deficit spending and increasing the money supply: among the asset portfolios of banks they served as

23. HF, K.V. Krogmann diaries, 11/K4, pp. 19f.
24. Klein, *Germany's Preparations for War*, p. 8f.
25. H. Schacht, *Account Settled*.
26. L. v. Schwerin v. Krosigk, *Es geschah in Deutschland: Menschenbilder unseres Jahrhunderts*, 3d ed. (Tübingen and Stuttgart, 1952), p. 191.

secondary reserves. Nevertheless, the technique appears to have achieved its aim of concealing the scope of rearmament and deficit spending.[27] Between 1933 and 1936, 9.5 billion reichsmarks' worth of Mefo-bills, representing more than 85 percent of the Reichsbank's direct money supply for deficit financing and rearmament, was issued (see appendix, table 4).

It follows that neither the financial technique the Nazis employed nor their assignment of deficit spending mainly to public consumption was their own invention. At least the Schleicher government had already prepared the initial blueprints. Even the autobahn project, later hailed as a special contribution of the Führer's genius, was not original. From the end of the twenties a company named Hafraba (Hamburg-Frankfurt-Basel) had conducted a propaganda campaign and designed basic blueprints for an autobahn between these cities, to serve as the initial artery of an extended road network. During the Great Depression the authors of the idea added the job-creation effect to their propaganda, closely cooperating with Dräger's research association and the circle around Gereke. The manager of this company, Willy Hof, was received by Hitler immediately after the Nazi takeover; according to Hof, Hitler praised the idea enthusiastically and promised to carry it out by means of Reichsbank financing.[28] However, I believe that the question of whether or not Nazi economic policy was original is secondary and is not relevant at the present stage of this discussion. In the preceding chapters I showed that, when the Nazis assumed power, they were not altogether unprepared with regard to an overall economic philosophy; they had even adopted proposals for immediate economic measures in order to relieve unemployment. The decisive element was the fact that they succeeded in realizing these proposals on a scale that exceeded all forecasts. There is no doubt that this success was crucial in recruiting majority support among the German people within a relatively short period of time and in winning their admiration for the Nazis' economic achievements, a phenomenon whose traces have not yet entirely disappeared.

What generated this success is to be found in the political as well as in the ideological-propagandist sphere. I have tried to show that what made the Nazis' employment policy feasible and successful was more than a convenient accident or the result of pragmatic

27. Erbe, *Die nationalsozialistische Wirtschaftspolitik*, p. 54.
28. Dräger-Materialsammlung.

intuition and that their success also arose from their ability to integrate new concepts in economic theory with their notion of the state's role in society and the economy. The Nazis succeeded where their predecessors had failed because they were able to secure absolute political power and they were given sufficient time. The Ermächtigungsgesetz (the law establishing plenipotentiary authority) of March 23, 1933, the subsequent dismantling of all parties that participated in the coalition government, and the purging of all government and public bodies and agencies enabled them to implement their economic policy by means of administrative decrees with minimal interference. They were not merely freed from the necessity of seeking parliamentary consent: their political power provided the means to exert sufficient pressure on various interest groups which had previously been strong enough to abort similar plans and had contributed to the toppling of the government involved in such plans.

The opposition of large-scale industry to public works did not cease after January 1933. In December 1933 the chairman of the branch association of iron-producing industries, Ernst Poensgen, complained at a confidential meeting of the board that industry, like banking, was up against "ideological difficulties." According to him, these surfaced in price policies as well as in the allocation of resources for works projects. He thought that labor-intensive public works were acceptable only as a temporary measure. The genuine solution to unemployment would be achieved only by allocation of resources to "capital-intensive objectives," that is, government orders for private industry (it is quite revealing that this paragraph in Poensgen's speech was marked in pencil "not to be copied").[29] Industrialists were quite right to treat employment as an ideological issue that was better not tampered with. Under the slogan of the "right to work," the Nazis had made full employment an ideological tenet to which they were fully committed before they seized power. Given the state of Germany's economy at the time, the relief of unemployment would have received top priority treatment from any government, and public support would have depended largely on the extent of success or failure in this sphere – the more so for a party that had conducted several election campaigns (especially the 1932 campaign) under the slogan of *Arbeit und Brot* (work and bread) and claimed to possess the only practical

29. BA, R 13/I, no. 106, pp. 34ff.

employment project, as presented by Gregor Strasser in the Immediate Program.

However, as part of Nazi ideology the principle of full employment went beyond its then-current usefulness, whether as a slogan to be used to achieve power or as an immediate goal for economic policy when they assumed office. It headed their list of economic objectives proclaimed as permanent to the extent that it became almost synonymous with what they called German socialism. As early as 1932 Bernhard Köhler had published an article in the paper of Goebbels's propaganda department, proclaiming the Nazi commitment to full employment: "The National Socialist state will guarantee that every one of our people finds work."[30] This, however, was not just a topical demand spawned by the scope of current unemployment but was the "Socialist Revolution" itself: "The creation of jobs is . . . more than an economic measure or restoration of the economy or better provision for those who wish to work: it is in itself the Socialist Revolution against the government of capital."[31] |1932

The Nazis retained their propaganda along the same lines after they assumed power. Otto Dietrich, the academically trained economist who headed Hitler's press bureau, explicitly identified German socialism with the right to work: "Our socialism is no utopia, alienated from the real world, but natural life, full of pulsating blood . . . the sole egalitarian economic demand it grants all the people is the right to work."[32] When a state of full employment was already in sight, success reinforced the propaganda effect: what could be more persuasive than the claim that German socialism was already there, fulfilling the promise of a job for everyone? Thus, an article published in 1936 by Köhler declared: "For the German people the battle for work is the turning point from capitalism to socialism because its intention is to provide every member of the nation once again with a job. . . . When he [Adolf Hitler] said 'We will liquidate unemployment by our own strength,' capitalism received its death blow."[33]

However, the more effective this claim was as propaganda, the greater was the commitment it implied. The Nazis knew that they could in no way survive a renewed employment crisis. Unfortunately

30. B. Köhler, *Unser Wille und Weg* 2 (1932): 132.
31. Ibid., p. 302.
32. O. Dietrich, *Das Wirtschaftsdenken im Dritten Reich* (Munich, 1936), p. 14.
33. A. Holtz, "Sozialistische Wirtschaft," *Der Aufbau* 4, no. 17 (1936): 6–7.

169

they were never put to the test, as rearmament and war preparations kept the German economy in a state of full employment until the war and certainly for its duration. This does not change the fact that full employment was from the outset and also in retrospect an ideological component of their policy and not a temporary measure introduced in order to overcome a current crisis. After their take-over this fact became prominent in economic theory, beyond the ideological-propagandist level. For instance, in 1936 Karl Brinkmann, a well-known professor of economics at Heidelberg University, wrote in a preface to a doctoral thesis by Karl Schiller: "Job creation is . . . not just the ignition of the economy by means of public money but also, as shown by its ties to transport, housing, and defense policies, the most important juncture and a precondition for the emergence of a new economic and territorial order for Germany."[34]

The author of the thesis himself (who after the war was to became West German minister of economics under the Social Democrats) argued along the same lines: "The battle for work has extended the notion of job creation beyond the objectively restricted sphere of public relief works; it has lifted it out of the sphere of restarting the economy, which was far-reaching but limited in time to the Great Depression; it has enhanced this notion until it embraces a comprehensive effort of all forces in the state, the movement, and the people, along the entire front of economic life."[35] If we remember that Schiller wrote this at a time when a state of full employment was already in sight, it is clear that these economists considered job creation by the state a permanent component of economic policy. This was not just an "initial restarting," as the economist Wilhelm Röpke called it in 1931, or "pump priming," as present-day economists would say. The promotion of full employment was no longer a passing emergency measure, to be followed by a return to reliance on the free-market mechanism which operates most efficiently without external interference. State direction of the economy through a system of controls that could be employed in accordance with the rulers' political goals had become a matter of principle. Within this economy, employment policy served as an important and permanent guideline. Since this tallied with the Nazi concept of the state's role in the economy, economic theory after 1933 kept in step.

34. Introduction to K. Schiller, *Arbeitsbeschaffung*.
35. Ibid., p. 1.

Beyond this statement of principle, one can point to ideological influence upon specific applications of employment policy. Besides deficit spending and public works, the Nazis sought to direct employment to sectors they preferred. A special law passed in May 1934[36] limited the employment of workers from villages in a number of large cities. This measure could have been justified by the fact that these cities had an extremely high unemployment rate, but the Nazis also emphasized the need to disperse the population and to prevent migration from villages.[37] Earlier decrees awarded special grants to newly married couples with the aim of promoting child-bearing. A special grant and a tax discount were also offered for the employment of female domestic servants. Fritz Reinhardt took the trouble to explain these decrees both in terms of the need to relieve the labor market and through arguments concerning the "role of German women": since marriage loans were awarded only to women who resigned from their jobs, he expected about two million jobs to become vacant within two years, as well as "a permanent shift in the position of our German women."[38] In a similar vein, the minister of finance explained these measures as true examples of "National Socialist finance policy, which together with the reconstruction of military power, was due to the personal merit of Adolf Hitler."[39] The head of the unemployment-insurance and labor exchanges praised the "desired changes in professional structure. They aim, on the one hand, at the expansion of a sound and stable class of agricultural workers . . . at the training of girls for their natural occupations as housewives and mothers, and on the other hand, at the liquidation of the chronic surplus in clerical and academic personnel."[40]

In this context one should also mention the Labor Service (Arbeitsdienst), which operated on a voluntary basis until June 1935, when it became compulsory. That the law making it compulsory was passed relatively late, close in time to the introduction of compulsory military service, provides evidence that the Labor Service was considered a framework for paramilitary training and ideological indoctrination rather than a solution for unemployment. Nevertheless, a decree of August 1934 created a kind of negative

36. Gesetz zur Regelung des Arbeitseinsatzes vom 15. Mai 1934, RGB1. I, p. 381.
37. Honigberger, "Wirtschaftspolitische Zielsetzung," pp. 40f.
38. Fritz Reinhardt, *Generalplan gegen die Arbeitslosigkeit* (Oldenburg, 1933), pp. 34f.
39. L. v. Schwerin v. Krosigk, *Nationalsozialistische Finanzpolitik* (Jena, 1936).
40. Mönckmeier, ed., *Jahrbuch*, pt. 2, p. 38.

incentive by granting workers above the age of twenty-five preference in the matter of new jobs, while directing younger ones to
agriculture and the Labor Service.[41] There is no doubt that the
Nazis at that time already valued the educational impact of this
service. Foreign observers were also impressed by a framework that
brought working youth together with high-school pupils and
trained them in manual labor, while they ignored the strong emphasis on the military aspect of the Labor Service.[42] All these decrees
stress the tendency to direct labor to villages or at least to prevent
migration to cities. At the same time opposing tendencies were at
work – for instance, the promotion of the automobile industry
through the abolition of special taxes.[43] Hitler's fondness for auto-
mobiles was well known and may have influenced this policy,
though military considerations were certainly of greater weight. In
March 1933 Blomberg, the minister of the armed forces, had already
informed the transport minister that he had a special interest in "an
efficient automobile industry for reasons of defence."[44] From an
economic point of view this confirms that right from the beginning
of the regime the tendency to prefer and promote agriculture was
pitted against the conflicting desire to prepare for war. What had
also already surfaced by then was the fact that by definition an
industrial society resists attempts to turn the clock back. Ultimately
these two factors were stronger than the ideological preference for
agriculture, in spite of the latter's initial successes.

Foreign Trade Policy

The realization of the goal of maximum independence from the
world economy proclaimed in early Nazi plans must be examined
primarily in the field of foreign trade. The investigation will show
that this economic sector also developed to a large extent according
to preconceived ideas, even if the proclaimed objectives were not
fully realized. A combination of objective economic and extra-
neous, that is, political-ideological, factors worked toward reduction of exports and imports, as well as substantial structural

41. Honigberger, "Wirtschaftspolitische Zielsetzung," p. 41.
42. For example, C.W. Guillebaud, *The Social Policy of Nazi Germany* (Cambridge, 1941), pp. 65ff.
43. Gesetz über Änderung des Kraftfahrzeugsteuergesetzes vom 10. April 1933,
RGBl. I, p. 192.
44. BA, Wi I F5/370, quoted by Ries, "Finanzpolitik," p. 35.

changes in German foreign trade.

German exports (at fixed 1928 prices) fell from 13.7 billion reichsmarks in 1929 to 8.1 billion in 1932 and remained at 8.0 billion in 1936; during the same period imports fell from 13.5 billion in 1929 to 9.5 in 1932 and 8.6 in 1936. The drop is even sharper at then-current prices because of the reduction in raw-material and agricultural produce prices on the international market, a situation that considerably improved Germany's terms of trade. German exports fell from 13.5 billion in 1929 to 5.7 billion in 1932. Imports decreased from 13.5 billion reichsmarks in 1929 to 4.7 in 1932 and 4.2 in 1936[45] (see appendix, table 10).

A partial explanation for this development lies in the overall decline in international trade. Between 1929 and 1932 its total volume shrank by more than 60 percent and continued to decline during the following years. However, within this general situation there were significant differences between various countries. England, for instance, succeeded in increasing its share of international trade during the same period, while the U.S. share fell considerably. In 1936 Germany's share was 8.5 percent of total international trade, only 1 percent less than in 1929.[46] But if we remember that Germany's GNP grew throughout this period much faster than the GNP of other industrial countries, we may safely assume that an export-oriented policy would have changed the picture substantially. The reasons for her failure to increase foreign trade were to a large extent extraeconomic considerations, which dictated orientation to the domestic market.

The influence of these considerations was unequivocal with regard to changes in the composition of imports and the geographical distribution of German foreign trade. Foodstuffs came to 47.7 percent of all German imports at current prices in 1932, sinking to 35.5 percent in 1936. Imports of raw materials, on the other hand, also at current prices, rose over the same period from 27.3 to 37.3 percent. There was a considerable drop too in imports of finished industrial products[47] (see appendix, table 10). One should remember that in Germany this was a period of prosperity, which generally boosts consumer demand, including the demand for imported goods. The statistical data therefore demonstrate a clear tendency to freeze private consumption, to seek self-sufficiency, and to channel

45. H.S. Ellis, *Exchange Control in Central Europe* (Westport, 1971), p. 381.
46. Fischer, *Deutsche Wirtschaftspolitik*, p. 74.
47. Ellis, *Exchange Control*, p. 382.

the limited amount of available foreign currency mainly into rearmament industries. The geographical distribution of Germany's foreign trade also reveals a significant political shift: the share of southeastern European and Middle Eastern countries increased between 1932 and 1938 from 4.8 percent to 15.7 percent of German exports and from 7.5 percent to 13.6 percent of German imports. This was the result of the introduction of Schacht's New Plan in 1934 (see appendix, table 11).[48] No one denies that this shift was the result of deliberate policy, though there are differences of opinion on the part played by economic as against political considerations.

Foreign trade had already been placed under direct and meticulous government control during the initial years of Nazi rule. Limited control of foreign currency had in fact been in effect since 1931, when the Brüning government was in office. The objective of the controls was to prevent the flight of capital since the withdrawal of short-term foreign loans had caused unrest within the German economy. The Brüning government tried to overcome these difficulties by preserving a fixed exchange rate for the reichsmark and legislating that all foreign currency had to be handed over to the Reichsbank. Foreign currency allocations were calculated on the basis of the 1930–31 fiscal year, initially in the full amount but later reduced in the course of 1932 to 75 percent and subsequently to 50 percent. The government also agreed with foreign creditor and suppliers on certain "frozen" accounts, which were only gradually released, mainly for export. In contrast to measures subsequently introduced by Schacht, who employed the same method, payments of interest to foreign creditors were not restricted. These decrees laid the foundations for the much tighter foreign currency controls introduced later. Nevertheless, the decisive factors in the reduction of imports were the international price slump in imported commodities and the decrease in domestic demand, not the foreign currency squeeze.[49] I do not know to what extent control regulations prevented the flight of capital. The system of fines and severe penalties introduced by the Nazis with regard to currency offenses imply that well-versed experts had previously succeeded in evading regulations.

A conflict of interest between industry and agriculture concerning desirable foreign-trade policy emerged immediately after Hitler attained power. Industrial circles demanded promotion of exports

48. Erbe, *Die nationalsozialistische Wirtschaftspolitik*, p. 76.
49. Ibid., pp. 69f.

for political reasons as well as to create employment. A memorandum presented by the DIHT on February 23, 1933, pointed out that export industries and related branches employed three million workers, so that any damage to exports would increase unemployment. They added the political argument that exports were "a vital foundation for the life of nationally conscious Germans abroad . . . in particular overseas." The same arguments reappeared in a spate of memoranda presented by the associations of export-import enterprises, based mainly in seaports.[50] Agricultural associations demanded the opposite – extensive customs protection and a clear-cut preference for the "national economy" over the "world economy." They stressed the ideological significance of their demands in all appeals, as, for instance, in a memorandum by the DIHT: "Mussolini's successful foreign policy is not based on trade concessions but on domestic economic measures that decidedly aid agriculture."[51]

In the Reichstag speech of March 23, 1933, in which Hitler presented his Ermächtigungsgesetz, he also announced his ruling on this controversy in favor of agriculture. He admitted that "the geographical position of Germany, poor in raw materials, did not allow for full autarky of our Reich . . . and that the Reich government was far from hostile to exports." Nevertheless, he accorded explicit preference to "the rescue of the German peasant, whatever the cost. . . . The restoration of profitability for agricultural enterprises may be hard on the consumer; but the fate in store for the entire people, if the German peasant perishes, would be incomparably worse. . . . The ruin of our peasants would not only cause the ruin of Germany's economy, but above all the ruin of the body of the nation [*Volkskörper*]. Preservation of his [the peasant's] health is also the primary condition for the growth and prosperity of our industry, domestic trade, and German exports. . . . The debt that our whole economy, export industries included, owes the sound spirit of the German peasant cannot be paid off by any economic sacrifice."[52] This ruling immediately caused considerable rises in customs duties on imported agricultural products; I have discussed the influence of this policy on agricultural prices and incomes in the preceding chapter. Export branches tried in vain to resist these

50. Quoted by H.J. Schröder, *Deutschland und die Vereinigten Staaten, 1933–1939: Wirtschaft und Politik in der Entwicklung des deutsch-amerikanischen Gegensatzes* (Wiesbaden, 1970), p. 39.

51. BA, R 43/II, 308a.

52. E. Klöss, ed., *Reden des Führers: Politik und Propaganda Adolf Hitlers, 1922–1945* (Munich, 1967), pp. 101f.

increases and failed to prevent their harming shipping and import-export businesses, especially those in cities like Hamburg, Bremen, and other seaports, where the damage was particularly severe.[53]

The orientation to the domestic economy subsequently damaged the trade balance and caused a severe shortage of foreign currency. In 1932 Germany's trade-balance surplus stood at 1,072 million reichsmarks; though in 1933 it had dropped to 667 million, there was still some surplus. In 1934 there was already a deficit of 284 million reichsmarks. An examination of the figures shows that the reason for this deficit was the reduction of exports, not, as one would assume, increased imports resulting from rising demand for foodstuffs, raw materials, and finished products. German imports of goods also dropped over the same period, from 4.7 billion reichsmarks in 1932 to 4.2 in 1933, and rose only slightly to 4.4 billion reichsmarks in 1934. In the light of accelerating economic activity at the time, this small increase is rather surprising. It was imposed by the lack of foreign currency that resulted from reduced exports. In 1932, at the lowest point of the depression, Germany still exported 5.7 billion reichsmarks worth of goods. Exports fell in 1933 to 4.9 billion and in 1934 to only 4.2. The balance of services was positive throughout this period, and the surplus rose by 200 million reichsmarks in the period 1932 to 1934. This was, however, not enough to compensate for the deteriorating trade balance, with the result that the overall balance of payments remained negative.[54]

When Schacht became Reichsbank president at the end of March 1933, foreign currency reserves were his most pressing problem. He began by applying existing control regulations more stringently and extending penalties for offenders. In June 1933 a law was passed prohibiting payment of dividends and interest in foreign currency to other countries. Following this, Schacht concluded a number of "agreements" with foreign creditors, postponing dates of payment for Germany's debts in foreign currency. These payments were kept by the Reichsbank in a special conversion fund in German currency, so that foreign creditors really had no choice but to accept the arrangements proposed by Schacht, thus securing at least a partial return of their money.[55] In this manner a whole set of special reichsmark accounts were created and could be utilized for export, tourism, and investment in Germany. Creditors also had the choice

53. HF, K.V. Krogmann diaries, 11/K5.
54. Ellis, *Exchange Control*, p. 380.
55. R. Stucken, *Deutsche Geld- und Kreditpolitik*, 2d ed. (Tübingen, 1953), p. 131.

of selling their rights in these accounts to a subsidiary of the Reichsbank at half their nominal value and receiving the amount due to them in foreign currency.[56] Nevertheless, all these measures turned out to be inadequate because Schacht refused to follow the sterling and dollar devaluation with devaluation of the reichsmark. Gold and currency reserves continued to decline, reaching a low point of 78 million reichsmarks in July 1934.[57] Additional restrictions were therefore inevitable; during the early months of 1934 currency allocations for imports were radically curtailed, dropping ultimately to 5 percent of the base year. In March of the same year currency control became discriminative instead of utilizing the limitations imposed on overall volume employed until then: foreign currency was allocated only for vital needs. As the situation continued to deteriorate, the Reichsbank proceeded to issue daily allocations according to the state of its currency supply.[58]

Schacht and his aides knew full well that all these measures could be no more than palliatives. The German economy could not entirely forego the importation of important raw materials and foodstuffs, which would have to be paid for by increased revenue in order to keep up with rising domestic demand resulting from a growth in production and income. The shrinking of foreign currency reserves also emphasized this state of affairs, which from the beginning of 1934 drove decision makers to look for a more radical solution. This was ultimately found in the New Plan proclaimed by Schacht on September 24, 1934, after he had replaced Schmitt as minister of economics with wide-ranging authority. Schmitt's inability to cope with the foreign currency situation was one of the major reasons for his dismissal.[59] The New Plan introduced comprehensive state control over all foreign trade. One of twenty-five control stations organized according to economic branches had to authorize every single import transaction, and foreign currency was allocated only on the basis of such an authorization.[60] On the other hand, the New Plan promoted exports through bilateral agreements with countries prepared to accept German industrial export products in exchange for the raw materials and agricultural produce

56. H. Schacht, *My First 76 Years* (London, 1955), pp. 315f.; Erbe, *Die nationalsozialistische Wirtschaftspolitik*, pp. 69ff.
57. Ellis, *Exchange Control*, p. 374.
58. Posse, *Deutsche Wirtschaft*, p. 27; Erbe, *Die nationalsozialistische Wirtschaftspolitik*, p. 71.
59. Schacht, *76 Jahre meines Lebens*, p. 403.
60. Wolf, *Staatskonjunktur*, p. 19.

Germany had to import. Up to 1938 Germany had entered upon such clearing agreements with twenty-five states, most of them in southeastern Europe and Latin America. Most of these countries had large sums to their credit in Reichsbank conversion funds from previous years. Now they had to accept German goods at a much higher price than they would pay on the international market, particularly after the devaluation of the pound and the dollar, which had not been accompanied by a parallel devaluation of the German mark. The result for Germany was that in 1937 exports rose to 5.9 billion reichsmarks, imports to 5.5 billion, and once again the trade balance showed a surplus of 40 million. However, foreign currency reserves did not increase substantially because part of the German exports were paid for in German money held in closed accounts, as mentioned above. In December 1936 Germany's supply of foreign currency still stood at only 71.9 million reichsmarks (see appendix, table 10).

The New Plan also employed a method of selective export promotion though differential premiums. Actually a different rate of exchange was fixed for each transaction. The control station for the involved branch examined each export transaction and determined the subsidy level necessary to make the price of exported goods competitive on the international market. Subsidies fluctuated between 10 and 90 percent, but were usually between 40 and 60 percent.[61] To finance subsidies, the Reichsbank utilized income from the purchase of foreign creditor rights at half-price,[62] as well as an export promotion levy imposed by the Ministry of Economics on domestic production as a global sum, to be paid by the various branch associations. The latter collected the levy from their members in three-month installments, according to an estimate of sales during the preceding quarter.[63] In practice the New Plan provided the state with an almost total monopoly in foreign trade, implemented through rather cumbersome bureaucratic procedures. Importers sometimes had to fill out forty forms in order to carry out a single import transaction. For export a report following shipment was sufficient, but there was a ban on the export of certain raw materials.[64] Yet because importers rapidly mastered all this red tape the system worked rather well, notwithstanding cumbersome procedures. Results were substantial, in the short run as well as the

61. Kroll, *Weltwirtschaftskrise*, p. 477.
62. Schacht, *76 Jahre meines Lebens*, p. 399.
63. BA, R 13/I, no. 238, p. 27.
64. Ellis, *Exchange Control*, pp. 211f.

long. In the short run, the system secured vital imports in spite of the strangling shortage of foreign currency; in the long run, the plan altered the structure of Germany's foreign trade: the import of finished and semifinished products and the export of raw materials, especially those needed for rearmament, were reduced. The geographical distribution of Germany's foreign trade was altered, principally toward penetration into southeastern Europe (see appendix, tables 10–11). In principle it was shown that foreign trade, which lends itself less than other sectors to sovereign state manipulation, can also be regulated internally and externally according to political objectives through a suitable control mechanism and administrative regulations.

From this point of view the New Plan was a full realization of the outlines drawn by the Nazis' Immediate Program of 1932: the import preference given to raw materials; the blocking of industrial and agricultural imports that competed with domestic production; the implementation of the principle of bilateral agreements; and the directing of the foreign trade to Southeastern Europe. The 1932 program presented these goals not merely as temporary measures aimed at relieving unemployment but as the basis for "the social liberation of the German worker. . . . By shifting emphasis to the domestic market the influence of capital will be automatically reduced because the importance of large capitalistic conglomerates will shrink and the importance of agriculture will rise." Although the demand for *Lebensraum* was not spelled out, the program denounced the current state of affairs "in which the majority of Germany's sources for raw materials are still overseas" and could be cut off in case of war. "National Socialist trade policy intends therefore to supply the needs of the German people to the largest possible extent by domestic production and to import the necessary raw materials by preference from friendly European states, in particular from those which are prepared to accept finished industrial products from Germany in exchange." In order to realize these aims, the state would have to control all movement of capital and monies between Germany and other countries, to ascertain "that the small amounts of foreign currency we still receive annually be used only for the purchase of raw materials needed in industry and additional foodstuffs . . . still . . . necessary for the sustenance of the German people and not available within the country."[65] Schacht's

65. *Sofortprogramm*, pp. 9, 17.

New Plan was therefore no more than a technically clever implementation of the Nazi platform, based on these political and ideological motives.

The question arises as to whether this policy was dictated by economic considerations; whether, in light of the situation in international markets, an alternative policy was feasible while open or covert import restrictions operated in most countries. Was there any chance of increasing exports instead of promoting the domestic market, rationing foreign currency, and strictly controlling foreign trade? Some sources even argue that under prevailing conditions Schacht's policy, at least until 1936, actually encouraged exports, in striking contrast to the proclaimed autarky trend of Nazi doctrine.[66] However, statistical data counter this claim: during 1933–35 German export shrank in absolute terms, rising only slightly in 1936, both in current and real values. During this period the German GNP grew and there were clear signs of recovery in international trade. It is unlikely that exports could have been expanded sufficiently to liquidate unemployment in Germany to the extent that this goal was achieved through the policy of public employment and rearmament. The collapse of the international market was a fact to be reckoned with; all industrial countries adopted measures to limit imports and promote exports, trying to export unemployment by means of the so-called beggar my neighbor policy.[67] The wish for self-sufficiency existed not only in Germany; in 1933 Keynes also spoke of "national self-sufficiency," of the need to produce a maximum of goods at home and of "state sovereignty" in monetary matters.[68] Nevertheless, most scholars agree that the foreign currency necessary for vital imports could have been obtained through expanding exports using conventional economic measures; that is, the authorities' drastic measures for regulating foreign currency and foreign trade arose principally from extraeconomic considerations. In his study of the subject, Ellis clearly states this view: "Since 1933 or thereabouts the German Exchange control is impossible to justify on economic grounds. . . . the institution persisted, because it was an instrument par-excellence of political power . . . not only over other states but

---

66. For example, Meinck, *Hitler und die deutsche Aufrüstung*, p. 159.

67. Ch.P. Kindleberger, *Die Weltwirtschaftskrise* (Munich, 1973), pp. 290ff.

68. J.M. Keynes, "National Self Sufficiency," *Yale Review* 22 (1933), quoted by Kindleberger, *Weltwirtschaftskrise*, pp. 271f.

equally significantly over vested economic interests within the country."[69]

Cautious criticism of the tight regulation of foreign trade and the reduction of its volume could even be discerned between the lines of contemporary German publications. Thus, in a summary of the year 1934, the economic editor of the *Frankfurter Zeitung* stated that "the ultimate goal remains renewed integration in frictionless international exchange. . . . Compensatory transactions in all their varieties can only serve as an emergency substitute. The best way is still to obtain foreign currency through export."[70] Devaluation of the German mark could have served as a patently economic measure toward this end. After the devaluation of the pound by England in the fall of 1931 and that of the dollar in April 1933, most countries adjusted their currency until the end of 1935. Germany avoided formal devaluation and its exports became expensive in comparison with those of other exporting countries.[71] Devaluation proposals circulated in business circles, and it seems that Schacht himself considered this possibility in 1936 but ultimately decided to continue his previous policy. It is noteworthy that at least one devaluation proposal from the electrical-engineering industries was bound up with the desire to sign a trade agreement with the United States and France, to seek an arrangement for international debts, to abolish foreign-trade controls, and to work toward an agreement on mutual arms reduction.[72] What is clearly recognized here is the significance of foreign-trade policy as an integral part of a politics which went far beyond the purely economic aspects of the problem.

There may be differences of opinion with regard to the purely economic benefit devaluation might have brought. After the war Schacht justified his policy by the size of Germany's international debt in foreign currency and the relative inflexibility of demand for German export goods. There is no doubt that the system of bilateral agreements also had economic advantages: by exerting political pressure and exploiting the wish of Germany's creditors to obtain at least part of their frozen deposits, German bilateral export achieved prices that were 12 to 20 percent higher than world-market prices. However, even the scholar who presents these arguments ultimately agrees that Germany did not attempt to reenter the system of

69. Ellis, *Exchange Control*, pp. 288f.
70. Wolf, *Staatskonjunktur*, p. 20.
71. Ziemer, *Inflation und Deflation*, p. 78.
72. Schweitzer, *Big Business*, pp. 308, 433.

international trade and continued to seek maximal self-sufficiency for reasons whose nature was noneconomic.[73] The *Staatsekretär* at the Ministry of Economics revealed the true reasons in a semiofficial paper. Having listed all the economic arguments against devaluation mentioned above, he wrote: "What could be more logical . . . than to seek a new orientation on regional economy? Tendencies toward closer geopolitical relationships are therefore the characteristic feature of German trade policy in its third phase after the war."[74]

The Nazis' foreign-trade policy was therefore an intrinsic part of their comprehensive method with regard to both objectives and means. Foreign currency regulations and the import monopoly should be viewed as complementary measures in a fiscal and monetary policy that sought full employment through the increase of public, and explicitly not private, demand.[75] A German scholar esteemed as a monetary expert under the Nazis admits in retrospect that state control was inherent to the method and was therefore also imposed in this sphere: "That Germany advanced during this period further toward dirigism in domestic economy as well as in economic foreign relations . . . was no doubt aided by the National Socialists' disposition to influence the economy by state guidance, if not to say, by commands of the state."[76] Zimmermann (writing as Ferdinand Fried) also explained the direction of foreign trade by the state as a consequence of granting the state absolute sovereignty over the economy. He once again referred his ideas to Fichte's *Geschlossener Handlesstaat*, whose author "may be regarded as the herald of National Socialist . . . thought." Absolute and sovereign dominance of the state, which according to Zimmermann, the Nazis achieved when they attained power, was possible only with regard to the domestic market. Subsequently they were able to circumvent the impediments facing such dominance on the international market "because revival of the economy by means of the domestic market was a principle of [National Socialist] economic policy anyway."[77]

The goals of this policy were political and ideological: on the one hand, self-sufficiency in vital raw materials and their substitutes for rearmament; on the other hand, autarky as an ideological goal in

73. K. Mandelbaum, "An Experiment in Full Employment: Controls in the German Economy, 1933–1938," in *The Economics of Full Employment* (Oxford, 1945), p. 188.

74. Posse, *Deutsche Wirtschaft*, p. 30.

75. Erbe, *Die nationalsozialistische Wirtschaftspolitik*, p. 81.

76. Stucken, *Geld- und Kreditpolitik*, p. 135.

77. Fried, *Die Zukunft des Außenhandels*, p. 10.

itself, as conceived by Darré and the adherents of the "new order" in Europe. These two aspects were not necessarily interdependent, but they complemented each other in Hitler's mode of thought, where "economic autarky was on the one hand an autonomous goal . . . [which] could be realized only in the distant future, when the large *Lebensraum* would be gained for the German people . . . but at the same time also a medicine urgently needed . . . in order to achieve the distant goal in the manner he decided upon, by war."[78]

Tax, Wage, and Price Policies

One of the arguments against devaluation was the fear of inflationary pressures, despite all the theoretical counterarguments the reformers presented to the effect that with prevailing unemployment these fears were groundless. There is a story that Lautenbach was sent in the summer of 1933 to persuade Hitler with regard to deficit spending on works projects: "Mr. Hitler," he allegedly said, "you are now the most powerful man in Germany. There is only one thing you cannot do: under prevailing circumstances you cannot cause inflation, however hard you try."[79] Yet the traumatic experience of 1922–23 was still very real in the public mind and served as a deterrent to exaggerated increases in disposable income, even when it was already clear that deficit spending could not be avoided. This explains why it was stressed time and again that any such spending should be "productive," namely, that the government-initiated projects financed in this manner had to be covered by genuine economic assets. The Nazis' Immediate Program of 1932 also attempted to defuse possible objections through its claim that the "creation of productive credit" would only be a complementary measure and that the amount spent in this manner would be offset by real economic gain. For the same reason Schacht and his collaborators tried from the very outset to accompany their expansive policy with a number of preventive measures intended to preempt any possibility of inflationary pressures. This tendency is demonstrated in taxation policies as well as in the steps taken to stabilize prices and freeze wages by means of administrative regulations. These measures were in fact implemented sporadically and inconsistently as long as economic circumstances made them unnecessary. The nearer the economy drew to full employment, the more

78. Fischer, *Deutsche Wirtschaftspolitik*, p. 75.
79. Lautenbach, *Zins, Kredit und Produktion*, p. x.

they became active and efficacious tools. Since regulation of wages, prices, and interest rates was in principle considered part of an economic system directed by the state for the good of the community, the regime endeavored to create a suitable operative mechanism from its very beginnings.

Tax policies showed a tendency not to increase the disposable income of the population. At first the tax-credit notes of the Papen Plan as well as a few selective tax discounts introduced during the first months of 1933 were retained. However, the discounts were rapidly redirected to branches to which the regime gave preference for reasons of job creation and rearmament, for example, by cancelling the tax on motor vehicles and promoting building of and investment in new equipment for industrial enterprises to further the development of war-related heavy industries. A law of July 15, 1933,[80] granted a 10 percent discount on income and corporate taxes for building construction or repair of industrial enterprises, on condition that the work be completed by January 1, 1935, and that the total wages paid exceed the total paid out during the preceding tax period. This law was clearly intended to increase employment in construction, a relatively labor-intensive branch. In order to boost sales of small- and medium-sized retail businesses, the law abolished taxes on that part of wages paid in purchase vouchers for clothing and household appliances. Another paragraph permitted tax authorities to grant discounts or tax exemption to enterprises that introduced innovative methods or new products "if a persuasive need for these [new products] is evident within the whole German national economy."[81] These regulations emphasized the wish to promote the production of substitutes for raw materials and other rearmament-oriented industries, though I believe it is an exaggeration to label them "a law for the promotion of rearmament industries,"[82] like the tax-exemption decree for air-raid shelter construction of October 1933.[83] Tax reductions for agriculture had unmistakable ideological significance. The second Reinhardt Plan of September 21, 1933, included a one-hundred-million-reichsmark reduction of property tax on agricultural land, in addition to considerable reductions of purchase taxes for agricultural products. The same law also reduced property tax on residential buildings. For the

80. Gesetz über Steuererleichterungen vom 15. Juli 1933, RGBl. I, p. 491.
81. Quoted by Ries, "Finanzpolitik," p. 38.
82. W. Sauer, in Bracher, Sauer, and Schulz, *Machtergreifung*, p. 800.
83. Ries, "Finanzpolitik," p. 39.

period of 1933–35 these tax discounts amounted to 250 million reichsmarks.[84]

For agriculture and other preferred branches these discounts no doubt brought substantial relief. For the economy as a whole their significance was rather marginal. The majority of the high tax rates introduced by the Brüning government as part of its deflationary policy remained at the same level. Until 1935 all tax reductions, including the discount of Papen's tax-credit notes, came to 1.76 billion reichsmarks. In contrast, the accumulated increase in revenue from taxes for the same period added up to 5 billion reichsmarks more than in 1932; already in 1933 the net revenue came to 400 million reichsmarks more than in the preceeding year.[85] As a result of high tax rates and the increase in the GNP, additional revenue from tax collection reached 7 billion reichsmarks by 1936. To this sum one must add another 2 billion, collected through various levies like "donations" to the *Winterhilfe* (winter aid) (see appendix, table 3). In October 1934 a National Socialist Tax Reform was proclaimed with considerable hullabaloo, though its main contents were continued high tax rates and even some increases in corporate taxes, plus intensified tax collection and tightened penalties on tax evasion. The tax-department chief of the Association of Industrialists (Reichsgruppe Industrie) emphasized that it was useless to attempt a precise comparison between new and old tax regulations because the important issue was "the new spirit of the reform, the spirit of National Socialism. The principle of the 'the common good precedes the good of the individual' stands above everything else. In the interest of the whole nation, everyone has to pay the taxes he owes according to the tax law."[86] In accordance with this principle tax authorities were instructed not to bother with too many details while assessing tax dues, that is, to "interpret" both old and new regulations with a view to stringency, as appropriate to a National Socialist weltanschauung. Thus, for the good of the community the German citizen was asked to act out the old German saying "Pay your taxes and shut up." The only flexibility assessment officials were permitted to employ was to choose, in case of doubt, the more severe possibility, thus pressuring the taxpayer even beyond his obligations under the law. Even an economic

84. Ibid., p. 87.
85. Ibid., pp. 88f.
86. Mönckmeier, ed., *Jahrbuch*, pt. 2, p. 152.

yearbook of the official Nazi publishing house questioned "whether it was desirable to restrict regulations for the taxpayer's legal protection so severely."[87]

The situation created by these measures seems, on the face of it, paradoxical: the government increasingly drew money from the public at a time of widespread unemployment, while simultaneously introducing a policy of deficit spending. We find, however, that this paradox was a result neither of mistaken economic calculation nor of a lack of theoretical skill: it followed from an overall policy that aimed to reduce unemployment by increasing the GNP through expansion of government demand, primarily for rearmament, and explicitly not by means of an increase on disposable private income, that is, the promotion of private consumption. This fact alone already invalidates the assumption still accepted by many, mainly German scholars, that the period under discussion consisted of an initial stage of job creation, followed by a stage of state prosperity (*Staatskonjunktur*), which began only after the former had been accomplished.[88] In fact the policy of a wage and price freeze complemented tax policies quite logically, deriving as it did from the same pattern of thought.

The official explanation for the wage freeze was that it would prevent inflation. It was accompanied by a commitment to price control in order to preserve the value of wages. Labor trustees were instructed to deviate from existing wage rates only in very special cases. Nevertheless, the wage freeze was not absolute even under the law, which permitted certain branches or enterprises to be released from existing agreements. Price control, which will be discussed below, was conceived as a necessary complement to the wage freeze. However as certain prices, in particular those of agricultural produce, rose nevertheless, the level of real wages sank. The level of real wages reached its lowest point in January 1934 and rose only slightly later. According to one assessment the level of real wages per work hour, using 1932, the worst year of the depression, as a base, rose only to 107.2 in 1936; however, even German economists admitted that the cost of living index that served as a basis for this assessment was deliberately set low. In addition, this calculation was based on the wage index before the deduction of taxes and other obligatory payments, which under the Nazis rose

87. Ibid., p. 160.
88. For example, Kroll, *Weltwirtschaftskrise*.

considerably, to as much as 15 percent of gross income.[89] It is therefore reasonable to assess that in 1933–34 net real wages per week dropped by 6 to 7 percent and returned to the 1932 level only at the end of 1936 (see appendix, table 12). On the other hand, the increase in work hours per employee and the expansion of employment raised the total amount of wages paid and, thus, the overall income of workers.[90]

Labor trustees were aware of the drop in real wages and even tried to neutralize it by preventing the rise of prices, especially for food. At a meeting with Backe, the *Staatssekretär* for agriculture, the Ministry of Labor representative also complained about the drop in real wages. He demanded that agricultural prices be lowered because under prevailing circumstances "current nominal wages are unbearable." Nevertheless, at this stage workers' demands "to share in the achievements of agriculture and those branches of the economy that have been favored by works projects" could not be met: "The battle against unemployment and the rearmament of the German people have priority and require preservation of current wage levels." But this could be achieved only by the lowering of food prices.[91]

The argument that the wage freeze was still necessary because of employment and rearmament policies recurs in all press publications of the period. As the achievement of full employment drew nearer, demands for higher wages increased; at times even party organs voiced these demands. An article of September 1936 begins by admitting that "the question of higher wages is closely bound up with our shortage of foodstuffs and raw materials. . . . It is therefore not yet time to attack the problem energetically." At the same time the article sharply attacks employers in heavy industry, who refuse to raise wages because doing so would influence prices: "Is it truly necessary for every rise in production costs to be shifted to prices? In the light of the large profits and high liquidity of the industry in question here . . . the iron and metal industry, this appears to us rather questionable." The paper concludes that wages could be raised without raising prices and that a highly profitable industry could even "afford to lower prices! This does not refute the tendency to strengthen purchasing power. This wage rise is not unjust,

89. Guillebaud, *Economic Recovery*, pp. 186f.; Kroll, *Weltwirtschaftskrise*, p. 583.

90. J. Kuczinski, *Die Geschichte der Lage der Arbeiter in Deutschland von 1789 bis in die Gegenwart*, vol. 2, pt. 1, 3d ed. (Berlin [East], 1953), p. 184.

91. BA, R 43/II, 318.

but for the good of the community."[92]

Price control was always presented as a complement to wage freezing in order to preserve the real standard of living. Like administrative wage freezing, price control was in fact unnecessary as long as the economy operated under conditions of partial unemployment and the fear of inflationary pressures was largely imaginary. What motivated both measures, besides this fear, was the same antiliberalist economic philosophy that included the objection to free-market price setting and the search for just prices as a matter of principle. The Nazis created a control mechanism, frequently utilizing previous laws and decrees, because it was a component of their preliminary plans. When it became obvious that under current conditions this mechanism was in fact superflous, they activated it only sporadically and in sectors in which external factors created upward pressures on prices; at the same time, they retained the legal and institutional framework of the control mechanism with an eye to future needs.

The Brüning government had already established a price-control agency. In 1931 the mayor of Leipzig, Karl Goerdeler, was appointed national price supervisor. The office was abolished in July 1933, but was reestablished in November 1934 and once again given to Goerdeler. It is noteworthy that after Goerdeler's resignation in the fall of 1935 a whole year passed before a new price supervisor was appointed, at a time when full employment had already been achieved. The new appointee was Joseph Wagner, the influential Nazi Gauleiter of Silesia, and his office was redefined as Reich commissioner for price formation (*Preisbildung*) instead of price supervision (*Preisüberwachung*), that is, not merely price control but *the setting of prices* by the government.[93]

Until November 1934 agricultural prices were in fact raised administratively, both because this sector was severely hit by sharp price slumps during the depression and because of its ideologically preferred status. Steps intended to stabilize and/or raise prices were also taken with regard to some weak industrial branches, mainly through a law of July 15, 1933 that introduced compulsory cartels.[94] It appears that these measures were primarily introduced in branches in which thousands of small, middle-class enterprises fought each other in cutthroat competition, thus endangering their

manda-tory cartels to prevent destructive competition

92. *Westdeutscher Beobachter*, Sept. 4, 1936.
93. Kroll, *Weltwirtschaftskrise*, pp. 55f.
94. Gesetz über die Errichtung von Zwangskartellen, RGB1. I, p. 480.

viability as businesses. The cartelization law compelled these enterprises to collaborate on marketing and price agreements, the result
of which was, of course, higher consumer prices.[95] It follows that
during this period administrative price controls were rarely employed to prevent price increases. The only exception was for some
imported raw materials, which were allocated to each branch or
enterprise according to precisely calculated quotas at fixed minimum prices, accompanied by strict administrative supervision.[96]

In spite of lax price controls, prices rose very little in 1935–36.
The index of wholesale prices (based on 1925–27) rose between the
first quarters of 1933 and 1937 from 66.1 to 76.6, that is, by 10.5
points; the cost of living index for the same period rose by 5.7
points, from 81.0 to 86.7 (see appendix, table 13). The difference
between the rise of wholesale prices and cost of living indexes
derived from reduced marketing margins, in particular in agriculture. This sector enjoyed a considerable increase in producer prices,
which for certain products rose by up to 30 percent over 1932
prices.[97]

The tendency to raise prices was not limited to agriculture. It
appears that certain industries had already tried to obtain increases
in 1933, after the first signs of economic recovery, justifying their
demands by citing the rising cost of raw materials, and so forth. At a
closed meeting of the RDI in December 1933, Schmitt, the minister
of economics, was sharply criticized for not permitting price increases in spite of rising production costs. According to the minutes
of this meeting, Schmitt was accused of being more radical than
Gottfried Feder and other Nazis and of demanding that enterprises
operate on the brink of profitability in order not to raise prices; in
the opinion of these industrialists, his position could only be
explained by political considerations. Association officials suggested
that enterprise owners avoid, as far as possible, involving the
authorities whenever their suppliers raised prices and try to arrange
matters within their own agencies instead of "running at once to
consult the attorney."[98] It seems that they sought to avoid providing pretexts for the state to intervene in their affairs since they still
thought in terms of corporate self-management. A confidential
internal circular of the Association of Chemical Industries also

95. Schweitzer, *Big Business*, p. 272.
96. Mandelbaum, "Full Employment," p. 191.
97. Guillebaud, *Economic Recovery*, p. 166; Kroll, *Weltwirtschaftskrise*, p. 538.
98. BA R 13/I, 625, Meeting of Nov. 11, 1933.

contains evidence of Schmitt's determination to keep prices stable: the circular warned members not to ignore the minister of economics because the government was determined "to use its authority in order to dismantle associations, syndicates, and groupings that defy its regulations."[99]

The more unemployment receded and private income rose, the stronger the tendency to raise prices became. The NSDAP also regarded the preservation of price stability as one of its duties. In November 1934 it was decided (probably by Bernhard Köhler's committee in Munich) to conduct a national price survey. The decision attracted criticism from members of the business community, who claimed that the source for price rises was mainly agriculture, which enjoyed party support. They resented the party's tendency to turn public opinion against them by publishing figures and random comparisons of price lists that the layman did not really understand. "To bring them together in a survey like the projected one is in any case difficult, but requires above all expert knowledge and a cautious hand. . . . In individual cases it remains to be seen whether what is not always correctly understood should at all cost be denigrated before everyone's eyes."[100]

The concern felt within the business community was not unfounded. Complaints by party and municipal bodies increased at the time, generating a series of appeals to Hitler, the Ministry of Economics, and the RNS. In July 1934 the minister of the interior informed the chancellor's office of a number of Gestapo reports (*Lageberichte der Staatspolizei*) from various regions that told of unrest following the rise in food prices. As we saw in the previous chapter, in August of the same year the Gauleiters met with *Staatssekretär* Backe to discuss the same matter, just a few days after Backe's meeting with labor trustees.[101] There was also press criticism of agricultural policy. In November 1934 the *Frankfurter Zeitung* devoted an editorial to Goerdeler's appointment as price commissioner. It praised the government for its wage-freeze policy but emphasized that this demanded price stability, which had not been sufficiently preserved. Once again the blame was put mainly on agriculture as well as on wholesale and retail trade in agricultural produce, which had caused a rise of about 24 percent compared to the low level of prices in the spring of 1933: "The price

99. NA, T-71, roll 139, fr. 653359f.
100. *Deutsche Führerbriefe*, Nov. 2, 1934.
101. BA, R 43/II, 317/18.

commissioner will no doubt extend his supervisory activity in this direction, but it appears that the price policy of agricultural corporations also requires reexamination."[102]

It soon became obvious that Goerdeler was the loser in the contest with Darré and party officials entrenched in agriculture. He held office for less than a year and was continuously embroiled in arguments, not only about the level of agricultural prices but also about the whole method of authorizing the RNS to determine prices. Hitler ultimately ruled in favor of Darré and agriculture, and not even industrial circles supported Goerdeler. It seems that the industrialists had meanwhile come round to the view that cartelization and administrative fixing of prices for government orders served their interests better than a return to free-market rules.

In 1931, when Goerdeler was appointed supervisor of prices for the first time, the lowering of prices was part of Brüning's overall policy and was in line with the general trend in the economy because of the Great Depression and unemployment. In 1934 the situation was different; he had to cope with a tendency for prices to rise within an expanding economy. Goerdeler held traditional liberal views on economics, believing that exaggerated cartelization, particularly in agriculture, made prices rise. However, his efforts to lead the economy back to free-market competition clashed with the Nazis' basic economic principles and were therefore doomed from the outset.

In a press interview of February 1935 Goerdeler explained that he approved of fixed prices for basic agricultural produce, but that one should seek "to keep the market regulation of food-processing industries and the accompanying trade free from damaging cartelization."[103] In March another interviewer from *Chemische Industrie* received the impression that Goerdeler's objections were not limited to agriculture and that he refused "to dictate prices or to set maximum and minimum prices; his only measure was an appeal to voluntary price discipline in the economy."[104] In January, Goerdeler had written in the same paper that although it was impossible to abolish price controls immediately, an effort had to be made to moderate price supervision and eventually abolish controls altogether.[105] In February Goerdeler tried to reintroduce free price

102. *Frankfurter Zeitung*, Nov. 7, 1934.
103. *Berliner Börsen Courier*, Feb. 7, 1935.
104. *Chemische Industrie*, Mar. 16, 1935.
105. Ibid., Jan. 12, 1935.

setting into construction work through a method of tenders, granting work contracts to the cheapest bidder. He soon found that in this matter industrialists were not prepared to follow his lead; they preferred the cost plus method (which they called "fair prices") in their relations with public authorities. At a meeting at the Berlin office of the Association of Industrialists on June 4, 1935, the industrialists decided to protest against Goerdeler's proposal, arguing that it would attract questionable elements to their branch, which had just then been heavily burdened by the export levy. They claimed that, having been promised compensation for the levy through profitable prices on the domestic market, Goerdeler's decree constituted a breach of this promise. Goerdeler's representative did not budge from his position and even refused to let association officials participate in later consultations. It is of interest that the circular distributed by the association after this meeting was addressed not only to their own members and the Ministry of Economics, but also to the Nazi leadership's Committee for Economic Policy in Munich and to the Gauleiters.[106] It appears that industrialists considered the issue a matter of principle that the party was certain to support, as indeed it did.

The matter of the export levy on domestic production reappeared in all discussions on price levels from June to September 1935, ultimately leading to Goerdeler's resignation. In his interrogation by the Gestapo following the assassination plot against Hitler of June 20, 1944, Goerdeler explained in detail what difficulties he had to cope with as price commissioner. His evidence shows beyond any doubt that his approach was diametrically opposed to the entire economic system prevailing at the time, including credit expansion by deficit spending and export levies:

Scarcity of goods [exists] only in a few spheres. The interference comes from the direction of money (artificial creation of money!). Very different methods [are] therefore necessary: 1. To stop the artificial creation of money. To raise output without raising wages through longer working time. 2. To liquidate gaps in the supply of goods. 3. To examine prices and release from price controls. . . .

Report on a controversy with Ley and interest groups that demand compulsory measures (already known):

As to paragraph 1, Schacht could be won over only very late. He is bound by his promise to the Führer to create money, a fact that became

106. BA, R 13/I, 238, pp. 50ff.

known to Goerdeler only in 1937. . . . There follows an easing of price controls. International obligations also have to be checked. Agreement on this with the minister of economy. . . . Fight against the inclination of business since 33, to demand directive measures. But the abuse of competition (dumping) is also to be fought. . . . All this was accomplished by May 1935. Now the money issue had to be regulated [point 1]. Here Goerdeler lacks adequate authority. Schacht cautiously refuses to stop the forwarding of further credit. The massive printing of paper money pushes prices upward, a situation Goerdeler tries to brake by an abundance of decrees. He thus arrives at the limits of what he can do; does not want a system of maximum prices. . . . Goerdeler makes stoppage of credit expansion a condition for continuing in office. Demands abolition of the export levy, which pushes prices up. A meeting with the Führer because the president of the Reichsbank and minister of economy [Schacht] rejected his demand at the end of July. No ruling, the Führer refuses to give it, but asks him to continue working. Goerdeler agrees provided that he is to receive additional authority. Talks that this may happen, but it does not because, as Goerdeler learned, some of the ministers opposed it.[107]

Goerdeler's account to his Gestapo interrogators on the eve of his execution following the assassination plot is fully confirmed by the correspondence on this issue from June to September 1935 kept in the files of the chancellor's office. The sharpest objections to enhanced authority for Goerdeler came from Darré, who insisted on RNS independence in the matter of prices. He claimed that he had supervised the lowering of bread and beef prices, while Goerdeler had agreed to raise them. In addition, he accused Goerdeler of the inclination to ignore the ministers concerned and make arrangements over their heads.[108] Three days later a letter whose contents were almost identical to these complaints reached the Reich chancellery (at Darré's request, according to various sources), signed by Martin Bormann in the name of Rudolf Heß. The letter conveyed the party's full support for Darré and opposed Goerdeler and his demand for more authority.[109] But a letter by Schacht expresses somewhat qualified support for the proposed law granting far-reaching authority to the price commissioner, on the explicit condition that a preliminary agreement with the minister concerned be achieved for every issue or that the issue be submitted to the Führer

107. BA, Nachlaß Goerdeler, no. 25.
108. BA R 43/II, 315a, Darré an Lammers vom 6.7.1935.
109. Ibid., Bormann an Lammers vom 9.7.1935.

for a final ruling.[110] Goerdeler rejected this condition out of hand and resigned.[111]

I have described this affair in detail because it clearly demonstrates: 1) that the regime favored the method of price control as an inherent component of a comprehensive economic system that combined ideological motivations with immediate political goals; 2) that business circles supported this method from 1933 on and opposed Goerdeler's attempts to return to a competitive market economy; and 3) that a policy of credit expansion and state-regulated foreign trade were part of this system, so that Schacht opted with Hitler against Goerdeler. Given the condition of the German economy in 1935, when about 2.5 million people were still unemployed, purely economic considerations were on their side; Goerdeler's proposals for a longer work day and reduction of government credit were not to the point. For the same reason the government had no difficulty in accepting the price commissioner's resignation and could afford not to appoint a new one as long as there was partial unemployment and the danger of inflationary pressures was imaginary. Prices did indeed rise in certain sectors where shortages were caused by external pressures like rising prices on the international market or lack of foreign currency. But these were controlled through existing cartel agencies and the fixed prices for government orders on which these agencies depended. Acute inflationary pressures did not appear as long as production increased and most enterprises still had reserves of unemployed capacity. In economic terms this enabled these enterprises to expand their output at a lower average cost per unit. During the initial years these reserves were sufficiently large to set off opposing pressures, mainly from international trade.[112]

The wage freeze to which price control was tied, on the other hand, had political significance and was designed "to win the confidence of property-owning classes."[113] There is no doubt that in 1933 as well as during the subsequent period Hitler still needed that group's support and voluntary cooperation; it is reasonable to assume that a proclaimed policy of wage freezing was part of this

The object was to zap labor

---

110. Ibid., Schacht an Lammers vom 15.7.1935.
111. Ibid., Goerdeler an Lammers vom 27.7.1935.
112. Schweitzer, *Big Business*, p. 186; H. Stuebel, "Die Finanzierung der Aufrüstung im Dritten Reich," *Europa-Archiv* 6 (1951): 4134; Mandelbaum, "Full Employment," p. 189.
113. Mandelbaum, "Full Employment," p. 191.

effort. The preservation of stable prices and, therefore, of real wages was emphasized as a balancing factor, aimed at public opinion and in particular at workers, who found themselves exposed and without legal protection after the abolition of trade unions. It follows that price control was a necessary complement to the wage freeze from a political angle as well. One should also remember that price control as an instrument for social justice was an ideological focal point of all early Nazi plans and platforms. An economist from the Othmar Spann circle who adjusted rapidly to the new regime from the start stressed the ideological approach to the matter of price policies: "A view of pricing which is causal-mechanistic is rejected *anti-* by National Socialism for there should be no domination by the *market* vagaries of the market. The economic fate of the individual must not *ideology* be abandoned to the free interplay of supply and demand. This means that price policy has priority over price theory and that price regulation by the state or by the estates is superimposed upon the price mechanisms that result from the movement of the market. The demand for just or fair prices was voiced from the very beginning."[114] Dietrich Klagges had already made a similar claim in 1929: "Comprehensive social justice can be brought to bear only by withdrawing the decision making on interest rates, prices, and wages from the sphere of economic power and transferring it to the sphere of justice and legal authority. . . . But in economic matters the sense of justice is not at all the same in both spheres, especially when particular interests are involved, which always happens with questions of prices and wages. Ultimately the regulation of wages and prices will therefore always become a matter for state decision."[115] This argument was the basis for Klagges's strange demand for a mathematical calculation of social justice and the common good.

It was thus no accident that in 1936, when the economy achieved full employment and the question of price control became economically acute, the office of price commissioner was given to a Nazi Gauleiter and not to an economist. The *Völkischer Beobachter* greeted the appointment with an editorial written by its economic editor, who celebrated the occasion as a victory for the party, which would from this point onward change "the whole structure of the economy. . . . When the Führer said, 'The party commands the state,' every National Socialist knew that in [the area of] economic

114. Bülow, *Ständestaat*, p. 51.
115. D. Klagges, "Soziale Gerechtigkeit durch Organisation und Berechnung," *Nationalsozialistische Briefe* 5 (1929–30): 29f.

policy also the movement and its spirit would be mobilized. We have awaited this, convinced that the call would, indeed, come." The author regarded the news of the appointment of Joseph Wagner as Reich commissioner for price formation and the appointee's announcement that he would call on party agencies not only for educational purposes, but also to take part in day-to-day control activities, as the final realization of the Führer's promise.[116]

Income and Capital Formation

Private consumption rose very little in proportion to production growth between 1933 and 1936; the savings level of households was low at least until 1935; private net investment was limited and at times even negative (see appendix, tables 1, 14, 19, 21). Public consumption and investment, on the other hand, rose considerably, and business savings in the form of undistributed profits grew. Today there is no doubt that this was the result of deliberate policies, intended to channel maximum resources into rearmament and the infrastructure of industry and transport, as dictated by the regime's political aims. The execution of these policies and the manner in which they were explained to the public were aided, or even guided, by a series of ideological norms.

The percentage of the national income spent on wages dropped between 1932 and 1936 from 64 to 59 percent.[117] Within households income from capital rose only slightly over the same period, while the growth of undistributed company profits was quite spectacular, shifting from a deficit of 450 million reichsmarks to profits of 2,330 million reichsmarks. These statistics reflect the regime's policy of curbing private income by means of wage freezing and limiting the distribution (though not the volume) of profits. The rise in relative volume of the income from capital can perhaps be explained by the expanded state of the economy despite continued unemployment; in addition, this trend was encouraged by the liquidation of trade unions and the regime's efforts to secure the support and cooperation of the business community.

Private consumption grew throughout this period by 15.5 percent

116. *Völkischer Beobachter*, June 14, 1936.
117. Erbe, *Die nationalsozialistische Wirtschaftspolitik*, p. 101. Slightly different data by W.G. Hoffmann and H. Müller, *Das deutsche Volkseinkommen; 1851–1957* (Tübingen, 1959), p. 56, show the same developments.

(at current prices) and consumption per capita by 11.4 percent.[118] If we remember that unemployment reached its peak in 1932, this growth is minute compared to the growth in the GNP. The regime deliberately channeled the fruits of this prosperity into public expenditures at the expense of private consumption. We will see below that the same policy was brought to bear on investment. The wage freeze was paralleled by the restriction of distribution of dividends through two bills passed in March 1934;[119] these compelled enterprises to invest surplus capital in public bonds in amounts equal to dividend payments exceeding 6 percent. The law of course had an additional aim, to sell government bonds, which was only partially achieved. The main result of this policy was the accumulation of surplus capital within enterprises, whether for renewal of equipment or increase in liquidity and reduction of debts, which was characteristic of economic policy at the time.

Statistical data and currently available research do not permit us to draw reliable conclusions on the functional composition of public consumption because publication of the national budget was stopped in 1934.[120] The meager evidence available shows clearly that the share of social services within the total of public consumption dropped to the same degree that military expenses rose. The rise in economic and general services paralleled the rise in total expenditure, remaining at the same level in proportion to the total.[121] State expenditure on goods and services rose from 1932 to 1936 from 9.5 billion to 21.9 billion reichsmarks, that is, by 130 percent (see appendix, tables 2, 3, 17, 18). Over the same period expenditure by the Reich, that is, the central government, rose steadily in contrast to expenditure incurred by individual states (the *Länder*) and municipal authorities, primarily because of rearmament expenses but also as a result of the general tendency to assign public sector activities increasingly to central Reich agencies and reduce *Länder* autonomy. Notwithstanding the fragmentary character of available data and the differences in calculations by various scholars, the

118. Calculated from W.G. Hoffmann, *Das Wachstum der deutschen Wirtschaft seit Mitte des 19. Jahrhunderts* (Berlin, 1965), p. 701, and idem, *Deutsche Volkseinkommen*, p. 56.

119. Kapitalanlagegesetz vom 29. März 1934, RGB1. I, p. 295; Anleihestockgesetz vom 4. Dezember 1933, RGB1. I, p. 1222.

120. For example, S. Andic and J. Veverka, "The Growth of Government Expenditure in Germany since the Unification," *Finanz-Archiv*, n.s. 23 (1963–64): 169–278.

121. Ries, "Finanzpolitik," table VI.

general direction is quite clear – a steep rise in public consumption as well as an increase in the share the public sector had in national income and the use of economic resources.

A similar tendency stands out in the sphere of investment. The data on gross investment and assessments of net investment made by various scholars conflict with each other and are thus unsuitable as a basis for reliable quantitative conclusions (see comparison in table 14 of appendix). However, all scholars believe that up to 1936 or 1937 private investment was rather limited. Net investment in industry was negative until 1934 according to official data, even if one takes into account real depreciation and deducts accelerated amortization write-offs granted to preferred enterprises. Only in 1935 did industry achieve a net private investment of 160 million reichsmarks, which rose to 430 million reichsmarks in 1936.[122]

From a purely economic viewpoint this was a rational course of action as long as the economy still performed at surplus capacity. In spite of this, the regime introduced administrative control measures right from the beginning in order to direct investment into preferred channels. The regulation of raw-material imports, introduced in March 1933 and tightened by a special law in July 1934, also served this aim, in addition to restricting the use of foreign currency reserves. Twenty-eight special bureaus allocated raw materials to various branches; their data pool served as the basis for special investment licenses issued by the Ministry of Economics.[123] An explicit ban was imposed on investment in or expansion of entire industrial branches like textiles, paper, cement, and glass, as well as a few branches of heavy industry, such as lead processing and pipes. However, the majority of prohibitions concerned consumer goods that had a high import component. In actuality, it appears that these prohibitions were unnecessary: there was no economic reason to fear a surplus of investment in these branches. In addition to unexploited capacity, the wage freeze and restrictions on income from capital imposed by the regime kept the rise of disposable income within limits that did not allow for any economic incentive to invest in these industries. On the other hand, government de-mand created sufficient incentives in heavy and chemical industries to attract investment; this was further enhanced by deliberate

122. Erbe, *Die nationalsozialistische Wirtschaftspolitik*, p. 114; Kroll, *Weltwirt-schaftskrise*, pp. 634f.
123. Gesetz über wirtschaftliche Maßnahmen vom 3. Juli 1934, RGB1. I, p. 565; Kroll, *Weltwirtschaftskrise*, p. 548.

special incentives like licensing accelerated amortization, raw-material allocations, and long-term government supply contracts.[124] And indeed, a specific study of private investment in Germany arrived at the conclusion that the partial and inconsistent extent to which these bans and control instructions were exercised rendered their significance as measures for the direction of investment negligible, at least until the end of 1936.[125]

Although some have tried to explain these contradictions by claiming that in many spheres the Nazis adhered to the principle that "to double-check is safer," I believe that this desire to double-check is at best a partial answer. I think that ideological motives operated in the sphere of investment as they did with regard to price control and wage freezing, in this case by considering institutional controls an important component of the economic system they wished to create. The Nazis acknowledged the significance of the investment factor for cyclical fluctuations within the economy and considered decisions on this issue too crucial to be left to private entrepreneurs. The 1937 *Jahrbuch für nationalsozialistische Wirtschaft*, in analyzing the impact of savings and investment on the state of employment, added the following, with explicit reference to Keynes: "What does investment, generated by purely private initiative, contribute to the preservation of economic equilibrium? The answer is unequivocal: private investment activity can by no means guarantee this equilibrium." The author goes on to say that more economic stability and ultimately, therefore, more general welfare could have been achieved during the preceding 150 years if some authority had existed to regulate the sphere of investment. The state alone can offer such authority and should not hesitate to act directly, on its own initiative, in the field of investment.[126] Specific research on investment policies has arrived at similar conclusions: the Nazi regime primarily sought to create a crisis-immune economy, meaning "a permanent state of full employment. . . . Cyclical fluctuations of privately motivated investment were to be eliminated by compensatory public investment, coupled with regulations of savings and investment in the economy."[127]

Until 1936 direct government investment did not amount to

124. W. Prion, *Das deutsche Finanzwunder: Die Geldbeschaffung für den deutschen Wirtschaftsaufschwung* (Berlin, 1938), pp. 32f.

125. Lurie, *Private Investment*, pp. 201f.

126. V. Wrede in Mönckmeier, ed., *Jahrbuch*, pt. 2, pp. 334f.

127. Lurie, *Private Investment*, p. 3.

much except in infrastructure-oriented public works – drainage, soil amelioration, and road construction – aimed at the creation of employment. For the development of new industries, in particular raw-material substitutes, the government preferred joint ventures by private industrialists, initiated by government agencies and aided by existing industrial self-management bodies. The need for legislative measures arose only in a few cases when it was considered necessary to disperse the risk and utilize the advantage of large-scale operations that went beyond the capacity of single enterprises. In this manner the government estabished "obligatory partnerships for joint financing" of new projects in industries producing synthetic fuel and textile substitutes.[128] A decree issued by the minister of economics on October 23, 1934, resulted in the creation of the Braunkohle Bearbeitungs A.G. (Brabag) for the development of coal-based synthetic fuel; the Ruhr Benzin A.G. was established for the same purpose in September 1935 without any legislation, but as the result of some pressure. The agreement between Gottfried Feder, *Staatssekretär* at the Ministry of Economics, and the I.G. Farben Company concerning synthetic gasoline production had already been signed in December 1933; it guaranteed reimbursement of possible losses by the government and the purchase of surplus production at a fixed price.[129] However, these were still limited and rather marginal occurrences. In general, economic motivation and a minimum of direct intervention were sufficient during the initial period. Nevertheless, the administrative and legal tools that had been created remained intact; later on they were effectively employed in order to steer investment in the direction the government wished it to go. The measures for direction of the money market, which will be discussed below, also acquired significance at the end of 1935; at that time private savings, especially in the business sector, became viable as a substantial source for investment. Only then did discriminating, commodity-oriented investment control become a dominant feature of investment policy.[130]

With regard to the money market, the regime also utilized the means at its disposal to prevent the investment of liquid capital reserves in the expansion of civil consumption. Such intervention had become necessary by the end of 1935, when savings had

128. Ibid., pp. 185f.; Gesetz über wirtschaftliche Pflichtgemeinschaften vom 28. September 1934, RGB1. I, p. 863.
129. Sauer in Bracher, Sauer, and Schulz, *Machtergreifung*, p. 820.
130. Mönckmeier, ed., *Jahrbuch*, pt. 2, p. 347.

accumulated as a result of more employment and the expansion of economic activity. From this point onward money-market policy deliberately strove to change the structure of savings to favor the business sector and nonvoluntary institutional savings that were invested in government bonds and poured into rearmament. This policy resulted in a decline in the position of commercial banks, which will be discussed below. During the initial years, tax and wage policies as well as dividend restrictions prevented a significant rise in disposable income, so household savings did not grow much. These savings were negative until 1934 and reached the sum of four million reichsmarks, about 6 percent of private income before taxes, only in 1936.[131] However, over the two following years private savings increased to about ten billion reichsmarks, most of which ended up in the government till. Even if we assume that these calculations are set slightly low, there is no doubt that up to the end of 1936 private savings did not constitute a substantial source for capital formation. In contrast, the amounts of nonvoluntary savings, in the form of considerable growth of social security funds and obligatory life insurance, increased over the same period (see appendix, table 19). The expansion of nonvoluntary institutional saving facilitated the transfer of accumulated sums to the state by means of what was called the noiseless procedure, namely, by investing the money in government bonds and turning a majority of the population, "apparently without [their] even having had a glimmer of what was going on, into indirect creditors of the state."[132] It is reasonable to assume that, under the conditions prevailing at the time, propaganda pressure and other means of "persuasion" would have achieved the same result if government loans had been put on the market. However, the fact remains that no one even bothered to try such means, preferring from the outset to use the "rolling procedure." As all saving and insurance agencies were members of a compulsory association (*Reichsgruppe*) and were attached to the central clearing house (Deutsche Girozentrale), the method was simple and economical. Loan certificates were not distributed and were not negotiable, so the great majority of savings was invested in government bonds with very little loss of time.[133]

131. Erbe, *Die nationalsozialistische Wirtschaftspolitik*, p. 105.
132. Stuebel, "Aufrüstung," p. 4132.
133. M. Moeller, "Schacht als Geld- und Finanzpolitiker," *Finanz-Archiv*, n.s. 11 (1949): 735f.; W. Dieben, "Die innere Reichsschuld seit 1933," *Finanz-Archiv*, n.s. 11 (1949): 687.

Nazi Economics

The savings of the man on the street were only a part, and not the most important part, of the private savings that the government collected. The savings of the business sector constituted a more substantial source of capital. It is therefore noteworthy that, precisely in the sphere of the money market and interest rates, state intervention was undisguised and underlined right from the beginning of Nazi rule. Among the means to channel business savings into the purchase of government bonds was the already mentioned law that made the purchase of these loans a condition for dividend distribution above the officially ratified rate, with the bonds held as a special fund by the enterprise. A complementary law passed in December 1934 withdrew this fund from the company's sphere of authority and transferred it to the Golddiskontbank, a subsidiary of the Reichsbank, as the implied "representative of all shareholders." This decree provided the bank with a measure of follow-up and control over profit distribution, for which tax agencies were also utilized. The law also determined the composition of assets, that is, the manner in which these funds were used. This law is characteristic of the Nazi inclination to mix topical economic considerations with ideological motives. If the intention was to boost business investment in government loans, it failed to achieve its aim: until April 1935 purchases of government bonds by business companies totaled only a little more than one million reichsmarks! As it was, companies preferred to accumulate undistributed profits which they could use in order to finance investments, increase their liquidity, or pay off old debts instead of paying higher dividends and purchasing the obligatory amount of government bonds, whose returns were lower than the interest they could save.[134] However, it seems that the law had a more important objective: industrial prosperity and increased profitability of enterprises caused a considerable rise in the market value of their shares, a trend that was enhanced by the restriction (in fact, ban) on the issue of stock. The law restricting dividend payments was clearly intended to curb the rise in share quotations and raise bond prices, as one means of lowering interest rates on the market. We will see below that it was not the only means to this end, but it did fulfill this role quite efficiently. As early as the end of 1934 the quotations for Reich and municipal bonds, which had previously undergone a severe decline, had climbed back to their nominal value. At the same time, although there was talk of

134. Frh. von Falkenhausen, "Das Anleihestockgesetz und seine Durchführung," *Bank-Archiv* 34 (1935): 283f.

a compulsory conversion of these bonds, the capital market was not effected by an excessive tendency to sell.[135]

The law also expressed the Nazis' basic objection to large-scale companies and anonymous capital stock. Only stock companies whose share capital exceeded 100,000 reichsmarks were subject to the law's restrictions. Private companies and partnerships were exempt. Moreover, any stock company that changed its legal status to that of a private or partnership company was automatically released from application of the law. An authoritative commentator explained that "this does not contravene the spirit of the law or the purpose of the legislator because the general . . . preferred tendency is to move toward the abolition of anonymity and a return to responsible leadership in suitable economic enterprises."[136]

If this was the way the law was interpreted in banking and stock-exchange periodicals, party publications were certainly even more eager to stress this aspect. The organ of the Nazi middle-class association NS-Hago tailored the law to a citation from *Mein Kampf*, where the phenomenon of severe economic degeneration caused the slow transfer of the whole economy to the hands of stock companies. The author of the article adds that, in the spirit of the above, stock companies had been forced to establish bonds funds and had been forbidden to pay exorbitant dividends. But at the same time, tax and registration-dues discounts made it easy for them to change their status to that of another kind of company: "These legal measures in the battle against phenomena of degeneration in the German economy initiate the return of German enterprises to private ownership. Dividends are reduced for the common good, preconditions in finance and taxation for the transformation of stock companies into personal companies are created, and the number of joint-stock companies is being reduced."[137] We have no data to measure how successful these laws were in changing owner-ship patterns of companies. One has the impression that if this was the purpose of the law, it remained but a pious wish. This prefer-ence for personal responsibility was soon to give way before the regime's more pressing needs and the voluntary cooperation it received from the big business associations. Nevertheless, the issue illuminates the overall context of economic policy and legislation in

135. Kroll, *Weltwirtschaftskrise*, pp. 593, 600; Stucken, *Geld- und Kreditpolitik*, p. 141.
136. Falkenhausen, "Das Anleihestockgesetz," p. 285.
137. *Der Aufbau*, no. 30 (1934), pp. 10f.

the regime's early days.

There is no doubt, however, that one of the major objectives of this legislation was the lowering of interest rates. From 1933 on the regime worked consistently toward this end, employing all means at the disposal of the government and the Reichsbank. Interest rates were lowered from 8 to 6 percent and in agriculture even to 4.5 percent while Hugenberg was still minister of agriculture. Payments were postponed and part of the debt on the principal was cancelled. The next stage was a general conversion incurred by municipal authorities: three billion reichsmarks' worth of municipal bonds were converted into new bonds at 4 percent interest. This conversion was "voluntary" and not imposed by decree, but those who did not convert had to forego payment of principal and interest, including arrears, for a period of five years. This was a sufficiently negative incentive for most bondholders to choose "voluntary" conversion.[138]

The next important step was again a "voluntary" conversion of all bonds issued by public agencies and banks, announced at the beginning of 1935. Bonds at 6 percent interest were converted into new bonds at 4.5 percent, with a tax-exempt bonus of 2 percent at the time of conversion. Conversion was carried out automatically unless the creditor explicitly announced his refusal. In that case he could keep the old bonds, but these were no longer negotiable, that is, they were frozen until their date of maturity. It is not surprising that success was complete – only 1 percent of the total debt was not converted. Eight billion reichsmarks in municipal debts and another two billion in various public loans were converted with no signs of a massive flight from these loans before the deadline. Saving banks and insurance companies "voluntarily" lowered their interest rates as a result of these transactions, so that on the face of it the road was clear for widespread dissemination of new state loans. But it was still possible to lend money on the private mortgage market at 7 to 8 percent interest. This led to an additional law, passed in July 1936, committing creditors to negotiations with their debtors in order to lower interest rates. If they could not reach an agreement, the decision was passed to a judge whose ruling determined the revised interest rate.[139] Party publications once again celebrated the new law as a triumph over "the slavery of interest . . . the core of the National Socialist economic philosophy. . . . Unfortunately on the

138. Stucken, *Geld- und Kreditpolitik*, p. 137; Kroll, *Weltwirtschaftskrise*, p. 598.
139. Stucken, *Geld- und Kreditpolitik*, pp. 145f.

private mortgage market circumstances have changed in such a way that the lowering of interest rates on private mortgages could not be felt. How far Jewish capital played a role in this remains an open question. . . . Further development of these decrees [will] . . . determine whether the involved creditors will become part of the community of the German people or whether they . . . have not yet grasped the great principles of National Socialist construction."[140]

The lowering of interest rates on mortgages was an old demand of middle-class homeowners, who had been hard hit by the price slump and the ensuing rise in actual value of debts and interest during the depression. Moreover, official economists spoke of the need to consolidate the Reich's short-term debts and to withdraw money from the public in order to preempt inflationary pressures while the economy was nearing full employment.[141] Such a state of affairs should, in fact, have caused the *raising* of interest rates in order to curb investment and reduce the money supply. However, the scope of investment in the German economy was dictated by the government, and private investment was being curbed, as we have seen, by administrative means. There was therefore no reason to fear the influence of low interest rates on private sector investment; the government, on the other hand, wished to reduce its payments to bondholders to save money as well as to limit the flow of income to the public. From a purely economic point of view this situation was paradoxical: the nearer the economy drew to full employment, the more effort was expended to lower interest rates instead of raising them. Nor should one ignore the ideological factor. Before the Nazis assumed power, "breaking the slavery of interest" and fighting "finance capital" had been major party-platform objectives. As we have seen with regard to other subjects, one should not accept the widespread claim that once the Nazis had seized power the ideological cargo was thrown overboard. German economists of the period also considered it necessary to underline ideological motivations: "The demand 'to break the slavery of interest' postulates, in any case, that the burden of interest debtors have to bear be made compatible with their income."[142] The *Staatssekretär* at the Ministry of Economics also emphasized this aspect of the interest-rate issue: "National Socialism devoted heightened attention to the question of interest for dogmatic and practical reasons. Besides the

140. *Der Aufbau*, no. 14 (1936), pp. 15f.
141. Prion, *Das deutsche Finanzwunder*, p. 83.
142. Stucken, *Geld- und Kreditpolitik*, p. 144.

return of confidence in the official exchange rate, the seizure of power was accompanied by progressive lowering of interest rates. . . . This movement was supported by . . . additional government measures."[143]

Success on this front was complete. The discount rate of private banks dropped from an annual average of 4.95 to 2.91 percent between 1932 and 1937. The interest rate for overnight loans dropped even more, from 6.23 to 2.93 percent.[144] The characteristic feature is the fact that in the course of time, that is, as the economy progressively approached full employment, interest rates sank rapidly instead of rising, as would be reasonable to assume. There can be no economic explanation for this phenomenon other than deliberate government policy that countered the natural economic process and was motivated, among other considerations, by ideological commitment. Other considerations, of course, were primarily the requirements of rearmament as well as the wish to finance that rearmament, as far as possible, by extensive public and banking loans. From 1935 on the regime did not bother to disguise its intentions. On the contrary, the propaganda campaign for government loans emphasized rearmament efforts. Schacht, in his famous Königsberg speech of August 1935, besides rearmament also emphasized the continuation of active employment policy and the necessity of utilizing all existing savings for government expenditure instead of steering those funds to the stock market or to investment in durable assets: "No one should forget that thanks to the government's employment project alone and, in particular, to rearmament, we have almost liquidated the large army of unemployed. . . . From time to time certain people are once again attacked by the so-called asset psychosis, namely, the attempt to escape an imaginary danger of devaluation by the purchase of durable assets, stock, and property partnerships. . . . We are all in the same boat and no one will have the opportunity to disembark. . . . For a German there is no better or more useful investment of his savings than putting them at the disposal of the German Reich as a loan toward the accomplishment of works projects. . . . Every individual must therefore contribute in his own interest so that the Führer's gigantic reconstruction work can be continued and completed, by harnessing his savings . . . to this urgent task, which is the most vital one for every individual."[145]

143. Posse, *Deutsche Wirtschaft*, p. 34.
144. Prion, *Das deutsche Finanzwunder*, p. 83.
145. Quoted by Krause, *Organisation*, pp. 77f.

This kind of persuasion brought results, and the very real and effective measures taken by the government probably more so than the widespread, vociferous propaganda launched by all levels of the general and party press: during the period 1935 to 1938 over fifteen billion reichsmarks in government loans were sold.[146] Only a small part, about 4.5 billion had been sold by the end of 1936. From about this time onward banking and industry accumulated very large liquidity surpluses, with no other outlet for investment once old debts had been paid and investment in their own enterprises financed.[147]

The Riddle of German Banking: Stagnation in an Expanding Economy

Banking in the Third Reich has still not been properly studied, in spite of its economic importance and the central place it held in Nazi ideology. The reason may be that so far no scholar has appeared who is as much at home with the specific body of knowledge concerning banking as with historical analysis. But even such a scholar would find it hard to assemble the necessary documentary evidence, most of which is hidden away in the restricted archives of German banks. Even the little that is known so far, however, raises some questions that are relevant to the present discussion.

The 1931 crisis hit German banking badly. At the same time, the crisis also created the tools later utilized by the Nazis to strengthen the position of the Reichsbank and state control over private banking. In September 1931 Brüning created the office of national banking commissioner through emergency legislation and placed the banks under tight control. To save the whole banking system from a complete breakdown, the state took over a considerable part of the share capital. Ultimately a consolidation agreement was reached with foreign creditors, deferring payments for a longer period of time, but only after five billion reichsmarks of foreign deposits had already been withdrawn. German banks had invested heavily in industry and were therefore severely hit by the slump and the ensuing drop of industrial stock rates in their portfolios. All

146. Erbe, *Die nationalsozialistische Wirtschaftspolitik*, p. 67.
147. A. Friedrichs, "Die Finanzierung der Staatskonjunktur," *Bank-Archiv* 37 (1938): 145.

these events greatly strengthened the strategical position of the Reichsbank, which became a major shareholder in some of the largest banks.[148]

After the Nazis assumed power, demands became obtrusively loud to realize one of the important paragraphs in their 1920 platform – nationalization of corporate banks and immediate lowering of interest rates. Schacht, who in April 1933 was once more appointed president of the Reichsbank, cleared this hurdle by creating a committee of inquiry headed by himself, with Hitler issuing explicit instructions that no steps be taken before the committee completed its report.[149] The committee only convened for the first time in September 1933 and conducted thorough research into German banking for a whole year. They received twenty-six written expert opinions and summoned 123 people to present oral evidence, usually at restricted sessions. The conclusions of the banking survey were subsequently published in two large volumes.[150] The main result was a new banking law, passed in December 1934.[151] The specifications of this law were not extraordinary by present-day standards, but at the time they greatly enhanced the stringency of control regulations, even in comparison with Brüning's emergency regulations. The supervisor of banks was authorized to license the establishment of new banks or new bank branches as well as to order the closure of a bank under certain conditions. Banks had to report any changes made in management or in the composition of their capital, mergers of various agencies, and loans above one million reichsmarks forwarded to a single debtor, with subsidiary firms and business groups to be treated as single debtors. There were also regulations for the legal volume of primary and secondary liquidity reserves: for 1935 10 percent primary liquidity (cash and deposits at the Reichsbank), plus 30 percent secondary liquidity in ordinary commercial bills whose exchange date did not exceed three months and/or in securities issued by the government or municipal authorities. Conditions for granting larger loans as well as loans to managers or board members of the bank itself were made much stricter. Such controls are nowadays accepted in most countries, and

148. Kroll, *Weltwirtschaftskrise*, p. 596; Lurie, *Private Investment*, pp. 92f.; K. Poole, *German Financial Policies, 1932–1939* (Cambridge, Mass., 1939), pp. 27f.

149. BA, R 13/I, 106, Hauptvorstand des Fachgruppenausschusses der eisenschaffenden Industrie vom 13. Dezember 1933.

150. Untersuchung des Bankwesens 1933/34, Berlin (Reichsbank) 1933/34.

151. Reichsgesetz über das Kreditwesen vom 5. Dezember 1934, RGB1. I, p. 1203.

even a paragraph authorizing the supervisor of banks "to intervene when it appears necessary" is not especially unusual. In any case, the influence of the law itself on the credit system should not be exaggerated: factors outside the banking system and deliberate government policies had greater impact. Had the regime wished to, it could have expanded banking activities even within this framework of control regulations, as indeed it did in the following years.[152]

The public treated the committee's work and the law it generated as a weighty matter of principle. The press gave prominent coverage to submerged skirmishes concerning the composition of the committee as well as to each stage of its work. Among its fifteen members, appointed by Hitler on advice from Schacht and Schmitt, were a few party members who had been connected to Otto Wagener's WPA before the Nazis assumed power: for example, Otto Christian Fischer from the board of the Reichskreditanstalt (National Credit Agency) and Professor Jens Jessen of Kiel University, appointed instead of the initially suggested Werner Sombart.[153] These, like Herbert Backe, who represented the Ministry of Agriculture, were appointed as representatives of banking, science, and government departments. The party was represented chiefly by Gottfried Feder and Wilhelm Keppler. In press reports on the committee's first sessions their utterances therefore received special attention. However, it soon became obvious that by shifting discussions away from the ideological plane, Schacht had succeeded in shunting them to the sidelines.[154] Ultimately he managed to dispose of Feder altogether, blaming him for leaks to the press from confidential committee meetings. This aroused the fury of party circles, who complained (in vain) to Rudolf Heß and the chancellor that party representatives were systematically being ousted from the committee.[155]

Arguments of ideological significance within the committee revolved mainly around three subjects: nationalization, the lowering of interest rates, and control regulations for public and corporate savings banks. Savings banks had already passed into the hands of Nazi management during the initial months of 1933, when Werner Daitz was appointed chairman of the National Association of

---

152. Lurie, *Private Investment*, p. 113.
153. BA R 43/II, p. 243.
154. O.C. Fischer, in BA R 13/I, p. 106.
155. BA, R 43/II, p. 243.

Savings Banks. In June 1933 that association decided to lower interest rates voluntarily, an event Daitz reported in a solemn letter to Hitler in which he expressed his hope that large as well as private banks would follow suit. As middle-class credit agencies, savings banks enjoyed party support. They were in general economically well established: following the 1931 banking crisis many individuals transferred their savings deposits from private banks to savings banks under the assumption that these offered greater security. Consequently savings banks recovered faster and thus were already able to repay the greater part of the 1.1 billion reichsmarks received as government aid by the end of 1933. In March 1934 the supervisor of banks loosened liquidity regulations for savings banks. In addition to lowering interest rates, these banks demonstrated their support for the regime by a loan to the party and the government.[156] Darré and Backe, his representative on the committee, aligned themselves with the savings banks because they sought to preserve the independent and preferred status of corporate credit associations in agriculture.[157]

Private banks which were members of the Centralverband des Deutschen Bank- und Bankiergewerbes (Central Association of the German Bank and Bankers' Profession) conducted their affairs prudently, being very much aware of their sensitive position. They apparently understood that for the time being they had better lie low because "a great number of ideological considerations . . . played a very powerful part. . . . From the outset the slogan of 'breaking the slavery of interest' was part of the political platform," a fact that made sober discussion very difficult. So Fischer described the situation at a restricted meeting of the RDI. He added that the public interpreted the presence of bank representatives on industrial boards of directors as representing the former's dominance over the entire economy and admitted that it was hard to argue with such a position: "A bunch of dethroned bank rulers were sitting there [at sessions of the Banking Committee] finding it very difficult to defend themselves."[158] Under these circumstances the committee's conclusions and the resulting law were an achievement for the large corporate and private banks, but it is an exaggeration to speak of a decisive victory connected, according to some scholars, to the

156. Schweitzer, *Big Business*, pp. 130f.; BA R 2/13643, p. 54.
157. BA 43/II, p. 243, Darré an Hitler vom 27. April 1934.
158. Fisher in BA R 13/I, 106.

suppression of the SA on June 30, 1934.[159] The committee ruled against the nationalization of banks and also imposed control regulations on savings banks. But the law it initiated tightened these regulations: banks had to publish their balance sheets and present detailed monthly reports on their transactions. The lowering of interest rates was included as a desirable trend, to be realized only gradually. On the other hand, Schacht's concluding report left no doubt that the primary objective of his regulations was to harness the capital market to the requirements of the state: "German socialism means that the development of national economic life is not left to its own devices but that the state, standing for the people, sees to it that economic tasks are carried out, even to some extent assuming responsibility for them itself. The new state therefore needs a much greater volume of liquid capital than the former one. . . . The core of the new order is the creation of a money and capital market that is adequate for the tasks of the National Socialist state."[160]

The committee's conclusions were a kind of compromise: the demand to forbid savings banks to forward short-term credit, leaving this sphere of business exclusively to large, commercial banks, was rejected.[161] The obligation to make balance sheets public, besides presenting them to Reichsbank controllers, went against the grain of banking officials "because the general public does not sufficiently understand the matter of scope."[162] The raising of legal liquidity rates evoked fears of reduced profitability resulting from credit restrictions.[163] On the other hand, it is obvious that the more radical demands voiced by the Nazis, who consistently followed the proceedings with mistrust and depicted them as a struggle against "the closed phalanx of bankers,"[164] were not satisfied either.

Given the general atmosphere at the time and the bankers' fears prior to the inquiry, banking circles had reason to be satisfied with the committee's conclusions, though these were a far cry from a victory for finance capital. The principal victor was the Reichsbank. The new control regulations and the authority the Reichsbank had

159. Schweitzer, *Big Business*, p. 134; Bettelheim, *L'économie allemande*, p. 101.

160. Bericht des Untersuchungsausschusses für das Bankwesen, Deutsches Nachrichtenbüro (DNB), 29.11.1934.

161. *Deutsche Allgemeine Zeitung*, Nov. 30, 1934.

162. *Vossische Zeitung*, Nov. 30, 1934.

163. *Deutsche Allgemeine Zeitung*, Nov. 30, 1934; *Deutsche Führerbriefe*, Nov. 13, 1934.

164. F. Fried, "Jugend und Wirtschaft," *Nationalsozialistische Landespost*, Dec. 9, 1933.

over management and board appointments enabled it to guide the development of banking with considerable flexibility, according to overall policies. Of course, the decision against nationalization caused satisfaction in banking circles, but that decision was also not in opposition to the regime's proclaimed intention "to lead the economy, but not to venture into independent economic activity."[165]

In order to find out who the real victor was, it is not enough to examine the committee's work or even the new law that resulted from its conclusions. It is necessary to examine events in the field, namely, the development of banking and savings banks during subsequent years. The law provided government agencies with the tools to guide this development at will and in the light of their political aims; what is needed, therefore, is a meticulous examination of the manner in which these tools were actually employed. As I mentioned above, this specific research still awaits attention, but even a glance at available statistical evidence, as well as at publications of the period, shows that the picture is not at all unequivocal. The claim that these decisions constituted a triumph for finance capital, popular especially among East German and also Western Marxist scholars, fails to distinguish between ownership, economic influence, and political power.[166] However, even the available data on the scope of transactions and profits do not point to a triumph, at least not until the war.

During the depression German banking, the large banks in particular, suffered more than other banks because they held very large foreign deposits. The assets in their combined balance sheet dropped from 16.7 billion reichsmarks in 1929 to 10.7 billion in 1932. The surprising feature is that these assets continued to shrink over the following years, reaching a low of 9.6 billion in December 1935. Only at the end of 1936 did signs of a slight rise (9.7 billion) appear, which continued in subsequent years. Even more striking is the drop in private-business credits in this balance sheet: if we join long- and short-term credits to the discount of regular commercial bills, these credits declined from 12.0 billion reichsmarks in 1929 to 7.6 billion in 1932 and to 6.4 billion at the end of 1935. The slight rise to 6.7 billion at the end of 1936 came mainly from discounts of bills, while regular commercial credit continued to decline through-

165. Mönckmeier, ed., *Jahrbuch*, pt. 1, p. 172.
166. T.W. Mason, "Zur politischen Relevanz historischer Theorien: Die Imperialismus-Diskussion im Schatten des kalten Krieges," in *Aus Politik und Zeitgeschichte: Beilage zu Das Parlament*, B 20/72 (May 1972): 37.

out the year. It appears, therefore, that during a period of general economic prosperity, the transaction volume of national and regional banks decreased and the credit they forwarded to business shrank, which meant that their profits and capital were reduced! In contrast, the volume of savings deposits increased considerably over the same period, from 14.8 in 1932 to 19.2 billion reichsmarks in 1936 (see appendix, tables 20–21). It is obvious that public and corporate savings banks were the main beneficiaries of this development.

Contemporary observers called attention to the decline in the importance of banking in Germany, emphasizing its minor contribution to the process of economic recovery.[167] Attempts were made to explain this phenomenon in economic terms, namely, by stating that business and especially industry had no need of credit because they did not invest much; to the extent that they invested at all, they were able to finance investment with the surplus they could not distribute in the form of higher dividends. The result was that, in addition to not needing new credit, they were able to pay off large parts of previous debt, thus reducing the volume of loans in the asset portfolios of large banks. Liquidation of production surpluses accumulated during the depression reduced their need for working capital, while the lack of foreign currency made it impossible to amass large stocks of imported raw materials.[168] Such objective economic arguments are certainly not negligible, and their true weight has not yet been sufficiently evaluated. Nevertheless, I do not believe that they provide a full explanation for this phenomenon, part of which was due to a deliberate government policy that sought to reduce the volume of banking credit as much as possible.[169] The principal reason for this policy was the government's wish to channel liquidity surpluses into employment and rearmament projects. From this point of view, greater liquidity was desirable in banks. The banks themselves were certainly not pleased by this state of affairs, since it reduced their income: "This liquidity was not at all what they wanted because it always came at the expense of profitability and because it resulted from their exclusion from important business transactions."[170]

---

167. Prion, *Das deutsche Finanzwunder*, p. 52; A. Friedrichs, "Die Finanzierung der Arbeitsbeschaffung," *Bank-Archiv* 33 (1933–34): 146; F. Reinhart, "Die volkswirtschaftliche Verwendung der Bankeinlagen," *Bank-Archiv* 35 (1935–36): 59.
168. G. Keiser, "Strukturwandel der Bankbilanzen," *Bank-Archiv* (1939): 239.
169. Lurie, *Private Investment*, pp. 96f.
170. Grotkopp, *Die große Krise*, p. 297.

It would perhaps be an exaggeration to define the policy Schacht had already announced in the committee's report as explicitly hostile to banking; nor was it an inevitable consequence of overall economic policy. Had the regime valued the banking system as it valued agriculture and industry, for example, it would have employed banking services in the implementation of deficit spending and credit expansion and, in one way or another, would have granted it a share in regulated credit. The regime could also have realized its policy of monetary expansion and lower interest rates while compensating banks and assuring their profitability through an increase in deposits and credit volume. In fact, they chose to support enterprises directly through an elaborate system of tax discounts, accelerated amortization, and government orders at fixed prices. Payments were usually made through bills of various descriptions, many of which never reached a bank for discount; they served as an immediate means of payment within the economy as well as a device to keep liquidity surpluses within the enterprise. This was by no means the only possible way to implement such a policy; nor was it a self-evident consequence of the economy's requirements or the given institutional system. On the contrary, a monetary expert had already emphasized at the time that the banking system's potential for contributing to the creation of money was, in fact, not utilized, although the new banking law provided the necessary procedures. The law left room for a discriminatory policy of discount rates and open-market operations by means of flexible and variable liquidity rates: "The tools for regulation of money creation by credit banks . . . had no doubt been brilliantly perfected. This framework should have been filled out by suitable implementation rules; this . . . never happened. . . . Given the National Socialist attitude to the question of interest . . . the utilization of discount policies as well as of open-market policies could eventually have become very inconvenient."[171] Another scholar wonders why banks were excluded from financing investments and engaging the capital market, notwithstanding their long tradition of investment in industry, their disposable reserves, and their high liquidity. He remarks that this attitude "was directly opposed to technical conditions in German banking. . . . With regard to the capital-market and to banking-credit this neglect of 'external' sources for financing appears rather as a result of

171. Stucken, *Geld- und Kreditpolitik*, pp. 110f.

deliberate policy, than as a necessity that arose from prevailing circumstances."[172]

The situation that arose from this policy was the exact opposite of the conventional model – economic prosperity without an increase in credit volume or rising interest rates, but a drop in both to the point where interest ceased to have significance in industrial outlays. Even if ideological motivations did not actually initiate this policy, there is no doubt that it exploited antibanking sentiments among the population at large. People were aware of the change that occurred in the role of banking as well as of the decline in its importance for the economy. The subject was discussed in banking circles, by economists associated with those groups, and by others in a spirit of criticism and exhortation where banks were accused of failing to fulfill their proper role and contribute adequately to economic recovery. A well-known economist simply announced that the leading role of German banks had come to an end once and for all. They neither fulfilled a noteworthy role in the liquidation of unemployment nor lived up to expectations in the purchase of government loans, preferring to invest their money in special bills. He recognized their reduced profitability but had no word of compassion to spare; nor did he envision a better future for banking. On the contrary, "Not long ago it was proudly said: The banks are the leaders of production. . . . It appears that in no other economic sphere has it become so obvious that the state has assumed leadership as in banking. . . . One can no more speak of active credit policy conducted by banks. . . . The National Socialist state will not let the guidance or the steering of the economy out of its hands."[173] This was written by a professor of economics at Berlin University and the Berlin Institute for Technology in 1938, long after Gottfried Feder had disappeared from the public arena and his diatribes against finance capital had, on the face of it, fallen into oblivion. Nevertheless, it appears that the above statement echoes the same concepts that had allegedly been thrown overboard together with other middle-class ideological equipment of Nazi origin.

Publications by banking circles cautiously voiced their concern at prevailing conditions while looking forward to better days. They explained the decline in deposits and credit transactions as a passing occurrence that would change when state prosperity, that is,

172. Lurie, *Private Investment*, pp. 216f.
173. Prion, *Das deutsche Finanzwunder*, pp. 54f.

prosperity in the public sector, would again give way to private prosperity: "With the expansion of prosperity in the private sector the economy will need greater financial resources. . . . It will need the means it has loaned to the government . . . for itself."[174] There are also defensive overtones and an attempt to demonstrate the contribution made by banks, which sold government loans and held government bills in spite of the fact that these resulted in the loss of interest and, consequently, in reduced profitability: "It follows that banking activity is fully geared to the purposes of the government, the economy, and the goals of the works projects program."[175]

It seems that, granted the caution imposed by the prevailing state of research, one may conclude that the period under discussion was not a happy one for German banking. It is true that many of its early fears did not materialize: no nationalization of banks occurred, and the Nazi regime even activated a kind of return to private initiative by selling the stock portfolios of the major banks owned by the Reichsbank since the 1931 debacle on the open market. This process was almost accomplished by October 1937: within no more than eleven days, 120 million reichsmarks worth of shares was bought by the public, characteristically not by the banks themselves or a banking consortium but mainly in small amounts by the general public. It appears that the forecast of 5 percent dividends was a sufficient incentive, given the conditions on the capital market at the time.[176] However, even though banks were not nationalized, they lost, at least for a transition period, much of their economic strength and political power. The regime dictated the manner of their activity according to its own conditions, harnessing them first to rearmament and later to the war effort. This was the situation while Schacht was Reichsbank president, and it remained so after his resignation in 1939. Contemporaries were aware of this state of affairs and even described it as "a historic turning point." Thus a major economic newspaper wrote in 1938:

> The Great Depression begot the banking revolution; National Socialism carried it out. In economic history this change has far-reaching import and its impact goes deep; it demonstrates the renunciation of the past with particular clarity. Previously the banker represented money in popular consciousness, today the state does. The state has applied

174. Friedrichs, "Finanzierung der Staatskonjunktur," p. 147.
175. Reinhart, "Bankeinlagen," p. 60.
176. *Deutsche Allgemeine Zeitung*, Oct. 5, 1937.

Knapp's theory of money. It not only creates currency and regulates exchange rates, but also generates credit, directs its flow, and employs banks as sluices, collectors, and subsidiary distributors. . . . Private banks have largely assumed the character of public banks without being nationalized. . . . [They] are obedient assistants of the Reichsbank.[177]

What occurred after 1936 considerably improved the economic position of banking but does not necessarily conflict with my basic argument. The substantial improvement of balance sheets that began in 1937 was a result of the increase in government bonds in banking portfolios, but real prosperity of gigantic dimensions came only during the war when banks took their full share from the plunder of assets in the occupied territories. It is quite revealing that the claim defended by Bettelheim and other orthodox Marxists – namely, that Hitler and the Nazis faithfully served the triumph of finance capital – relies mainly on statistical evidence from these later years. The fact that from 1933 to 1939 banking was discriminated against in comparison with other economic branches is either ignored or halfheartedly recognized, with no attempt to explain it.[178]

War Economy in Peacetime?

Of about 27.5 billion reichsmarks poured into the economy by the German government from 1933 to 1936, about 21 billion went straight into rearmament. A considerable part of the 5.5 billion reichsmarks devoted to civil employment projects went into road construction and other strategically important infrastructure projects. The total expenditure on rearmament and war preparations therefore comprised nearly 90 percent of all additional government expenditure, the primum mobile of Germany's economic miracle in these four years. This or similar estimates feed the widely accepted claim that the German economy, at least from 1934 on, was "a war economy in peacetime."[179] The liquidation of unemployment is attributed solely to the rearmament boom; the growth in employment and the increased GNP are considered marginal products, cleverly exploited in propaganda, of expansionist war preparations conducted by the Nazis from the very start of their rule.[180]

177. Ibid., May 8, 1938.
178. Lurie, *Private Investment*, p. 98.
179. Erbe, *Die nationalsozialistische Wirtschaftspolitik*, p. 163.
180. Fischer, *Deutsche Wirtschaftspolitik*, pp. 62f.; Schulz, in Bracher, Sauer, and Schulz, *Machtergreifung*, p. 672; Schweitzer, *Big Business*, pp. 341f.

Today there is no doubt that war was a central political goal for Hitler, consistently pursued from the time he attained power or even earlier. On February 3, 1933, three days after his appointment as chancellor, he revealed his plan at a closed meeting of army chiefs:

> 3. Economy! The peasant must be saved! [Hence a] settlement policy! Settlement provides the only possibility to once again harness parts of the army of unemployed. But time is needed and no radical change is to be expected because the *Lebensraum* is too small for the German people.
> 4. The building up of the armed forces as the most important precondition for achievement of this goal, reconquest of political power. Compulsive military service must be reinstalled. . . . How should political power, once gained, be utilized? Now there is yet nothing to say. Perhaps capture of new export outlets, perhaps even better, the conquest of a new *Lebensraum* in the east and its ruthless Germanization. What is certain is that economic situations can be changed only by political power and struggle.[181]

These examples of Hitler's utterances at government meetings confirm once more that he strove to harness government-initiated public works to rearmament as well.

The statistical evidence also refutes claims made by certain German historians and economists who support the apologetics of some of the individuals involved, Schacht in particular. According to them, one should distinguish between a period of civil works projects, which ended approximately at the beginning of 1935, and the period of rearmament.[182] Nevertheless, the fact that rearmament and war preparations were undoubtedly a *political* objective of the Nazi regime from its very beginnings does not necessarily imply that from an *economic* point of view Germany conducted a "war economy in peacetime," as René Erbe, for example, claims. A year after the publication of Erbe's book (but without referring to it), Burton Klein presented the opposite thesis, that in contrast to the widespread opinion, held mainly in the West, that Germany's economy was totally harnessed to war preparations, the economy was in fact far from being fully mobilized, and rearmament expen-

181. Notes of Generalleutnant Liebmann, in T. Vogelsang, "Neue Dokumente zur Geschichte der Reichswehr, 1930–1933." *Vierteljahreshefte für Zeitgeschichte* 2 (1954): 434f.

182. Schacht, *My First 76 Years*, p. 367; Stucken, *Geld- und Kreditpolitik*, pp. 123f.; Kroll, *Weltwirtschaftskrise*, pp. 460f.

diture did not exceed the military budgets of other countries by much.[183] Nowadays most scholars agree that Klein's estimates of German rearmament, based on the American Strategic Bombing Survey, were too low. Nevertheless, one should not deny him the merit of having been the first to point out a considerable measure of improvisation and inefficiency in German war preparations. The German economy was totally mobilized for war to a much lesser extent than was assumed at the time, inside and outside the country.[184] Klein's thesis served as the basis for the provocative claim by the British historian A.J.P. Taylor that Hitler had initially not intended to trigger a world war.[185] But the copyright for this thesis is all Taylor's own. Klein himself interpreted his findings as indicating that Hitler had only planned a short blitzkrieg, which in his opinion made long-term and total economic mobilization unnecessary, and that Hitler had been influenced by the fear of inflation harbored by "far too conservative" German economists.

A war economy not "totally" mobilized for military purposes is, of course, possible. The whole discussion remains shallow unless one tries to define clearly what turns any economy into a war economy. I believe that one can define the principal criteria as follows: 1) quantitative parameters of rearmament and military expenditure in relation to the GNP and total state expenditure; 2) the existence and actual utilization of institutional control and steering agencies that channel economic resources into rearmament.

To determine reliable quantitative parameters for the relation of rearmament to the GNP and state expenditure is not an easy task – and not because there is a scarcity of data for rearmament expenses. Today these figures are more or less accepted by the majority of scholars as totaling about 60 billion reichsmarks for the period 1933 to 1939 (see appendix, table 22). In contrast, there are great differences in estimates of the GNP, gross and net investment, and government expenditure during the prewar years. As a result, there are also great differences in estimates of the part of the national product spent on rearmament (see appendix, table 21). Minimalists like Klein and Milward arrive at 3 percent of the GNP and 9 percent

---

183. Klein, *Germany's Preparations for War*, pp. 17f.

184. See Milward, *The German Economy at War*; Carroll, *Design for Total War*; Speer, *Inside the Third Reich*, pp. 299ff.

185. A.J.P. Taylor, *The Origins of the Second World War* (London, 1964), pp. 17ff.

of government expenditure for rearmament costs in 1934, which rose to 18 percent and 42 percent respectively in 1938. Stuebel's estimate, considered to be the most realistic, arrives at about 8 percent of the GNP and about 40 percent of Reich expenditure (without individual states and municipalities) in 1934, with rates of 21 and 60 percent respectively in 1938. The wide gap in estimates arises from different definitions of state expenditure (see appendix, table 22, for the author's attempt to calculate military expenses in proportion to total state expenditure on goods and services).

Berenice Carroll tried in a later study (1968) to set quantitative criteria for a war economy. She came to the conclusion that a fairly wide intermittent region exists between total war economy (in which over 50 percent of the GNP is military expenses) and peacetime economy (up to 3 percent of the GNP). She believes that the distinguishing line beyond which a given economy becomes a war economy, though not yet a total one, lies between these two poles. The placement of this watershed lends itself to a variety of arguments and evaluations. If we accept Carroll's assessment that the dividing line between peacetime and war economy is breached when 15 percent or more of the GNP is allocated to military expenses, the following picture emerges: according to calculations of maximalists like Stuebel and Hoffmann the decisive year is 1936, while according to Klein and Milward the German economy reached this stage only in 1938. Mandelbaum arrived at a similar conclusion based on the calculation of employment indexes, that is, that the German economy reached the stage of "over-employment inherent to war-economies" only by the end of 1937.[186]

I believe there is another dividing line, namely, when 50 percent of total state expenditure on goods and services flows into military and related expenses. It is difficult to draw an exact line because scholars use varying definitions of state expenditure in their calculations. But in a general way this criterion will also yield the year 1936 according to Stuebel and Hoffmann and a later date according to the minimalists. Thus both quantitative criteria show Germany's economy entering upon a stage of accelerated war preparation at the earliest in 1936. This turning point was documented by the proclamation of the Four-Year Plan and Hitler's memorandum announcing the guidelines for this plan.[187] Carroll arrives at a similar

186. Mandelbaum, *Full Employment*, p. 182.
187. W. Treue, "Hitlers Denkschrift zum Vierjahresplan," *Vierteljahreshefte für Zeitgeschichte* 3 (1955): 184ff.

conclusion: "In 1933 the economy of the Third Reich was still . . . peace-oriented. From 1934 on it was moving in the direction of war-economy, but in this and the following year it was still quite some distance from the objective. Beginning in 1936 Germany's economy was 'dominated' in certain key respects . . . by armaments but it should not be called a war economy. From 1938 on, however, that designation can legitimately be used."[188] This description reflects the gradual and dynamic development very well, though I still believe that, according to Carroll's own criteria, the end of 1936 is a more reasonable date than the later one she suggests.

The picture is more complex with regard to institutional criteria. We have seen that the legislative and administrative control mechanism was already set up in 1933 but was brought to bear only partially and sporadically before mid-1936, except in foreign trade. Only after the proclamation of the Four-Year Plan did the authorities begin to keep a tighter rein on price controls and labor-force mobility, as well as on the expansion of direct government activity. This took place within the administration of the Four-Year Plan headed by Göring, mainly in the sphere of fuel substitute industries. Yet this plan also included only parts of the economy. At least until 1942, when Albert Speer was appointed minister for armament and munitions production, there was no central planning agency in Germany, not even for strategically important sectors.[189] It is clear in any case that until the end of 1936 the German economy could not be defined as a war economy in institutional terms either.

This distinction is significant not because the claim that rearmament was the main factor in the liquidation of unemployment is mistaken, but because I do not believe it offers an adequate explanation. Rearmament and preparation for war were *political* goals of the Nazi regime, but with regard to method the criteria under discussion are saliently *economic*. The economic impact of these policies arose from the manner in which additional government expenses were financed and not from the way they were specifically allocated. From the aspect of economic theory, allocation for rearmament was not inherent in the method of massive deficit spending. The same effect – the liquidation of unemployment – could have been achieved by spending that money on civil projects for the private and public welfare. The Nazis acted differently because of their political objectives, not because war was the only possible

188. Carroll, *Design for Total War*, p. 189.
189. Ibid., pp. 248f.

way out of the depression. In other words, they chose rearmament because they were Nazis and aspired to an expansionist war, not because their economic method dictated rearmament.

Theoretically the opposite claim is also viable: rearmament could also have been accomplished by means of conventional fiscal and monetary policies although, under conditions prevailing at the time, certainly not with the same speed and on the same scale. It would have meant a drastic lowering of living standards, with the financing of rearmament through additional taxes, compulsory loans, or any other means available to extract money from the public. The regime would have achieved rearmament in this case as well but without the economic effect of liquidating unemployment. It is self-evident that it would also have relinquished the effect of their political propaganda which was instrumental in gaining majority support among the German people for the regime's internal policy and its external political objectives.

I have tried to show in the preceding chapters that the Nazis chose their economic tools not by accident but because these intrinsically suited their ideology and their economic philosophy. Furthermore, expansion of *Lebensraum* was also inherent to their mode of thinking. War and the preparation it required had double significance within this ideological fabric: for the Nazis war was a goal per se, rooted in Hitler's social-Darwinist world picture, and a means for realizing their vision of the future, where their sound society, firmly set in the vast and fertile plains of central and eastern Europe, provided a basis for the domination of Europe, and perhaps the entire world, by the master race. The stable, crisis-immune German economy beckoning on the distant horizon was to provide every pure Aryan German with the right to work within the Nazi Thousand-Year Reich. The postponement of this ultimate goal until the war was won did not prevent the Nazis from incorporating some ideological and administrative elements of "the new order" at an early stage in the development of their economic system. This system did not encroach on capitalist ownership or the profit incentive but did impose restrictions on entrepreneurs with regard to their freedom in decision making; like other sectors of the population, they were subject to the primacy of politics. The proclaimed objectives were not maximum production or profit, but national power and stability. From 1933 to 1936 this primacy demanded the liquidation of unemployment and the initiation of rearmament as immediate goals. From 1936 on, when full employment had been achieved, the next objective was to prepare for a war of expansion. These immediate goals caused the postponement of more distant ideological objectives like resettlement or reagrarianization, but this does not imply that they were altogether abandoned or forgotten. Today we know quite a lot about the plans made by Hitler, Himmler, and the SS for the time after the achievement of military victory. There is no doubt that they considered the new economic system they had created a durable instrument for the realization of ideological and political goals, in the short as well as in the long run.

This argument can be corroborated by countless Nazi publications and speeches by Nazi leaders as well as by professional economists of the period. As additions to what has been said in preceding chapters, however, three excerpts here will suffice. The first quotations are taken from a speech Goebbels delivered at a mass meeting of youths participating in a "battle week" under the heading "Youth in the Service of German Socialism":

> Even when unemployment is liquidated by us National Socialists, the economy will on account of this not simply have become National Socialist.... The economy must be molded in a National Socialist pattern because this is the only guarantee that in future we will be spared economic catastrophes like those we experienced under liberalism and Marxism.... An idea can live and exert influence only through norms it creates in order to realize itself. The reconstruction of the economy ... will be durable only if its structure is altered, that is, if National Socialist spirit spreads within the economy.... If the National Socialist idea does not acquire a firm design through certain shapes and norms, a breach will be left in the wall defending the German people. We National Socialists will fill this breach too and thus realize the demand for totality inherent in our weltanschauung.[190]

It is true that this was propaganda and ideology, but I believe one should not belittle these either. The more so as it appears that professional economists, who regarded the improvement of economic and managerial efficiency as their principal task, wrote in the same spirit. The National Institute for Economic Efficiency (Reichskuratorium für Wirtschaftlichkeit) was a veteran semiofficial agency supported by the Ministry of Economics from the time of the Weimar Republic. In 1933 the institute's economists sum-

190. *Der Aufbau*, Jan. 15, 1934, pp. 5f.

marized the first year of Nazi rule in the following manner:

> The variety of contemporary economic tasks, even the weighty ones like liquidation of unemployment, are ultimately partial and secondary to this most important of all economic problems, namely, the stabilization of an unalterably distinct corporate economic order; for the entire question of unemployment ... will be truly solved only when we succeed in creating a corporate order which both satisfies the principle of concordance and totality and makes impossible, as a matter of principle, the reappearance of crisis phenomena of any kind. ... The solution to these decisive economic questions has at all times to come from the economic order because only such a solution can be guaranteed to last.[191]

Such utterances do not belong only to the initial period of Nazi rule. They also recur consistently, though in slightly different versions, after corporate terminology had been abandoned. The continuity of this attitude is demonstrated, for instance, in the following paragraph written by the economic editor of one of the large nonparty newspapers: "In the long term, it is not the economy with maximum output that is nationally sound, but the economy with optimum output, backed by a well-balanced order in the life of a productive and working people." The author adds that this goal is not to be achieved easily or all at once, but that its time would indeed come "when policy has ultimately expanded the breakthrough to national power and greatness and to a new European order in the spirit of a Pax Germanica and has consolidated its outer circumference."[192]

The claim that explanation of the Nazis' economic policy during the early years cannot be reduced to the notion of a war economy in peacetime therefore does not subtract from the importance of rearmament or the Nazis' aggressive intentions. On the contrary, if the German economy up to 1936 was by economic and institutional standards less of a war economy than many assumed, it was at the same time more than just a war economy. It was an attempt to mold a new economic order based on ideological norms that were to some degree rooted in the German past. It appears that because of its historical roots the attempt had considerable persuasive power within German society of that period.

191. Reichskuratorium für Wirtschaftlichkeit (RKW), Publication no. 99, p. 65.
192. J. Winschuh, *Gerüstete Wirtschaft* (Berlin, 1940), p. 30.

Chapter 5

The Economy of War and Conquest, 1937–1945

In August 1936 Hitler composed a confidential memorandum requesting the army and all government branches in Germany to prepare the armed forces and the economy for war within four years.[1] Full employment had already been achieved, and there were signs of shortages in skilled labor and raw materials, primarily imported ones. German exports, reduced partly because of conditions on the international market and partly by deliberate government policy, were incapable of providing the necessary foreign currency. Hitler demanded that these difficulties be met by allocating top priority to rearmament and by coordinating the activity of all involved authorities. He also specified particular, immediate objectives: an increase in synthetic fuel and rubber production as well as the output of iron and coal mining, irrespective of production costs.

In September 1936 Göring was made responsible for the execution of these tasks. In addition to the offices he already held , he was appointed plenipotentiary for the execution of the Four-Year Plan (*Beauftragter zur Durchführung des Vierjahresplan*). Göring thus arrived at the peak of his power in the Nazi hierarchy, though his appointment did not cause substantial changes in the economy and its management.[2] A number of branches were pinpointed within the Four-Year Plan administration in order to award them the priority outlined in Hitler's memorandum. Another directive agency with wide-ranging but unspecified authority was added to the existing control mechanism. The appointment of Joseph Wagner, Gauleiter for Silesia, as price commissioner was among the first measures taken to tighten price administering. Göring also appointed a number of authorized general deputies for various production branches

1. Treue, "Hitlers Denkschrift," pp. 184–210.
2. Broszat, *Der Staat Hitlers*, pp. 349, 370ff.

like the steel, iron, chemicals, construction-work, and automobile industries. At the top of the pyramid stood the General Four-Year Plan Council headed by Göring himself and composed of the *Staatssekretäre* for economy, agriculture, labor, and transport. On the face of it these officials were appointed to the council with the aim of facilitating coordination between government departments, but at the same time they encroached on the authority of their respective ministers. Schacht was replaced as minister of economics in November 1937, first by Göring himself and later, at the beginning of 1938, by Walter Funk, who in January 1939 also took over Schacht's position at the Reichsbank. Prior to this time Funk was already a member of Göring's entourage, but he had much less experience, authority, and effective drive than his predecessor in this office.

In spite of its apparently powerful status, the Four-Year Plan administration never reached the level of a comprehensive planning agency;[3] its activity centered mainly on a few strategically important sectors plagued by shortages. Special attention was paid to the production of substitutes for rubber, fuel, and fibers for textile industries. Karl Krauch, an experienced chemist/industrialist and a board member of I.G. Farben, the leading chemical industry group in Germany, was put at the head of the department for chemical industries. Krauch had already served as Göring's adviser at the Air Force Ministry in 1933; in 1934 he was instrumental in the establishment of an industrial combine for the extraction of gasoline from coal. Now he was assigned as well to the development of synthetic rubber (*Buna*). His close cooperation with the I.G. Farben group facilitated participation of the group's administrative machinery in activities of the Four-Year Plan administration. Similar cooperative arrangements were established with other industrial branches connected to rearmament or production for its infrastructure, and these were progressively expanded during the war. Göring also established new state-owned enterprises directly managed by his administration. Outstanding among these was the Hermann Göring Werke, which started production in 1937 at Salzgitter near Braunschweig and processed iron ore whose quantitative and qualitative inferiority made it unattractive to private industry. Paul Pleiger, an industrialist from Westphalia and a friend of Göring's, headed this group of enterprises. During the war years he succeeded

3. Petzina, *Autarkiepolitik.*

in establishing new plants and in annexing existing ones in Austria and in occupied countries. In the course of time the Hermann Göring Werke became a giant industrial complex involved in the production of machinery, mining of various kinds, and even shipping, its functions extending far beyond its assignments within the framework of the Four-Year Plan.[4]

From the beginning of 1937 Göring, in his capacity as head of this plan, played a major role in hastening the ousting of Jews from the few economic activities in which they were still engaged. Following the pogrom of November 1938, he directed all expropriation and seizure of Jewish property. It was Göring who ordered compulsory Aryanization and payment of the "indemnity" of one billion reichsmarks imposed on German Jewry. This indemnity was collected as a personal levy of 20 to 25 percent payable by every Jew whose registered property exceeded 5,000 reichsmarks. After the invasion of Poland, it was only a natural sequel for the Four-Year Plan administration to authorize establishment of the Haupttreuhandstelle-Ost (Head Trusteeship East), empowered to manage all Jewish and Polish industrial enterprises in occupied territories.[5]

Strategy and Rearmament, 1936–1940

Postwar research has tended to depreciate the success in planning and performance of Germany's armament industries. The basis for these evaluations was a survey conducted by the U.S. Strategic Air Command in the fall of 1945. Two economists who took part in this survey (parts of which remain restricted even today) used it in works they published on this subject. Thus, for instance, N. Kaldor claims that "although everything was 'controlled' (on paper) right from the beginning of the war, the actual administration of controls was often clumsy and amateurish in the extreme."[6] Burton Klein, in the study mentioned above, went even further, claiming that the planning itself was not geared to a lengthy war. According to Klein, although the production of consumer goods had reached pre-depression level, that is, the level of 1928, in 1937, it continued to expand right up to the outbreak of war. His conclusion was that "in

4. Broszat, *Der Staat Hitlers*, pp. 374f.
5. Ibid., p. 376.
6. N. Kaldor, "The German War Economy," *The Review of Economic Studies* 13 (1945–46).

the prewar period the German economy produced both 'butter and guns' – much more of the former and much less of the latter than has been commonly assumed."[7]

Klein explained this surprising phenomenon by a distinction between "rearmament in depth" and "rearmament in width." The former bases arms production on a firm industrial infrastructure and stable raw material supply, which insure continuous production for war purposes and the renewal of reserves over lengthy periods. In contrast, rearmament in width calls for the production of a wide range of war equipment in large quantities in order to achieve an immediate advantage at the initial stage of war. In Klein's opinion the Nazis considered the creation of a large-scale infrastructure for long-term armament production unnecessary because their military and strategic planning was aimed at one short blitzkrieg or a consecutive series of such "lightning wars." They planned to insure quick victories by conducting rapidly moving campaigns based on the grouping of quantitatively and qualitatively superior forces and armament supplies, thus overpowering the enemy within a short span of time. They did not exclude the possibility that decisive victory would not be achieved in a single, rapid campaign and the war would therefore have to move to additional fronts. However, their planning for such an eventuality relied on the exploitation of the raw-material resources and industrial capacity of occupied territories. These territories were also to supply food for Germany's population in order to avoid the hardship of shortages of the type still recalled from World War I. As it turned out, such expectations were not exaggerated.

We have already shown that Klein's calculations were too low with regard to the proportion of rearmament costs to the GNP and total government expenditure until the war. We have now to examine the performance of the German economy at the stage of accelerated war preparations (1936–39) and subsequently during the war itself. First, Klein and Kaldor underrated Nazi successes at these stages. Multiple competing authorities as well as individual or group rivalries were indeed characteristic of the Nazi regime; at all levels of the administration decision making did not always adhere to obligatory and permanent managerial norms. The surprising fact is that the system nevertheless worked efficiently and achieved its objectives in this as well as in other spheres. The confusion of

7. Klein, *Germany's Preparations for War*, p. 76.

authority and the existence of parallel or competing agencies represented conflicting economic and social interests which the totalitarian regime did not permit to contend with each other in any other arena. This infighting generated friction, which damaged efficiency and no doubt also caused economic losses. It is possible, on the other hand, that this method of ad hoc decision making also provided a greater measure of flexibility and adaptability to rapidly changing conditions in the course of the war.

Surplus demand for skilled labor, in particular in branches working for rearmament, emerged on the labor market even before full employment was achieved. The existing law permitted labor trustees to authorize wage rises in enterprises that could demonstrate enhanced productivity. Plants working for rearmament, especially in metal-processing industries, had already utilized this permit in 1934 to attract skilled workers from other enterprises. In this manner they even succeeded in recruiting workers from other districts, in particular from those to the west of the Rhine, where arms production was prohibited until the German army occupied those areas in March 1936. At the same time the construction and building industries, which played a leading role during the initial stage of unemployment relief, recruited thousands of agricultural workers in spite of the authorities' efforts to restrict migration from villages. In response to these pressures, an obligatory, personal *Arbeitsbuch* (work book) was introduced in which every change of workplace had to be confirmed by the local labor exchange. Nevertheless, freedom of movement between workplaces was not yet restricted, even after the proclamation of compulsory military service in March 1935. The nearer the economy drew to full employment, the more the signs of labor shortages increased; these were exacerbated by the Nazi policy of returning women to their "natural role," that is, housekeeping.

Beginning in 1936 this state of affairs generated upward pressures on wages, thus also imperiling price policies. Nevertheless, an absolute prohibition against wage increases was postponed until 1938, probably in order not to deter highly skilled workers from moving to rearmament industries. Even after this date competition among enterprises over such workers continued, though by different means: enterprises granted various fringe benefits, officially or somehow disguised – improved working conditions, aid in housekeeping, permanent use of light vehicles (usually motorcycles) owned by the firm, higher wages for overtime, and so forth. These benefits yielded considerable added income in spite of the total wage freeze officially in effect.

The fever of war preparations reached its first peak in the summer of 1938, when about four hundred thousand workers were enlisted to build fortification works on the western frontier, the famous Western Wall. The method of recruitment, legalized by special decree, called for the issuing of individual summonses for a restricted period of time. From March 1939 the law forbade a worker to leave his workplace without permission from the labor exchange; thus militarization of the labor force within the framework of the Four-Year Plan was completed.

A shortage of imported raw materials had already appeared during the first years of Nazi rule. In 1928 Germany imported 95 percent of the raw materials for its textile industry and 60 percent of all mineral ores for heavy industry. Supervision Bureaus for the allocation of scarce raw materials had already been established in 1934. The Four-Year Plan accorded top priority to the production of raw materials and/or substitutes and united the Supervision Bureaus under a central authority. The use of certain raw materials like nickel, copper, and other noniron metals was altogether prohibited in industries producing consumer goods. In addition, a massive scrap-metal collection was launched with the aid of party agencies, including women's associations, youth associations, and schools. (The refuse dumps of 150 towns yielded 55,000 tons of discarded tin cans between September 1937 and July 1938.)[8]

The efforts invested in the Four-Year Plan were of course not limited to rationing existing raw materials. They were aimed also at increasing the output of key industrial branches through the establishment of new enterprises and investment in the expansion of existing ones. The data in the table on p. 231 show that these efforts yielded results in a number of spheres.[9]

Labor shortages became increasingly apparent in agriculture, where between 1933 and 1939 the number of employed fell from 9.3 to 9.0 million, or from 28.9 percent to 25.9 percent of the total

8. F. Blaich, "Wirtschaft und Rüstung in Deutschland, 1933–1939," in K.D. Bracher, M. Funke, and H.A. Jacobsen, eds., *Nationalsozialistische Diktatur, 1933–1945: Eine Bilanz* (Bonn, 1983), pp. 292ff.; Fischer, *Deutsche Wirtschaftspolitik*, pp. 83ff.; H. Aubin and W. Zorn, *Handbuch der deutschen Wirtschafts- und Sozialgeschichte*, vol. 2 (Stuttgart, 1976), relevant chapters.
9. R. Wagenführ, *Die deutsche Industrie im Kriege, 1939–1945* (Berlin, 1963), p. 18.

Production of Strategic Raw Materials (In Thousands of Tons)

	1936	1939	Growth in percent
Iron ores	2,259	3,928	73.9
Aluminum	95	194	104.2
Buna (synthetic rubber)	1	22	
Synthetic fibers	43	192	346.5
Aircraft gasoline	43	302	602.3
Regular gasoline	1,214	1,633	34.5

number of employed.[10] It appears that, its ideological commitment notwithstanding, the regime had resigned itself to the flight of workers from agriculture to the armament industries and tried to offset the losses in the labor force in various ways. Once the administration for the Four-Year Plan was established, the *Staatssekretär* at the Ministry of Agriculture also became an affiliated general plenipotentiary in order to "insure the sustenance of the German people." In March 1937 a special law authorized the RNS to determine what crops were to be grown in order to increase the output of scarce produce, in particular vegetable fats. In July of the same year peasants were ordered to hand over all wheat and rye harvests to official purchase agencies, while the feeding of these grains to livestock was strictly forbidden. From August 1938 grains were stockpiled in specially requisitioned gymnasiums and dance halls; up to 35 percent of the construction costs for the building of granaries was subsidized.

To counter labor shortages students were recruited at harvesttime and girls were committed to a year of duty in agriculture after graduating from school. The Labor Service, from 1935 on a compulsory year of premilitary training, was also partially utilized at harvesttime. Peasants received considerable aid for mechanization and the purchase of chemicals like fertilizers and pesticides. Jointly, these efforts yielded an increase in the output of some vital crops and the almost complete independence from bread-grain imports as early as 1938.[11] However, the shortage in animal and vegetable fats remained acute; it generated a propaganda campaign against the consumption of butter even before the war and was responsible for

10. D. Petzina, W. Abelshauser, and A. Faust, *Sozialgeschichtliches Arbeitsbuch, III: Materialien zur Statistik des Deutschen Reiches, 1914–1945* (Munich, 1978), pp. 55ff.

11. Petzina, *Autarkiepolitik*, p. 95.

the familiar cliché of "guns instead of butter." The output of beef
and pork, on the other hand, grew between 1936 and 1939 by 25
percent and 10 percent respectively, reflecting the rise in living
standards resulting from increased employment and income.[12]

The shortage of raw materials was quite prominent in the textile
industries. To meet rising consumer demand, synthetic fibers of
poor quality were added to fabrics, thus diminishing the product's
quality and shortening its life span. Consumer complaints were met
with decrees and restrictions for the producer: quality specifications
like "pure wool" were prohibited, as were cleaning instructions that
were liable to reveal the poor quality of the product.

It is interesting that in spite of these restrictions, caused mainly
by the state of foreign trade, the output of consumer goods grew
throughout these years and declined only slightly even after the
outbreak of war. The per capita production index for consumer
goods returned in 1936 to the level of 1928 and rose by 8 percent
until 1939; by the beginning of 1942 it had returned to the 1936 level
and only in 1944, when what was left of the German economy made
its final rearmament efforts, did the index drop by 18 percent. The
production of capital goods grew at a much faster pace over the
same period: their per capita production index, which in 1936
already stood at 110 compared to 1928, rose in 1939 to 121 and to
150 in the middle of 1944.[13] There is therefore no doubt that
industrial production directly or indirectly connected to rearmament enjoyed preference even before the war, but only to a small
extent at the expense of current civil consumption, although the
growth of the latter was slowed down.

Even without going into details with regard to specific products,
it is clear that the situation described above arose from deliberate
government policy. The Nazis did not scorn public opinion and
followed with concern every sign of public dissatisfaction, even
when their success in foreign and economic policy resulted in
widespread and sometimes enthusiastic support among the majority
of the German people. This attitude left its mark on the sphere of
consumer goods: the production of certain goods, at the time
classified all over the world as luxury items, was explicitly encouraged. Thus, for example, a considerable effort was invested in the
production and sale of a cheap, uniform model of radio receiver.
Awareness of its propaganda value caused production to continue

12. M. Rolfes in Aubin and Zorn, *Handbuch*, p. 771.
13. W. Fischer in Aubin and Zorn, *Handbuch*, p. 807.

even during the war. A popular refrigerator was also produced and sold in considerable quantities as part of a propaganda drive against the waste of perishable food products.

Another campaign, accompanied by a clamorous propaganda drive, pursued an entirely different aim. In May 1938, with a great deal of publicity, Hitler laid the cornerstone for the plant that was to produce the popular Volkswagen. Even before the ceremony numerous Germans had begun to pay savings-installments toward future purchase of such a car. It is reasonable to assume that at the time, with accelerating war preparations, no one seriously intended to begin production of such cars in the foreseeable future. Instead, it was a measure directed toward the withdrawal of disposable income from the public, whose earnings had grown throughout the period of prosperity, wage restrictions notwithstanding. Hitler himself mentioned the issue in his foundation ceremony speech: "If the German people spend all their wages on consumer goods, we cannot . . . produce without limits, it will cause disaster. It is therefore vital to guide the purchasing power of the German people in other directions."[14] In this case the direction was toward recruiting savings for armaments, with an additional incentive to work overtime in order to realize the dream of owning a car. By the end of March 170,000 savers had deposited the sum of 110 million reichsmarks in the Volkswagen account for the popular model. However, when the plant began operating, it produced military vehicles and aircraft parts exclusively.[15] Ferdinand Porsche's clever invention, the horizontal "boxer engine," achieved recognition and was mass-produced only some years after the war had ended.

Can we conclude from all this that Nazi Germany did indeed not prepare for war and that the nation produced more butter than guns? We know today that such an evaluation is mistaken. Actually, from 1936 or 1937 on Germany pursued a regimen of covert austerity with regard to numerous consumer goods, with the explicit purpose of directing its scarce production resources to rearmament. There seems to be some justification for Blaich's view that during these years Germany produced not "guns as well as butter," but "guns and jam" instead of butter and bunkers and fortifications instead of residences. Blaich is also right to claim that confusion and

14. M. Domarus, *Hitler-Reden und Proklamationen* (Würzburg, 1962–63), pp. 867f.
15. P. Kluke, "Hitler und das Volkswagenprojekt," *Vierteljahreshefte für Zeitgeschichte* 8 (1960): 341f.

rivalries within the Four-Year Plan administration "should by no means obscure the fact that by September 1, 1939, the foundations for centralized planning and the direction of the economy, based on private business initiative and private capital, had already been laid."[16] Autarky was only partial; given the prevailing conditions it is doubtful whether it could have been expanded. Yet achievements on the road to self-sufficiency were still impressive, and the hope of compensating for shortages quickly by rapid conquests in Europe and the exertion of pressure on neutral countries like Sweden were not groundless, as it turned out.

At the outbreak of war, rationing was at once expanded to additional products, though this was explicitly proclaimed to be a temporary measure and the rations fixed were only slightly smaller than the average consumption.[17] Jews still living in Germany generally received much smaller rations or, for certain products, none at all. They were forbidden to buy clothing or footwear and received no rations for meat, fish, white bread, fruit, sweets, and cigarettes.[18] In the initial stages of war, the general population's consumption was much less restricted than it had been during World War I; later on the Germans even enjoyed abundance when the spoils of war were removed from the occupied territories.

Economic activity during the war was clearly divided into two periods. The first, until the end of 1941, was still dominated by blitzkrieg strategy, that is, industrial production directed toward the short-term goals described above. On the face of it, military successes in Poland, France, the Netherlands, and Scandinavia justified Hitler's reasoning that an in-depth infrastructure for long-term war production was not necessary: the mass production of the armaments necessary for the next stage of the blitzkrieg was sufficient to achieve a decisive power advantage and quick victory.[19] The Germans immediately seized all stocks of raw materials, such as mineral ores, in occupied countries and transferred large quantities of them to Germany even before they harnessed local production capacity to their own requirements. Substantial quantities of some materials gained in this manner were instrumental in relieving severe shortages in Germany's war industry. In Poland and France alone, 355,000 tons of noniron metals plus 272,000 tons of iron ore, along

16. Blaich, "Wirtschaft und Rüstung," p. 315.
17. H. Kellenbenz, *Deutsche Wirtschaftsgeschichte*, vol. 2 (Munich, 1981), p. 458.
18. W. Scheffler, *Judenvervolgung im Dritten Reich* (Berlin, 1964), p. 42.
19. Milward, *The German Economy at War*, pp. 30ff.

with substantial quantities of aircraft and other kinds of fuel as well as various chemical products vital in armament industries, fell into the hands of the Germans.[20] These, combined with the regular supply of high-quality iron ore from Sweden, enabled Germany to increase steel production by 26 percent between the end of 1939 and the end of 1940, almost without detracting from civil production; 40.8 percent of its industrial output was still directed to civil consumption, as compared to 41.5 percent in the last quarter of 1939.

These data imply not merely stagnation but even a certain drop in the production of armaments in the summer of 1940 following the surrender of France. Loyal to their blitzkrieg strategy, German planners made substantial changes in their production plans in accordance with the specific requirements of the next campaign. In the summer of 1940, while the invasion of the British Isles was still on the agenda, production was directed to aircraft and shipping. At the end of that year and during the beginning of 1941, when the Barbarossa decision – to invade the USSR – had been made, production was shifted to tanks, guns, ammunition, and infantry equipment. It turned out that it was precisely the absence of rigid preliminary planning that provided the military and industrial system with a considerable measure of flexibility – as long as war objectives and the manner in which the war was conducted were almost exclusively determined by Germany.[21]

1941–1945: Toward Total War

The blitzkrieg strategy had already come to an end in the fall of 1941, with the failure of the German army to capture Moscow before winter closed in. Nevertheless, a few more months were needed to make Hitler and his generals realize that they were in for a lengthy war. In December 1941, when the United States entered the war, the Germans faced superior military, human, and economic resources, while the halt of their military advance at the gates of Moscow had put an end to their hopes of a quick victory. The signal for the change in direction was given by the Führerbefehl Rüstung, Hitler's order of January 10, 1942, on armaments production.[22] His instructions granted equal priority to the construction of armored

20. Ibid.; Kellenbenz, *Deutsche Wirtschaftsgeschichte*, p. 460.
21. Milward, *The German Economy at War*, pp. 38ff.
22. "Führerbefehl Rüstung," see A.S. Milward, *War Economy and Society, 1939–1945* (Berkeley and Los Angeles, 1977), pp. 56f.

vehicles for the eastern front and of submarines for the Atlantic. Intensifying the maritime blockade of Britain was perceived as the only means of defeating that nation before the United States could mobilize all of its resources for the war effort and send substantial forces to Europe. From this point on Hitler too realized that in order to cope with all these tasks, the long-term capacity of the rearmament industries had to be expanded considerably through heavy investment in additional development projects.

This assignment was given to Fritz Todt, minister for armament and munitions production, a capable engineer and veteran Nazi who before the war had been in charge of construction of the autobahn network and the Western Wall. Choosing from the Western Wall administration's personnel pool, he formed the Organisation Todt, a kind of independent engineering force run like any military unit. Todt was initially attached to the Four-Year Plan administration under Göring, but was appointed minister for armament and munitions production heading an independent government department, in March 1940. In this capacity he laid the foundations for the reorganization of the entire armaments production system. The impressive achievements of this system are often and somewhat misleadingly attributed to the man who succeeded Todt following his death in an aircraft accident in February 1942. Albert Speer, Hitler's architect, in fact continued Todt's work according to the organizational guidelines his predecessor had drawn up. He was nevertheless a talented administrator in his own right, and his ties with Hitler, who fully backed him, enabled Speer to circumvent bureaucratic pitfalls in order to achieve his objectives.

The organizational principles laid down by Todt and implemented with a great deal of technocratic efficiency by Speer were based on mobilization and coordination of the initiative, the know-how, and the profit motive of private industrial enterprises. Actually this was merely a continuation of the Nazi method of guiding the economy without too much rigid central planning. Yet because circumstances had changed, it was necessary to impose more restrictions on private entrepreneurship as well as to pinpoint from the top precise objectives as they extended over longer periods of time. From this time on central planning was conducted through branch committees with wide-ranging authority which determined production quotas and allocated raw materials as well as the use of the labor force. Initially such committees had been established only for ammunition supply, to coordinate production with the planned

stages of warfare. From the end of 1941 Todt added such coordinating committees for all kinds of armaments. Thus Ferdinand
Porsche was appointed chief of the committee for the production of
tanks. These committees issued technically specific orders to each
enterprise, supervised production of the items ordered, and ratified
the transfer of skilled labor between enterprises whenever necessary, as well as vital investments in mechanical equipment and
buildings. In the course of time a supreme committee was added at
the top to coordinate the activities of the branch committees.
Gradually the minister for armament and munitions production
gathered far-reaching authority over all economic sectors into his
own hands, circumventing other government departments, including the Ministry of Economics and the Four-Year Plan administration.

Within the framework of comprehensive planning, enterprises
still had fairly wide discretion. Until the end of 1941 enterprises
operated on a cost-plus basis, that is, they presented cost calculations and were permitted to add 3 to 6 percent profit. This method
of course neutralized any incentive to save materials and labor in
order to reduce costs, since profits rose in accordance with expenses. Todt replaced this by a method of fixed prices determined
by his department in consultation with branch coordinating committees. The management of each enterprise was responsible for
improving efficiency in production and internal administration,
which from then on was the only way to increase their profits. His
successor, Speer, encouraged more centralized production in large
enterprises instead of its distribution among a great number of
smaller ones scattered all over the country and in the occupied
regions. Although he achieved higher efficiency by utilizing the
advantage of size, he also made production centers more vulnerable
to attacks from the air once the Allies began their massive bombing
campaign.[23]

The planning of armaments production depended to a great
extent on the availability of skilled labor, in particular from 1942,
when more than thirteen million Germans were mobilized to serve
in the armed forces. In order to direct the flow of required labor, in
particular forced labor from the occupied territories, Hitler appointed the Gauleiter of Thuringia, Fritz Sauckel, general plenipotentiary for labor allocation. Hitler's proposition was quite

23. Speer, *Inside the Third Reich*, pp. 292ff.; Milward, *The German Economy at War*, pp. 54ff.

simple: since Germany ruled over a population of 250 million people in Europe, the very notion of labor shortages was a contradiction in terms! Loyal to his master, Sauckel tried to exploit this pool ruthlessly and through all possible means, fully coordinating his activities with Speer and his committees. For this he was condemned to death at the Nuremberg trials. The separation of labor force supervision from the authority of the minister for armament and munitions production may have caused functional difficulties at the time,[24] but it enabled, or at least aided, Albert Speer to come out of his trial with no more than a period of imprisonment.

The changes made in planning and direction at the beginning of 1942 to organize the economy for a drawn-out war effort yielded immediate results. The output of the armaments industries had already risen by 55 percent between February and July 1942, but only partly at the expense of civil production – proof that previously unexploited reserves still existed. Up to mid-1944 ammunition production had increased by 3.5 and tank production by 6 times their levels compared to 1941. Production of other armaments increased 3.6 times over the same period. The Germans went on with accelerated production of a few types of weapons until the beginning of 1945,[25] in spite of their losses in territory and raw-material sources as well as Allied bombing. Had the German economy been fully mobilized before 1942, such an increase in output would have been impossible. In fact, armaments and ammunition production came only to 16 percent of overall industrial output in 1941; in 1944 it came to 40 percent. Over the same period construction work dropped from 13 to 6 percent, consumer goods from 28 to 22 percent, and the rest of the industrial branches from 18 to 11 percent. However, merely comparing the production of various branches could lead to incorrect conclusions because of the increase in total production, resulting primarily from plundering the occupied countries. A separate examination of each branch reveals that the construction industry alone shrank substantially over this period, declining in 1944 to 25 percent of its prewar output. The output of consumer goods dropped only by 15 percent and even rose temporarily in 1943 to 90 percent of its prewar level.[26]

We see that Nazi rulers were sensitive to the damage shortages

24. Speer, *Inside the Third Reich*, pp. 305ff.
25. Milward, *War Economy*, pp. 80f.; Kellenbenz, *Deutsche Wirtschaftsgeschichte*, p. 461.
26. Fischer in Aubin and Zorn, *Handbuch*, pp. 824f.

might have caused to civil population morale, even at the peak of
their war effort. This is the sole explanation for the fact that the
workday in industry was hardly lengthened and that the majority of
factories, vital armaments producers included, operated on a single
shift up to the end of the war, while in England, for instance,
factories had already operated on two or three shifts from the
beginning of the war. The number of women employed in industry
remained almost the same – 2.5 million – throughout the war. The
Germans made no effort to recruit more female labor, even supporting the families of soldiers at a level that permitted them to
preserve a relatively high standard of living while the wife remained
at home.[27]

The European War Economy

All this was made possible, of course, by unbridled exploitation of
the occupied countries. The men who went into the army were
replaced by prisoners of war and workers brought from those
countries, a small contingent of whom came voluntarily because
there were no opportunities for work at home, though the majority
were coerced. The number of these workers, as well as of prisoners
brought from concentration camps, increased steadily thanks to the
efforts of Plenipotentiary Sauckel and his administration. According
to official data, over seven million such workers were employed
within Germany itself in May 1944, more than 20 percent of the
total German labor force at the time.[28] These figures do not include
prisoners from concentration camps outside Germany who were
employed by various enterprises in the occupied countries. Nor do
these calculations account for Jews working for German enterprises
especially established in the ghettos to produce for the German
market and the army, enterprises that became a source of rapidly
accumulated wealth for their owners.

The independent economic empire the SS had established, primarily in the occupied regions but also in Germany itself, was also
not included in statistics on the recruitment of labor for the war
effort. Subject to the SS-Wirtschafts- und Verwaltungshauptamt
(Economic and Administrative Head Office of the SS), this empire

27. K. Borchardt in Aubin and Zorn, *Handbuch*, p. 716; Kellenbenz, *Deutsche Wirtschaftsgeschichte* p. 464.
28. Milward, *War Economy*, pp. 222ff.; idem, *The German Economy at War*, pp. 113ff.

operated about 150 firms in all spheres of production – from the mining of minerals and building materials, through production of special armament systems for Waffen SS units, to the extraction of mineral water! With the exception of a small number of engineers, these enterprises were manned by forced labor and inmates of concentration camps. Their exact numbers are not known, but there can be no doubt that they added up to hundreds of thousands. The largest among these companies, Deutsche Erd- und Steinwerke GmbH, began with earthworks and construction early in the war, but over the course of time switched to the production of armaments and ammunition. During the final years of the war the firm produced aircraft for the Messerschmidt Company in subterranean shelters inside concentration camps.[29]

The plundering of resources in the occupied countries was, of course, not limited to the exploitation of their labor forces. Initially, during the blitzkrieg phase, the Germans regarded these countries primarily as a convenient and easy source of looted raw materials and goods required by the immediate war effort. This was so as long as they believed that the war would be short. They changed their attitude in the winter of 1941–42, following the shift in strategic outlook. From then on they began to harness the capacities of the occupied countries to the war effort within the framework of their self-styled "European war economy." The basic Nazi concept of a *Großraumwirtschaft* was already being realized in wartime, though initially it had been planned as the crowning touch after final military victory. However, even under these conditions, the policy of exploitation in the occupied countries was not dictated by purely economic considerations and was by no means consistent. Ideological notions arising from racial theory as well as from plans for the future tied to this theory often cancelled strategic or economic considerations. The extermination of millions of Jews and Russian prisoners of war, as well as the allocation of human resources for the execution of these tasks even during crucial stages of the war, are merely the most extreme examples of this attitude.

Nevertheless, there can be no doubt that Germany's ability to hold out for such a long time, while her own population was required to expend only relatively limited efforts with regard to austerity in consumption and additional work, was due to the exploitation of the occupied countries. France, the richest and most

29. Milward, *The German Economy at War*, pp. 156ff.

advanced among these, was apparently also the most profitable from this point of view. Germany collected "occupation expenses" to the tune of 20 million reichsmarks a day, a calculation based on an inflated exchange rate of the mark against the franc. The principle of collecting occupation expenditure from the occupied country was implemented everywhere. Germany's war expenses were assessed at 685 to 850 billion reichsmarks, of which only 25 percent was covered by taxes paid by the Germans themselves throughout those years. The financial contributions of the occupied countries covered a substantial part of the remainder.[30]

To these direct payments, levied regularly and continuously in defeated countries, one must add their "exports" to Germany, at prices dictated by the conqueror. Even the reduced price of this mandatory foreign trade, conducted at enforced exchange rates, was not paid in full; a large part was credited to exporting countries in a clearing account at Berlin, through which occupied countries were compelled to settle trade transactions among themselves as well. These countries accumulated considerable amounts in their Berlin accounts during the war, which in reality served as an additional contribution to the German economy. For instance, only 57 percent of Germany's coal output, which reached its peak in 1943–44, came from German prewar territory. The figures for fuel and noniron metals were still lower. Thus in 1943–44, the French contribution alone amounted to almost a third of the French GNP in 1938. Yet since the French GNP had been greatly reduced by war losses and compulsory transfer of part of its labor force to Germany, this contribution was actually much higher in proportion to the French GNP of 1943–44. These estimates for France and the other occupied countries do not include either consumption by occupation forces or direct plunder, like looted Jewish property or Belgian gold, which continued to flow into Germany. Nor is the contribution of prisoners of war and forced labor inside Germany included.[31]

Ultimately it is impossible to assess the scope of industrial and agricultural output, the raw materials, and the labor of occupied countries that were utilized for the German war effort, all of which simultaneously enabled the German population to preserve a living standard only slightly lower than that of the years 1936–39. "Here the ideology of the master race found very concrete expression –

30. Borchardt in Aubin and Zorn, *Handbuch*, p. 716; Kellenbenz, *Deutsche Wirtschaftsgeschichte*, p. 462.
31. Fischer in Aubin and Zorn, *Handbuch*, p. 826.

their own energy was spared because the strength of others was at their disposal. Thus the war of expansion bore fruit even after the Germans were forced to abandon parts of the occupied territories."[32] It remains a matter of conjecture how much of this fruit was left in German hands after their military defeat, rescued and preserved to contribute to the country's speedy recovery through the second German economic miracle.

32. Ibid., p. 830.

Conclusion

Notwithstanding the abundance of scholarly studies devoted to the analysis of Nazism, differences of opinion about its basic character still exist. Was it part of a universal or pan-European phenomenon, one of the forms that totalitarianism or fascism assumed, or was it specifically German? Was Nazi rule that of a gang of criminals, lusting for power and devoid of conscience, who overran Germany through political intrigue and undisguised terror, or the state-monopoly stage of capitalism, defending the system in the face of the threat of Socialist revolution from the East? There are still no generally accepted answers to these questions, and it is also doubtful that research could arrive at such universal solutions. It appears, however, that any serious modern attempt to expose the roots of this phenomenon must make the effort to understand Nazi ideology and its implications for all spheres of society and regime in the Third Reich.

Nazi ideology was not a unified and consistent conceptual system that rates comparison with coherent schools of thought like liberalism or Marxism; it was a mixture of archaic resentments and irrational longings that germinated in the soil of a late industrial revolution and a social revolution that perished in infancy. It was generated by the frustration and misery of a nation defeated in war at the very moment it had imagined itself near the peak of national power and glory. This ideology was not conceived by spiritual giants, and it contributed nothing to lift the spirit or fire the imagination beyond its time and place. In spite of all this, millions of Germans regarded it as a genuine reflection of their innermost social and national aspirations and adopted it faithfully and fanatically.

The Nazi party was unquestionably an ideological movement, even though its ideas were a jumble collected from here, there, and everywhere without any worthwhile original contributions. Hitler's genius lay in his unfailing instinct for the heartfelt yearnings of

243

millions among his people, as well as in his talent for assembling fragments of traditional and *völkisch* ideas into a sufficiently comprehensive system in which almost every German could identify with some element of the whole. The lack of originality and vague definition of ideological norms in this ideological system were an advantage rather than a failing. One should not belittle its importance by labeling it "mere propaganda." The distinction between ideology and propaganda belongs to the sphere of psychology and the propagandist's motivations. There is no doubt that Hitler and the Nazis were totally unrestrained demagogues, even if they believed in their own propaganda. The success of any propaganda depends on its ability to touch the hidden dreams and aspirations of the masses to whom it is addressed. Nazi propaganda certainly knew how to arouse these sentiments better than any other ideology that existed in Germany at the time.

It is true that Nazism was part of the general political/ideological development in Europe between the two world wars and cannot be understood outside that context. Feelings of disappointment with parliamentary democracy and, even more important, a fear of Bolshevism were not uniquely German. Nevertheless, Nazism cannot be fully explained by generalizing epithets like totalitarianism and fascism, which blur its specific characteristics. Nazi ideology appealed to the masses of German people who had grown up in a social and spiritual atmosphere created by a specific historical past. The images and norms they carried in their minds had been molded by generations of thinkers and teachers. At first this ideology appealed primarily to the middle classes: yearning to distance themselves from the proletarian masses, they adopted national and social values that were the hallmark of the traditional German elite whom they wished to emulate. As the *simplificateurs terribles* that they were, the Nazis selected a few of this traditional and exclusive elite's ideological norms and effectively turned them into the propagandist platform of a mass movement. The Nazis very lack of originality was therefore actually a source of strength, and during the stormy thirties – before and after 1933 – they successfully used their ideology to rally different classes and social strata behind their banner.

I believe that the same principle applies to Nazi concepts in economics. It is not true that the economy was neglected within their ideological system. The Nazis were sufficiently aware of its social and political significance to grant it a well-defined place in this system which, eclectic as it was, presumed to constitute a comprehensive weltanschauung. I have shown that these concepts were rooted in the traditional strain of antiliberalist nationalist etatism that had dominated German social and economic thought for a long period of time and have demonstrated how this tradition was adapted to suit the Nazi party's ideological and political requirements.

[handwritten margin note: *Nazi econ concepts*]

The soil on which this school of thought fed was the specific economic evolution that took place in Germany, a latecomer to the Industrial Revolution, during the second half of the nineteenth century. German industry was established and grew powerful through the active aid and encouragement of the government, which did not limit its share to infrastructure. It became directly involved in numerous economic branches, thus creating a public sector whose relative importance was unparalleled in any other country at the time. The class behind these developments was an aggressive industrial bourgeoisie, intermingled with traditional agrarian interests and "investment-happy" banking. The alliance of rye and steel, that is, of Prussian Junkers and industrial magnates from the Rhine and Ruhr regions, left its stamp on the economic as well as the political development of the German Reich founded by Bismarck. Not only did that alliance produce a system of protective tariffs for grain plus accelerated industrialization, but to a large extent it also determined interior as well as foreign policy and the shape of German society and government before 1914. Views of nationalist etatism were not limited to economists at universities – they were also adopted by businessmen and politicians. Thus the status and influence of a large governmental bureaucracy – a bureaucracy whose members came in most cases from the same combined social class that fostered the tradition of the German *Obrigkeitsstaat* – was greatly enhanced. In Bismarck's own time this etatism emerged in the "stick and carrot" policies of the law against Socialists on the one hand and in a highly progressive social security system on the other. Later on the same etatism largely determined the objectives of foreign policy and the aggressive colonial drive that characterized young German imperialism before World War I.

[handwritten margin note: *inst'l and historical context*]

Economic difficulties between the wars and the worldwide Great Depression generated the revival of these economic principles, yet at the same time they were adapted to contemporary realities. Although not cut off from relevant developments in other countries, this was an independent theoretical trend that demonstrated awareness and acknowledgment of its ties to the particular German tradition. On the whole this trend was nurtured outside the Nazi party or parallel to it. But its basic assumptions, as well as the importance accorded to its roots in German tradition, made it eminently suitable for adoption by the party. And indeed, from about 1932 on, the Nazis realized how well this economic theory and its accompanying practical proposals suited their party's own ideological and economic principles. They now had at their disposal a complementary system that consisted of comprehensive economic and social concepts accompanied by operational proposals which could be translated into an economic platform for the liquidation of unemployment.

anti-
liberal
ism

No one can be certain what would have become of these concepts if conditions had differed from those prevailing during the Great Depression of 1929–33. Under conditions of full employment and peaceful growth within the international economy they would probably have faded into oblivion. However, as matters stood at the time, by adopting them the Nazis unfortunately became almost the only party in Germany that had the right answers and could therefore point to an effective way out of the depression. The ruling parties as well as the Social Democrats were held captive by conservative economic principles and shied away from new ideas already in the wind. Thus they may have facilitated the Nazi takeover, though they probably could not have prevented it even by employing a less conservative and more daring economic policy. It was not merely a question of choosing between different economic theories. Toward the end of the Weimar Republic political parties were embroiled in a struggle of conflicting social forces as well as economic and political interests that had brought the government to a standstill. Hitler's rise to power was certainly not inevitable, nor was it merely the result of a passing political blindness. The basis of the January 1933 conspiracy was an alliance between related forces, in the face of which the Socialist and democratic forces on the scene turned out to be the lesser opponent, not only with regard to economic theory.

The initial foundations for the economic policy implemented from the beginning of 1933 were laid earlier, and it is not true that the Nazis were totally unequipped in the sphere of economic policy when they seized power. The short-lived economic policies of both preceding right-wing governments had come from the same think tank that provided the Nazis with theoretical and operational equipment for their economic projects. Continuity was therefore natural – the Nazis simply had to proceed along the same road. Once their dictatorship was firmly established, they could suppress the opposition of vested economic interests with much greater ease than could previous governments. When their first measures, introduced cautiously and with some hesitation, began to yield results in the form of reduced unemployment, without the greatly feared by-product of inflationary pressures, confidence increased; the policy of economic expansion and deficit spending rapidly gained momentum. Success not only brought scientific esteem for their policy and an image of broad theoretical horizons, but also enhanced the Nazis' power and stature in the eyes of the general public, the business community, and university economists.

Economists, most of them from outside the Nazi camp, supplied the tools and plans for their economic policy and even participated actively in its execution. In the short term the objectives of this policy arose from the state of the economy and the urgent needs generated by the recession in agriculture and industry. However, long-term ideological and political objectives also played a considerable role from the very beginnings of Nazi rule. My attempt to trace these influences in various sectors of economic activity has shown that at times these objectives conflicted with each other, so that the regime was compelled to forego some and set up an order of priorities, which rapidly placed rearmament and war preparations at the head of the list. This does not imply that ideology concerning economic matters was altogether abandoned. In the first place, war itself was an objective of ideological significance. Among other targets, it was to achieve *Lebensraum* in order to lay the foundations for a future German *Volkswirtschaft* within the framework of the European "new order." Second, the economic and institutional tools designed to serve these aims also embodied specific social and political principles, namely, the direction of the economy and the subjection of particular interests to state authority as an ideological norm. Only if one turns a blind eye to these facts can one view the Nazis' economic policy as purely pragmatic improvisation, utterly untouched by ideological norms.

The mixture of short-term pragmatic maneuvering with fanatical adherence to ultimate goals characteristic of Hitler and his regime appears to have shaped economic as well as other policies. The difficulty in this sphere is that, unlike political issues, economic objectives were never finally and comprehensively defined either by Hitler himself or by an official and binding party document. We have seen that before and immediately after the seizure of power this deliberate "vagueness" was intended to gain the support of as many social groups and interests as possible. But even though this ideological platform was never explicitly formulated as mandatory, it nevertheless existed and carried great significance.

I have tried to outline the main features of this plan as it appears in programmatic statements and executive actions of the Nazi regime, a system that, besides general objectives, incorporated the principles and means for institutional organization as well as for executive practice. I believe that it is permissible to speak of a Nazi economic system as well as of the attempt to realize it, despite the fluctuations and inconsistencies the evidence reveals.

sum re Nazi econ objectives in their political context

The particular features of this system, apart from the general goals of *Lebensraum*, preference for agriculture, and maximum independence from the world economy, were the principles of guided production and distribution of income and consumption by the state without encroachment on private ownership or the profit incentive and without a central planning authority. This required a highly ramified control system which, in purely economic terms, was bound to cause many distortions and losses. However, the basic guiding principle of this method was not optimal allocation of production factors, aimed at maximal yields. Its proclaimed primary goal was maximum stability as distinguished from maximum production. Nevertheless, in spite of all the talk about "German socialism" and the fact that the term "capitalism" was a dirty word in party publications, there is no doubt that Germany's economy was capitalistic, though controlled and guided from above. The

"state organized capital- ism"

individual firm still operated according to the principle of maximum profit. The market still existed but was not a free market, and most decisions taken by the owners of enterprise were not "free" either. The term "organized capitalism" suits this economic method, subject only to the reservation that organization was imposed from above by extraeconomic, that is, political, factors; it was these factors that were responsible for directing the economy in accordance with basically noneconomic considerations. It was therefore a capitalist economy in which capitalists, like all other citizens, were not free even though they enjoyed a privileged status, had a limited measure of freedom in their activities, and were able to accumulate huge profits as long as they accepted the primacy of politics.

248

I have no answer to the question of how long such a system could have worked under peaceful conditions. It worked fairly well as long as there was unemployment and the economy had unexploited reserves. When full employment was achieved the clash between conflicting interests became more acute, necessitating tighter controls and more coercion. However, from then on economic activity was increasingly harnessed to the dominant political objective – war and military victory. The Nazis conducted the war at the expense of other peoples as long as possible. Their own people were permitted to share in some of the spoils and were promised riches and welfare after final victory and the establishment of the "new order."

It can be stated with certainty that a continuation of the economic system introduced by the Nazis would have been possible only under a permanent and increasingly severe dictatorship. If economic problems could have been solved at all by this system in the long run, the price would have been exacerbated coercion at home as well as harsher racist and imperialistic oppression outside Germany. The oppression of other peoples and a strong regime are the oxygen that also activates populist movements at present. They too accord top priority to national power and the stability of the regime. The material welfare of the individual, restricted to those who belong to the dominant people, is at best of secondary importance as long as it safeguards those primary objectives. A socioeconomic system of this kind leaves no room for the personal liberty and the safeguarding of individual rights granted under a democratic government. This is the reason why only those who believe that economic recessions and mass unemployment belong once and for all to the past will be able to relegate the lesson of Nazi economics to scholarly seminars on economic history.

You can be anti-liberal (anti-neoclassical) without also being a Nazi — or a Bolshevik. And you can solve a lot of economic problems by being anti-neoclassical.

Appendix
Statistical Tables

Table 1. Indicators of German Economic Development, 1932–1936

	1932	1936	Percentage of growth	Average annual rate of growth (%)
1. GNP at current prices (in billions of reichsmarks)	58	83	43	9.5
2. GNP at 1928 prices (in billions of reichsmarks)	71.9	101.2	41	9.0
3. Net national product at current prices (in billions of reichsmarks)	50.8	78.9	55	11.6
4. Per capita income at current prices (in reichsmarks)	633	922	46	9.8
5. Crafts and industry: production index (1913 = 100)	72.8	137.1	88	17.2
6. Average annual employment (in millions)	12.6	17.1	36	8.0
7. Average annual unemployment (in millions)	5.6	1.6		
8. Net investment at current prices (in billions of reichsmarks)	–2.1	9.0		
9. Private consumption at current prices (in billions of reichsmarks)	44.9	51.9	16	3.6
10. Public expenditures (Reich, Länder, municipalities) for goods				

Table 1. *continued*

	1932	1936	Percentage of growth	Average annual rate of growth (%)
and services at current prices (in billions of reichsmarks)	9.5	21.9	130	18.7
11. Wholesale price index for the last quarter of the year (1925–27 = 100)	67.8	75.8		
12. Cost of living index for the last quarter of the year (1925–27 = 100)	82.3	86.4		

Sources: 1: B.A. Carroll, *Design for Total War: Arms and Economics in the Third Reich* (The Hague, 1968), p. 184 (R. Erbe, *Die nationalsozialistische Wirtschaftspolitik, 1933–1939, im Lichte der modernen Theorie* [Zurich, 1958], p. 100 cites almost the same calculation); 2: B.H. Klein, *Germany's Preparations for War* (Cambridge, Mass., 1959), p. 10; 3: W.G. Hoffmann, *Das Wachstum der deutschen Wirtschaft seit der Mitte des 19. Jahrhunderts* (Berlin, 1965), p. 826; 4: W.G. Hoffman and H. Müller, *Das deutsche Volkseinkommen, 1871–1957* (Tübingen, 1959), p. 56; 5: Hoffmann, p. 393; 6 and 7: C.W. Guillebaud, *The Economic Recovery of Germany* (London, 1939), p. 277; 8 and 9: Hoffmann, pp. 260 and 701, respectively; 10: calculated according to Hoffmann, p. 721 and Erbe, p. 25; 11 and 12: H.S. Ellis, *Exchange Control in Central Europe* (Westport, Conn., 1972), p. 378.

Table 2. Public Expenditures for Goods and Services, 1932–1936, at Current Prices (In Millions of Reichsmarks)

	1932	1933	1934	1935	1936
1. Total public consumption	7,508	8,850	10,927	13,928	17,689
2. Military expenditures (budget and Mefo-bills, as part of item 1)	520	1,900	4,000	6,700	10,300
3. Public investments (Reich, Länder, municipalities), excluding armaments	1,970	2,430	3,460	3,890	4,220
Totals for goods and services (1 + 3)	9,478	11,280	14,387	17,818	21,909

Sources: 1 and 2: Hoffmann, pp. 720f.; 3: Erbe, p. 25.

Appendix

Table 3. Additional Public Expenditures and Their Financing, 1933–1936 (In Billions of Reichsmarks)

Total additional expenditures[1]		Additional income	
1. Armaments	20.8	4. Additional tax revenues	6.7
2. State investments for civilian purposes	6.1	5. "Donations" and export levies	2.2
3. Other expenditures	0.6	6. Loans from financial institutions and the general public	3.3
		7. "Savings" from unemployment insurance	4.0
		8. Reichsbank financing	11.3
Total additional expenditures	27.5	Total additional income	27.5

1. Calculated by subtracting the respective expenditure items for 1932 from the expenditures for each of the individual years from 1933 to 1936 and adding the totals.

Sources: 1–3: table 2; 4–7: Reichskreditgesellschaft A.G., quoted in H.E. Priester, *Das deutsche Wirtschaftswunder* (Amsterdam, 1936), pp. 217ff.; 8: calculated as the remainder. The result is confirmed by H. Stuebel's calculations in "Die Finanzierung der Aufrüstung im Dritten Reich," *Europa-Archiv* 6 (1951): 4129.

Table 4. Public Expenditures on Works Projects, 1933–1934 (In Millions of Reichsmarks)

Purpose of expenditure	Until the end of 1933	Cumulative until the end of 1934
1. Public construction (Waterways, roads, public buildings, bridges, etc.)	855.6	1,002.4
2. Housing construction	723.3	1,280.0
3. Transport network (Autobahns, as part of that network)	950.8 (50.0)	1,683.9 (350.0)
4. Agriculture and fishing (soil amelioration, agricultural settlements, etc.)	337.4	389.2

Table 4. *continued*

Purpose of expenditure	Until the end of 1933	Cumulative until the end of 1934
5. Promotion of consumption	70.0	70.0
6. Other expenses	164.0	568.0
Total	3,101.1	4,994.0
7. For comparison: armaments	1,900.0	5,900.0

Sources: 1–6: K. Schiller, *Arbeitsbeschaffung und Finanzordnung in Deutschland* (Berlin, 1936), pp. 158f.; 7: table 2.

Table 5. Income, Expenditures, and Net Gains in German Agriculture, 1928–1938, at Current Prices (In Billions of Reichsmarks)

Year	Total income	Total expenditures	Net gains
1928–29	10.2	8.6	1.6
1930–31	8.6	7.4	1.2
1932–33	6.4	5.9	0.5
1933–34	7.4	5.9	1.5
1934–35	8.3	6.0	2.3
1935–36	8.8	6.3	2.5
1936–37	8.9	6.4	2.5
1937–38	9.5	6.9	2.6

Source: J.E. Farquharson, "The NSDAP and Agriculture in Germany, 1928–1938" (dissertation, University of Kent, Canterbury, 1972), p. 540.

Table 6. Annual Rate of Growth of Agricultural Income in Comparison with Other Economic Sectors, 1933–1938 (Percentage Compared to the Previous Year)

Economic sector	1933–34	1934–35	1935–36	1936–37	1937–38
Agriculture	17.1	16.9	1.0	3.8	2.8
Other economic sectors combined	6.8	12.2	12.3	9.6	6.4

Source: Farquharson, p. 540.

Table 7. German Import of Foodstuffs, 1929–1939

	1929	1933	1934	1935	1936	1937	1938	1939
1. In billions of reichsmarks (1928 prices)	5.5	3.6	3.7	3.3	3.1	4.1	5.0	4.4
2. Percentage of total imports	40.0	38.8	34.7	—	35.5	37.5	38.8	—

Source: Farquharson, p. 542.

Table 8. German Self-production in Foodstuffs, 1927/28–1938/39 (In Percentages of Total Domestic Consumption)

Product	1927–28	1933–34	1938–39
All foodstuffs	68	80	83
Bread grain	79	99	115
Potatoes	84	90	91
Meat	91	98	97
Fats	44	53	57

Source: Farquharson, p. 541.

Table 9. German Foreign Trade, 1929–1936, at Current Prices (In Millions of Reichsmarks)

	1929	1932	1933	1934	1935	1936
1. Total goods imports	13,449	4,667	4,204	4,451	4,159	4,218
2. Total goods exports	13,483	5,739	4,871	4,167	4,270	4,768
3. Foodstuffs, percentage of total imports	40.0	45.7	38.8	34.7	34.5	35.5
4. Raw materials, percentage of total imports	29.2	27.3	32.5	34.6	37.7	37.3
5. Finished products, as a percentage of						

Table 9. *continued*

	1929	1932	1933	1934	1935	1936
total imports	13.1	11.9	12.0	12.9	9.8	9.4
6. Trade balance surplus (+) or deficit (−)	+36	+1,072	+667	−284	+111	+550
7. Balance of payments deficit	−165	−256	−447	−424	−30	—
8. Gold and currency reserves (as of December 31 of the year)	2,660	918	400	83	89	72

Sources: 1–6: Ellis, *Exchange Control*, pp. 380ff.; 7: W. Fischer, *Deutsche Wirtschaftspolitik, 1918–1945*, 3d ed. (Opladen, 1968), p. 103; 8: Ellis, pp. 373ff.

Table 10. Geographical Redistribution of German Foreign Trade, 1929–1938

	Percentage of total exports				Percentage of total imports			
	1929	1932	1935	1938	1929	1932	1935	1938
Southeastern Europe	4.3	3.5	5.9	10.3	3.8	5.0	7.7	9.8
Egypt, Turkey, the Near East	1.4	1.3	3.4	5.4	1.4	2.5	3.8	3.8
Latin America	7.3	4.1	9.1	11.7	11.7	9.6	13.1	14.9
Northern Europe	10.2	9.4	11.4	12.9	7.3	6.4	9.9	11.4
Total	23.2	18.3	29.8	40.3	23.9	23.5	34.5	39.9
Western Europe	26.2	31.9	26.1	20.8	15.7	15.1	14.1	11.9
Great Britain	9.7	7.8	8.8	6.7	6.4	5.5	6.2	5.2
United States	7.4	4.9	4.0	2.8	13.3	12.7	5.8	7.4
All others	33.5	37.1	31.3	29.4	40.7	43.2	39.4	35.6
Total	76.8	81.7	70.2	59.7	76.1	76.5	65.5	60.1

Source: Vierteljahreshefte zur Konjunkturforschung des Instituts für Konjunkturforschung, n.s. 14, no. 1 (1939–40): 75ff., as cited in Erbe, p. 76.

Table 11. Indexes of Real Wages, 1933–1936 (1932 = 100)

Year	Real wage scale wages		Real weekly wages	
	Gross	Net[1]	Gross	Net[2]
1933	99	95	98	94
1934	97	93	100	96
1935	99	91	103	99
1936	94	89	107	102

1. After taxes and compulsory deductions.
2. Ibid.

Source: J. Kuczynski, *Die Geschichte der Lage der Arbeiter in Deutschland von 1789 bis in die Gegenwart* (Berlin [East], 1953), vol. 2, pt. 1, pp. 132ff.

Table 12. Price Trends in Germany, 1931–1938, for the First Quarter of the Year (1925–27 = 100)

	1931	1932	1933	1934	1935	1936	1937	1938
1. Wholesale price index	83.0	72.4	66.1	69.8	73.2	75.2	76.6	76.7
2. Cost of living index	96.9	85.7	81.0	83.5	85.0	86.5	86.7	87.0

Source: *Institut für Konjunkturforschung*, as cited in Ellis, p. 378.

Table 13. Different Estimates of Net Investments in Germany, 1932–1936, at Current Prices (In Billions of Reichsmarks)

	1932	1933	1934	1935	1936
1. Erbe	−2.3	−1.1	1.2	1.3	4.6
2. Hoffman	−2.1	1.9	4.7	7.5	9.0
3. Official data (1938)	−1.6	−0.75	2.4	5.6	7.6

Sources: 1: Erbe, p. 114; 2: Hoffmann, p. 826; 3: Reichskreditgesellschaft, Report 1937–38, quoted in Guillebaud, *Economic Recovery*, p. 275.

Table 14. Distribution of National Income in Germany, 1929–1938, at Current Prices (In Millions of Reichsmarks)

Year	Total national income	Wages and salaries	Percentage	Employers' income[1]	Percentage	Undistributed profits (Corporations)	Percentage	Others[2]	Percentage
1929	70,880	43,045	60.7	21,608	30.5	882	1.2	5,345	7.6
1932	41,086	25,711	61.9	12,973	31.1	–450	—	2,852	7.0
1933	42,552	25,960	61.0	13,628	32.0	175	0.4	2,789	6.6
1934	48,953	29,183	59.6	15,782	32.2	735	1.5	3,253	6.7
1935	55,341	32,252	58.3	17,954	32.4	1,365	2.5	3,770	6.8
1936	62,098	35,260	56.8	20,404	32.9	2,330	3.6	4,104	6.7
1937	69,887	38,907	55.7	23,470	33.6	3,000	4.3	4,150	6.4
1938	78,268	42,958	54.9	26,710	34.1	3,900	5.0	4,700	6.0

1. Household income from assets and self-employment.
2. Income from public companies, pension funds, employers' payments for social insurance, and interest on the national debt.

Source: Hoffmann and Müller, pp. 43, 47, and 56.

Table 15. Distribution of Income from Assets and Self-employment in Germany, 1929–1938, at Current Prices (In Millions of Reichsmarks)

Year	Total income	Income from trade, industry, professions, rentals, and leases	As a percentage of national income	Income from agriculture and forestry	As a percentage of national income	Capital assets	As a percentage of national income
1929	21,608	12,857	18.1	5,487	7.8	3,264	4.6
1932	12,973	6,980	17.0	3,695	9.0	2,298	5.6
1933	13,628	7,360	17.3	3,865	9.1	2,403	5.6
1934	15,782	8,238	16.8	4,975	10.2	2,659	5.2
1935	17,954	9,560	17.2	5,750	10.4	2,644	4.8
1936	20,404	11,840	19.1	5,840	9.4	2,724	4.4
1937	23,470	14,580	20.9	6,110	8.7	2,780	4.0
1938	26,710	17,330	22.1	6,400	8.2	2,980	3.8

Source: Hoffmann and Müller, p. 47.

Table 16. Functional Distribution of Public Consumption, 1932–1935
(Reich, Länder, Municipalities, in Percent)

Purpose	1932	1933	1934	1935
1. General services	13.3	12.7	11.5	10.5
2. Security expenditures	3.3	4.8	16.1	20.7
3. Economic services	8.0	13.1	11.9	10.7
4. Social services	55.6	49.8	41.9	38.4
5. Other	19.8	19.6	18.6	19.7

Source: B. Ries, "Die Finanzpolitik im Deutschen Reich von 1933 bis 1935" (dissertation, Freiburg i. Br., 1964), app., table 6.

Table 17. Public Consumption, by Administrative Sectors, 1932–1936
(In Percent)

Year	Reich	Länder	Municipalities
1932	49.0	20.1	30.9
1933	51.3	19.5	29.2
1934	59.6	16.7	23.7
1935	63.6	14.0	22.4
1936	67.1	12.3	20.6

Source: S. Andic and J. Veverka, "The Growth of Government Expenditure since the Unification," *Finanz-Archiv*, n.s. 23 (Tübingen, 1963–64): 246.

Table 18. Composition of Private Savings, 1924–29 and 1933–38

Type of savings	1924–29		1933–38	
	In billions of reichsmarks	Percentage	In billions of reichsmarks	Percentage
1. Savings deposits	12.3	44.5	8.4	43.5
2. Private depositors' investments	11.6	41.9	4.7	24.2
3. Life insurance	1.6	5.8	2.7	13.9
4. Public social insurance	2.2	7.8	3.6	18.4
Total for each five-year period	27.7	100.0	29.4	100.0

Source: S. Lurie, *Private Investment in a Controlled Economy (Germany, 1933–1939)* (New York, 1947), p. 82.

Table 19. Combined Balance Sheet Data for the Major Corporate and Regional Banks, 1929–1938 (In Millions of Reichsmarks)

	1929 Dec.	1932 Dec.	1933 Dec.	1934 Dec.	1935 Dec.	1936 Dec.	1937 Nov.	1938 Nov.
Total assets[1]	16,673	10,679	9,773	9,667	9,631	9,726	10,350	11,649
Short-term loans	9,020	6,108	5,370	4,929	4,496	4,157	4,178	4,406
Regular commercial credit	3,015	1,429	1,425	1,767	1,873	2,460	3,241	2,860
Treasury notes and government loans	496	1,072	1,066	923	1,199	1,078	978	2,278
Total deposits	14,459	8,804	7,937	7,807	7,787	8,027	8,597	9,725
Private capital	1,350	851	823	809	789	794	806	813

1. After deduction of loans and mortgages.

Source: G. Keiser, "Strukturwandel der Bankbilanzen," *Bank-Archiv* (1939): 237.

Table 20. Armament Expenditures, 1932–1939 (In Millions of Reichsmarks)[1]

	1932	1933	1934	1935	1936	1937	1938	1939	Total[2]
High commands (Army, Navy, Air Force administrations)	—	—	3	5	128	346	452	258	1,192
Army	457	478	1,010	1,392	3,020	3,990	9,137	5,611	24,160
Navy	173	192	297	389	448	679	1,632	2,095	5,491
Air Force	—	76	642	1,036	2,225	3,258	6,026	3,942	17,128
Total	630	746	1,952	2,772	5,821	8,273	17,247	11,906	49,971
Mefo-bills	—	—	2,145	2,715	4,452	2,688	—	—	12,000
Total (including Mefo-bills)	630	746	4,197	5,487	10,273	10,961	17,247	11,906	59,971

1. For the fiscal year from April 1 to March 31 of the following year. Deviations from tables 2–4 are partially explained by calculations based upon a different fiscal year and by discrepancies between delivery and payment dates.
2. From April 1, 1932 to August 31, 1939.

Source: Stuebel, p. 4129.

Table 21. Various Estimates of Armament Expenditures in Relation to the National Product and Public Expenditures, 1933–1938

A. Proportion of the National Product Expended on Armaments (In Percent)

Author	In relation to	1933	1934	1935	1936	1937	1938
1. Klein	GNP	3.2	2.9	5.4	7.0	8.8	17.7
2. Stuebel	national income	1.5	7.8	9.3	15.7	15.0	21.0

Table 21. *continued*

Author	In relation to	1933	1934	1935	1936	1937	1938
3. Milward	GNP	3.2	3.4	5.5	7.6	9.6	18.1
4. Erbe	GNP	1.2	5.0	7.0	11.1	11.9	15.2
5. Hoffmann	net national product	3.3	6.2	9.3	13.0	12.4	17.5
6. Carroll	GNP	3.0	6.0	8.0	13.0	13.0	17.0

B. Proportion of Public Expenditures on Armaments (In Percent)

Author	In relation to	1933	1934	1935	1936	1937	1938
7. Klein	public consumption and transfer payments	12.4	10.9	21.2	25.2	30.0	46.7
8. Stuebel	Reich budget and Mefo-bills	11.1	39.8	48.0	58.2	55.0	60.0
9. Milward	public expenditures for goods and services	8.7	8.8	15.8	22.6	28.2	42.7
10. Erbe	public consumption	5.0	26.0	24.0	49.0	47.0	50.0
11. Hoffmann	public consumption	21.6	36.7	48.6	58.2	58.0	66.6
12. Carroll	public expenditures for goods and services	21.0	33.0	43.0	62.0	55.0	52.0

Sources: 1 and 7: Klein, pp. 251–54; 2 and 8: Stuebel, p. 4129; 3 and 9: A.S. Milward, *The German Economy at War* (London, 1965), p. 16; 4 and 10: Erbe, p. 114; 5 and 11: Hoffmann, pp. 721 and 826, respectively; 6 and 12: Carroll, pp. 184 and 187, respectively.

Table 22. Armament Expenditures in Relation to Public Expenditures for Goods and Services, 1933–1938 (In Billions of Reichsmarks)

	1933	1934	1935	1936	1937	1938
1. Total public consumption (not including armament expenditures)	7.0	6.9	7.2	7.4	7.9	8.6
2. Public investments (not including armament expenditures)	2.4	3.5	3.9	4.2	4.6	5.5
3. Armament expenditures (budget and Mefo-bills)	0.7	4.2	5.5	10.3	11.0	17.2

Table 22. *continued*

	1933	1934	1935	1936	1937	1938
4. Total public expenditures for goods and services (1 + 2 + 3)	10.1	14.6	16.6	21.9	23.5	31.3
5. Proportion for armament expenditures (3:4)		6.9	28.8	33.1	47.0	46.8	55.0

Sources: 1: Hoffman, p. 721; 2: Erbe, p. 25; 3: Stuebel, p. 4125.

Bibliography

Archival Materials and Unpublished Sources

BA   Bundesarchiv, Koblenz: Akten der Reichskanzlei (R 43/I, R 43/II), Reichsfinanzministerium (R 2), Reichswirtschaftsministerium (R 7), Verein Deutscher Eisen- und Stahlindustrieller/ Wirtschaftsgruppe Eisenschaffende Industrie (R 13/I), Reichsarbeitsministerium (R 41), Deutscher Industrie- und Handelstag (DIHT) (R 11), Beauftragter für den Vierjahresplan (R 26), Reichsleitung der NSDAP (NS 22), Nachlässe: W. von Moellendorff, Gustav Stolper, Silverberg, Karl Goerdeler, miscellaneous

BDC   Berlin Document Center: Personalakten in NSDAP-Zentralkartei, Parteikorrespondenz, Oberstes Parteigericht, Wirtschaftspolitische Abteilung, miscellaneous

HF   Forschungsstelle für die Geschichte des Nationalsozialismus in Hamburg: K.V. Krogmann diaries, Nachlaß Albert Krebs, miscellaneous

IfZ   Institut für Zeitgeschichte, Munich: Aufzeichnungen Otto Wagener (ED 60), Walter Darré (ED 110), Zeugenschrifttum Schwerin von Krosigk (ZS/A-20), unpublished documents from the Nuremberg trials, assorted documents on microfilm

NA   National Archives, Washington, D.C.: assorted documents on microfilm

Breiting-Hugenberg, unpublished interview of May 1933 (kindly placed at my disposal by Prof. Dr. Friedrich Zipfel)

Dräger-Materialsammlung: unpublished letters of R. Friedländer-Prechtl, miscellaneous

Published Sources and Secondary Materials

Abendroth, W., ed. *Faschismus und Kapitalismus*. Frankfurt a.M., 1967.

Abraham, D. *The Collapse of the Weimar Republic: Political Economy and Crisis*. Princeton, 1981.

Aubin, H., and Zorn, W. *Handbuch der deutschen Wirtschafts- und Sozialgeschichte*. Vol. 2. Stuttgart, 1976.

263

Bibliography

Barkai, A. *Vom Boykott zur "Entjudung": Der wirtschaftliche Existenz-kampf der Juden im Dritten Reich, 1933–1943.* Frankfurt a.M., 1988.
Bettelheim, Ch. *L'économie allemande sous le Nazisme: Un aspect de la décadence du capitalisme.* Paris, 1946.
Böhm, F. *Die Ordnung der Wirtschaft als geschichtliche Aufgabe und rechtschöpferische Leistung.* Stuttgart and Berlin, 1937.
Boelcke, W.A. *Die deutsche Wirtschaft, 1930–1945.* Düsseldorf, 1983.
Bracher, K.D. *Die deutsche Diktatur.* Cologne and Berlin, 1965.
Bracher, K.D.; Sauer, W.; and Schulz, G. *Die nationalsozialistische Macht-ergreifung: Studien zur Errichtung des totalitären Herrschaftssystems in Deutschland, 1933/34.* Cologne and Opladen, 1960.
Bräutigam, H. *Wirtschaftssystem des Nationalsozialismus: Probleme neu-zeitlicher Wirtschaftsgestaltung.* 3d ed. Berlin, 1936.
Broszat, M. *Der Staat Hitlers.* Munich, 1974.
Buchner, H. *Grundrisse einer nationalsozialistischen Wirtschaftstheorie.* Munich, 1930.
Bülow, F. *Der deutsche Ständestaat: Nationalsozialistische Gemeinschafts-politik durch Wirtschaftsorganisation.* Leipzig, 1934.
———. *Gustav Ruhland – Ein deutscher Bauerndenker im Kampf gegen Liberalismus und Marxismus.* Berlin, 1936.
Calic, E. *Ohne Maske: Hitler – Breiting Geheimgespräche, 1931.* Frankfurt a.M., 1968.
Carroll, B.A. *Design for Total War: Arms and Economics in the Third Reich.* The Hague, 1968.
Clapham, J.H. *The Economic Development of France and Germany, 1815–1914.* Cambridge, 1951.
Czichon, E. *Wer verhalf Hitler zur Macht? Zum Anteil der deutschen Industrie an der Zerstörung der Weimarer Republik.* Cologne, 1967.
Dahrendorf, R. *Gesellschaft und Demokratie in Deutschland.* Munich, 1965.
Dietrich, O. *Das Wirtschaftsdenken im Dritten Reich.* Munich, 1936.
Domarus, M. *Hitler-Reden und Proklamationen.* Würzburg, 1962–63.
Dräger, H. *Arbeitsbeschaffung durch produktive Kreditschöpfung – Ein Beitrag zur Frage der Wirtschaftsbelebung durch das sogenannte "Federgeld."* Nationalsozialistische Bibliothek, Heft 41. Munich, 1932. New ed. Düsseldorf, 1956.
Dräger, H., et al. *Arbeitsbeschaffung: Eine Gemeinschaftsarbeit.* Berlin, 1933.
Ellis, H.S. *German Monetary Theory, 1905–1933.* Cambridge, Mass., 1937.
———. *Exchange Control in Central Europe.* Westport, 1971.
Erbe, R. *Die nationalsozialistische Wirtschaftspolitik, 1933–1939, im Lichte der modernen Theorie.* Zurich, 1958.
Esenwein-Rothe, I. *Die Wirtschaftsverbände von 1933 bis 1945.* Berlin, 1965.

Europäisches Wirtschaftszentrum. *Reden und Vorträge auf dem 6. Großen Lehrgang der Kommission für Wirtschaftspolitik der NSDAP.* Munich, 1939.

Farquharson, J.E. *The Plough and the Swastika.* London, 1976.

Feder, G. *Das Manifest zur Brechung der Zinsknechtschaft des Geldes.* Munich, 1919.

——. *Der deutsche Staat auf nationaler und sozialer Grundlage.* Munich, 1923.

——. *Kampf gegen die Hochfinanz.* 5th ed. Munich, 1934.

——. *Wirtschaftslenkung im Dritten Reich.* Munich, 1934.

Fichte, J.G. *Der geschlossene Handelsstaat* (1st ed. 1800). Leipzig, n.d.

Fischer, F. *Germany's War Aims in the First World War.* London, 1967.

Fischer, W. *Deutsche Wirtschaftspolitik, 1918–1945.* 3d ed. Opladen, 1968.

Frauendorfer, M. *Der ständische Gedanke im Nationalsozialismus.* Munich, 1932.

Frei, R. *Die theoretischen Grundlagen der deutschen Währungspolitik während des Nationalsozialismus.* Bern, 1947.

Fried, F. [Friedrich Zimmermann]. *Das Ende des Kapitalismus.* Jena, 1931.

——. *Die Zukunft des Außenhandels: Durch innere Marktordnung zur Außenhandelsfreiheit.* Jena, 1934.

Friedländer-Prechtl, R. *Wirtschafts-Wende – Die Ursachen der Arbeitslosen-Krise und deren Bekämpfung.* Leipzig, 1931.

Genschel, H. *Die Verdrängung der Juden aus der Wirtschaft im Dritten Reich.* Göttingen, 1966.

Gereke, G. *Ich war königlich-preußischer Landrat.* Berlin (East), 1970.

Gerschenkron, A. *Bread and Democracy in Germany.* Berkeley and Los Angeles, 1943.

Gossweiler, K.; Kühnl, R.; and Opitz, R. *Faschismus – Entstehung und Verhinderung.* Antifaschistische Arbeitshefte No. 4. Frankfurt a.M., 1972.

Grotkopp, W. *Die große Krise: Lehren aus der Überwindung der Wirtschaftskrise, 1929/32.* Düsseldorf, 1954.

Grunberger, R. *A Social History of the Third Reich.* London, 1971.

Guillebaud, C.W. *The Economic Recovery of Germany.* London, 1939.

——. *The Social Policy of Nazi Germany.* Cambridge, 1941.

Gurland, A.; Kirchheimer, O.; and Neumann, F. *The Fate of Small Business in Nazi Germany.* Senate Committee print no. 14. Washington, D.C., 1943.

Hahn, L.A. *Volkswirtschaftliche Theorie des Bankkredits.* Tübingen, 1920.

Hallgarten, G.W. *Hitler, Reichswehr und Industrie.* Frankfurt a.M., 1955.

Hamerow, T.S. *Restoration, Revolution, Reaction, Economics, and Politics in Germany, 1815–1871.* Princeton, 1958.

Hardach, G. *Der Erste Weltkrieg.* Munich, 1973.

Hayes, P. *Industry and Ideology: IG Farben in the Nazi Era.* Cambridge, 1987.

Heinrich, W. *Das Ständewesen mit besonderer Berücksichtigung der Selbstverwaltung der Wirtschaft.* Jena, 1932.

Henderson. W.O. *The State and the Industrial Revolution in Prussia.* Liverpool, 1958.

Herbert, U. *Fremdarbeiter: Politik und Praxis des "Ausländer-Einsatzes" in der Kriegswirtschaft des Dritten Reiches.* 2d ed. Berlin and Bonn 1986.

Herbst, L. *Der Totale Krieg und die Ordnung der Wirtschaft: Die Kriegswirtschaft im Spannungsfeld von Politik, Ideologie und Propaganda, 1939–1945.* Stuttgart, 1982.

Herrmann, A.R., *Verstaatlichung des Giralgeldes: Ein Beitrag zur Frage der Währungsreform nach den Grundsätzen G. Feders.* Munich, 1932.

Hitler, A. *Mein Kampf.* Munich, 1933.

Hock, W. *Deutscher Antikapitalismus: Der ideologische Kampf gegen die freie Wirtschaft im Zeichen der großen Krise.* Frankfurt a.M., 1960.

Hofer, W., ed. *Der Nationalsozialismus: Dokumente, 1933–1945.* Frankfurt a.M., 1959.

Hoffmann, W.G. *Das Wachstum der deutschen Wirtschaft seit der Mitte des 19. Jahrhunderts.* Berlin, 1965.

Hoffmann, W.G., and Müller, H. *Das deutsche Volkseinkommen, 1851–1957.* Tübingen, 1959.

Hüttenberger, P. *Die Gauleiter: Studie zum Wandel des Machtgefüges in der NSDAP.* Stuttgart, 1969.

Jäckel, E. *Hitlers Weltanschauung.* Tübingen, 1969.

James, H. *The German Slump.* Oxford, 1986.

Kamenetsky, T. *"Lebensraum": Secret Nazi Plans for Eastern Europe.* New York, 1961.

Kehrl, H. *Krisenmanager im Dritten Reich.* Düsseldorf, 1973.

Kellenbenz, H. *Deutsche Wirtschaftsgeschichte.* Vol. 2. Munich, 1981.

Keynes, J.M. *Vom Gelde.* Munich and Leipzig, 1932.

——. *Allgemeine Theorie der Beschäftigung, des Zinses und des Geldes.* Berlin, 1936.

Kindleberger, Ch.P. *Die Weltwirtschaftskrise.* Munich, 1973.

Klagges, D. *Reichtum und soziale Gerechtigkeit.* 2d ed. Leipzig, 1933.

——. *Idee und System: Vorträge an der Deutschen Hochschule für Politik über Grundfragen nationalsozialistischer Weltanschauung.* Leipzig, 1934.

Klein, B.H. *Germany's Preparations for War.* Cambridge, Mass., 1959.

Klemperer, K. von. *Konservative Bewegungen zwischen Kaiserreich und Nationalsozialismus.* Munich, 1962.

——. *Germany's New Conservatism: Its History and Dilemma in the 20th Century.* Princeton, 1968.

Klöss, E., ed. *Reden des Führers: Politik und Propaganda Adolf Hitlers, 1922–1945.* Munich, 1967.

Knapp, G.F. *Staatliche Theorie des Geldes* (1st ed. 1905). Munich and Leipzig, 1918.

Knies, K. *Die politische Ökonomie vom geschichtlichen Standpunkte.* Braunschweig, 1883.

Köhler, B. *Das Dritte Reich und der Kapitalismus.* Munich, 1933.

Krause, A.B. *Organisation von Arbeit und Wirtschaft.* Berlin, ca. 1935.

Krause, W. *Wirtschaftstheorie unter dem Hakenkreuz.* Berlin (East), 1969.

Krebs, A. *Tendenzen und Gestalten der NSDAP: Erinnerungen an die Frühzeit der Partei.* Stuttgart, 1959.

Kroll, G. *Von der Weltwirtschaftskrise zur Staatskonjunktur.* Berlin, 1958.

Kuczynski, J. *Die Geschichte der Lage der Arbeiter in Deutschland von 1789 bis in die Gegenwart.* Berlin (East), 1953.

———. *Klassen und Klassenkämpfe im imperialistischen Deutschland und in der BRD.* Frankfurt a.M., 1972.

Kuhn, A. *Hitlers außenpolitisches Programm.* Stuttgart, 1970.

Kühnl, R. *Formen bürgerlicher Herrschaft: Liberalismus und Faschismus.* Hamburg, 1971.

Lautenbach, W. *Zins, Kredit und Produktion.* Edited by W. Stützel. Tübingen, 1952.

Lebovics, H. *Social Conservatism and the Middle Classes in Germany, 1914–1933.* Princeton, 1969.

Lindenlaub, D. *Richtungskämpfe im Verein für Sozialpolitik, Wissenschaft und Sozialpolitik im Kaiserreich, vornehmlich vom Beginn des "Neuen Kurses" bis zum Ausbruch des Ersten Weltkrieges (1890–1914).* Vierteljahresschrift für Sozial- und Wirtschaftsgeschichte, Beihefte 52–53. Wiesbaden, 1967.

List, F. *Das nationale System der politischen Ökonomie* (1st ed. 1841). 5th ed. Jena, 1928.

———. *Schriften, Reden, Briefe.* 10 vols. Berlin, 1932–35.

Lorenz, O. *Die Beseitigung der Arbeitslosigkeit.* Berlin, 1932.

Ludwig, K.H. *Technik und Ingenieure im Dritten Reich.* Düsseldorf, 1974.

Lurie, S. *Private Investment in a Controlled Economy (Germany, 1933–1939).* New York, 1947.

Meinck, G. *Hitler und die deutsche Aufrüstung, 1933–1937.* Wiesbaden, 1959.

Meyer, H.C. *Mitteleuropa in German Thought and Action, 1815–1945.* The Hague, 1955.

Milward, A.S. *The German Economy at War.* London, 1965.

———. *The New Order and the French Economy.* Oxford, 1970.

———. *War Economy and Society, 1939–1945.* Berkeley and Los Angeles, 1977.

Mises, L. von. *Omnipotent Government: The Rise of the Total State and Total War.* New Haven, 1948.

Moellendorff, W. von. *Deutsche Gemeinwirtschaft.* Berlin, 1916.

———. *Von Einst zu Einst.* Jena, 1917.

Mönckmeier, O., ed. *Jahrbuch für nationalsozialistische Wirtschaft.* Pt. 1,

Die nationalsozialistische Wirtschaftsordnung. Stuttgart and Berlin, 1935, pp. 3–450. Pt. 2, *Das nationalsozialistische Wirtschaftsrecht.* Stuttgart and Berlin, 1937, pp. 453–625.

Mommsen, H.; Petzina, D.; and Weisbrod, B., eds. *Industrielles System und politische Entwicklung in der Weimarer Republik: Verhandlungen des Internationalen Symposiums in Bochum vom 12.–17.Juni 1973.* Düsseldorf, 1974.

Mottek, H. *Studien zur Geschichte der industriellen Revolution in Deutschland.* Berlin (East), 1960.

Müller, A. *Vom Geiste der Gemeinschaft* (1st ed. 1810). Leipzig, 1931.

———. *Ausgewählte Abhandlungen.* Edited by J. Baxa. Jena, 1921.

Müller-Armack, A. *Staatsidee und Wirtschaftsordnung im neuen Reich.* Berlin, 1933.

Naftali, F. *Demokratia Kalkalit – Mivkhar Ktavim.* In Hebrew. N.p., n.d.

Nathan, O. *The Nazi Economic System: Germany's Mobilization for War.* Durham, 1944.

Naumann, Fr. *Neudeutsche Wirtschaftspolitik.* Berlin, 1906.

Neebe, R. *Großindustrie, Staat und NSDAP.* Göttingen, 1981.

Neumann, F. *Behemoth: The Structure and Practice of National Socialism.* London, 1942.

Nonnenbruch, F. *Die dynamische Wirtschaft.* 4th ed. Munich, 1939.

Petzina, D. *Autarkiepolitik im Dritten Reich: Der nationalsozialistische Vierjahresplan.* Stuttgart, 1968.

Petzina, D.; Abelshauser, W.; and Faust, A. *Sozialgeschichtliches Arbeitsbuch, III: Materialen zur Statistik des Deutschen Reiches, 1914–1945.* Munich, 1978.

Pieck, W.; Dimitroff, G.; and Togliatti, P. *Die Offensive des Faschismus: Referat auf dem VII. Kongress der Kommunistischen Internationale (1935).* Berlin (East), 1957.

Pinson, K.S. *Modern Germany: Its History and Civilization.* New York, 1954.

Poole, K. *German Financial Policies, 1932–1939.* Cambridge, Mass., 1939.

Posse, H. *Die deutsche Wirtschaft.* Berlin, ca. 1936. Vol. 3 of H.H. Lammers & H. Pfundtner, eds. *Grundlagen, Aufbau und Wirtschaftsordnung des nationalsozialistischen Staates.*

Prager, L. *Nationalsozialismus gegen Liberalismus.* Nationalsozialistische Bibliothek, Heft 49. Munich, 1933.

Priester, H.E. *Das deutsche Wirtschaftswunder.* Amsterdam, 1936.

Prion, W. *Das deutsche Finanzwunder: Die Geldbeschaffung für den deutschen Wirtschaftsaufschwung.* Berlin, 1938.

Der Prozeß gegen die Hauptkriegsverbrecher vor dem Internationalen Militär Gerichtshof (International Military Tribunal), Nürnberg, 14. Nov. 1945–1. Okt. 1946. 42 vols. Nuremberg, 1947–49.

Rathenau, W. *Gesammelte Schriften.* Berlin, 1929.

Rauschning, H. *Gespräche mit Hitler, 1932–1934*. New York, 1940.

Reinhardt, Fritz. *Generalplan gegen die Arbeitslosigkeit*. Oldenburg, 1933.

Reupke, H. *Der Nationalsozialismus und die Wirtschaft: Erläuterung der wirtschaftlichen Programmpunkte und Ideenlehre der nationalsozialistischen Bewegung*. Berlin, 1931.

Rist, Ch. *History of Monetary and Credit Theory from John Law to the Present Day*. London, 1940.

Robertson, E.M., ed. *The Origins of the Second World War: Historical Interpretations*. London, 1967.

Roscher, W. *Grundriß zu Vorlesungen über die Staatswirtschaft nach geschichtlicher Methode*. Göttingen, 1843.

———. *Die Grundlagen der Nationalökonomie*. Stuttgart, 1857.

———. *Geschichte der Nationalökonomie in Deutschland*. Munich, 1874.

Roll, E. *A History of Economic Thought*. London, 1966.

Schacht, H. *Grundsätze deutscher Wirtschaftspolitik*. Oldenburg i. O., 1932.

———. *Account Settled*. London, 1949.

———. *76 Jahre meines Lebens*. Bad Wörishofen, 1953.

———. *My First 76 Years*. London, 1955.

Scheffler, W. *Judenvervolgung im Dritten Reich*. Berlin, 1964.

Schiller, K. *Arbeitsbeschaffung und Finanzordnung in Deutschland*. Berlin, 1936.

Schmoller, G. *Umrisse und Untersuchungen zur Verfassungs-, Verwaltungs- und Wirtschaftsgeschichte, besonders des preußischen Staates*. Leipzig, 1898.

———. *Zur Literaturgeschichte der Staats- und Sozialwissenschaften*. Leipzig, 1888.

———. *Walther Rathenau und Hugo Preuß: Die Staatsmänner des neuen Deutschlands*. Munich and Leipzig, 1922.

———. *Zwanzig Jahre deutscher Politik*. Munich and Leipzig, 1920.

Schmoller, G.; Sering, M.; and Wagner, A., eds. *Handels- und Machtpolitik*. Berlin, 1900.

Schneider, M. *Das Arbeitsbeschaffungsprogramm des ADGB: Zur gewerkschaftlichen Politik in der Endphase der Weimarer Republik*. Bonn-Bad Godesberg, 1975.

Schneller, M. *Zwischen Romantik und Faschismus*. Stuttgart, 1970.

Schoenbaum, D. *Hitler's Social Revolution: Class and Status in Nazi Germany, 1933–1939*. London, 1967.

Schröder, H.J. *Deutschland und die Vereinigten Staaten, 1933–1939: Wirtschaft und Politik in der Entwicklung des Deutsch-Amerikanischen Gegensatzes*. Wiesbaden, 1970.

Schumann, H.G. *Nationalsozialismus und Gewerkschaftsbewegung*. Hannover, 1958.

Schumpeter, J.A. *History of Economic Analysis*. New York, 1954.

Schweitzer, A. *Big Business in the Third Reich*. Bloomington, 1964.

Schwerin v. Krosigk, L.v. *Nationalsozialistische Finanzpolitik.* Jena, 1936.
——. *Es geschah in Deutschland: Menschenbilder unseres Jahrhunderts.* Tübingen and Stuttgart, 1952.
Sombart, W. *Die deutsche Volkswirtschaft im 19. Jahrhundert und im Anfang des 20. Jahrhunderts* (1st ed. 1903). Darmstadt, 1954.
——. *Händler und Helden: Patriotische Besinnungen.* Munich and Leipzig, 1915.
——. *Die drei Nationalökonomien: Geschichte und System der Lehre von der Wirtschaft.* Munich and Leipzig, 1930.
——. *Die Zukunft des Kapitalismus.* Berlin, 1932.
——. *Deutscher Sozialismus.* Berlin, 1934.
Sontheimer, K. *Antidemokratisches Denken in der Weimarer Republik: Die politischen Ideen des deutschen Nationalismus zwischen 1918 und 1933.* Munich, 1962.
Spann, O., *Der wahre Staat: Vorlesungen über Abbruch und Neuaufbau der Gesellschaft.* 3d ed. Jena, 1931.
——. *Gesellschaftslehre.* 2d ed. Leipzig, 1923.
Speer, A. *Inside the Third Reich.* London, 1971.
Spengler, O. *Preußentum und Sozialismus.* Munich, 1920.
Stolper, G. *German Economy, 1870–1940: Issues and Trends.* New York, 1940.
——. *Deutsche Wirtschaft, 1870–1940.* Stuttgart, 1950.
Stucken, R. *Deutsche Geld- und Kreditpolitik* (1st ed. 1937). 2d ed. Tübingen, 1953.
Taylor, A.J.P. *The Origins of the Second World War.* London, 1964.
Thyssen, F. *I Paid Hitler.* London and New York, 1941.
Treue, W., and Frede, G. *Wirtschaft und Politik, 1933–1945: Dokumente mit verbindendem Text.* Braunschweig, 1953.
Turner, H.A., Jr. *Faschismus und Kapitalismus in Deutschland: Studien zum Verhältnis zwischen Nationalsozialismus und Wirtschaft.* Göttingen, 1972.
——. *German Big Business and the Rise of Hitler.* New York and Oxford, 1985.
——. ed. *Hitler aus nächster Nähe: Aufzeichnungen eines Vertrauten (Otto Wagener), 1929–1932.* Berlin, 1978.
Uhlig, H. *Die Warenhäuser im Dritten Reich.* Cologne and Opladen, 1956.
Wagemann, E. *Geld- und Kreditform.* Staatswissenschaftliche Zeitfragen No. 1. Berlin, 1932.
——. *Zwischenbilanz der Krisenpolitik.* Berlin, 1935.
——. *Wo kommt das viele Geld her?* Berlin, 1940.
Wagener, O. *Das Wirtschaftsprogramm der NSDAP.* Munich, 1932.
——. *Nationalsozialistische Wirtschaftsauffassung und berufsständischer Aufbau.* Berlin, 1933.
Wagenführ, R. *Die deutsche Industrie im Kriege, 1939–1945.* Berlin, 1963.
Wagner, A. *Agrar- und Industriestaat.* Berlin, 1901.

Weinberg, G.L., ed. *Hitlers Zweites Buch: Ein Dokument aus dem Jahre 1928.* Stuttgart, 1961.

Weippert, G. *Der späte List: Ein Beitrag zur Grundlegung der Wissenschaft von der Politik und zur politischen Ökonomie als Gestaltungslehre der Wirtschaft.* Erlangen, 1956.

Winkler, H.A. *Mittelstand, Demokratie und Nationalsozialismus – Die politische Entwicklung von Handwerk und Kleinhandel in der Weimarer Republik.* Cologne, 1972.

Winschuh, J. *Gerüstete Wirtschaft.* Berlin, 1940.

Wirsing, G. *Zwischeneuropa und die deutsche Zukunft.* Jena, 1932.

Wirtschaftliches Sofortprogramm der NSDAP. Munich, 1932.

Wolf, Fr. *Umschwung: Die deutsche Wirtschaft, 1933.* Frankfurt a.M., 1934.

———. *Staatskonjunktur: Die deutsche Wirtschaft, 1934.* Frankfurt a.M., 1935.

Ziemer, G. *Inflation und Deflation zerstören die Demokratie.* Stuttgart, 1971.

Dissertations

Farquharson, J.E. "The NSDAP and Agriculture in Germany, 1928–1938." University of Kent, Canterbury, 1972.

Gossweiler, K. "Die Rolle des Monopolkapitals bei der Herbeiführung der Röhm-Affäre." Berlin (East), 1963.

Honigberger, R. "Die wirtschaftspolitische Zielsetzung des Nationalsozialismus und deren Einfluß auf die deutsche Wirtschaftsordnung, dargestellt und kritisch untersucht am Beispiel des deutschen Arbeitsmarktes von 1933 bis 1939." Albert Ludwig Universität, Freiburg i. Br., 1949.

Rämisch, R.H. "Die berufsständische Verfassung in Theorie und Praxis des Nationalsozialismus." Freie Universität, Berlin, 1957.

Ries, B. "Die Finanzpolitik im Deutschen Reich von 1933 bis 1935." Freiburg i. Br., 1964.

Siegfried, K.J. "Universalismus und Faschismus: Zur historischen Wirksamkeit und politischen Funktion der universalistischen Gesellschaftslehre und Ständekonzeption Othmar Spanns." Philipps-Universität, Marburg, 1973.

Articles

Barkai, A. "Sozialdarwinismus und Antiliberalismus in Hitlers Wirtschaftskonzept: Zu Henry A. Turner Jr., Hitlers Einstellung zu Wirtschaft und Gesellschaft vor 1933," *Geschichte und Gesellschaft* 3 (1977): 406–17.

———. Wirtschaftliche Grundanschauungen und Ziele der NSDAP: Ein unveröffentlichtes Dokument aus dem Jahre 1931," *Jahrbuch des Instituts für Deutsche Geschichte*, 7 (1978): 355–85.

——."Die deutschen Unternehmer und die Judenpolitik im 'Dritten Reich.'" *Geschichte und Gesellschaft* 15 (1989): 227–47.

Blaich, F. "Wirtschaftspolitik und Wirtschaftsverfassung im Dritten Reich." *Politik und Zeitgeschichte: Beilage zur Wochenzeitschrift Das Parlament*, no. B 8/71, Feb. 20, 1971.

——. "Wirtschaft und Rüstung in Deutschland, 1933–1939," In K.D. Bracher et al., eds. *Nationalsozialistische Diktatur, 1933–1945: Eine Bilanz.* Bonn, 1983, 285–316.

Borchardt, K. "Ein neues Urteil über die deutsche Währungs- und Handelspolitik von 1931 bis 1938." *Vierteljahresschrift für Sozial- und Wirtschaftsgeschichte*, 46 (1959): 526–40.

Curth, H. "Das erste Scheitern des deutschen Sozialismus." *Die Tat* 24 (1932): 593–606.

Czichon, E. "Der Primat der Industrie im Kartell der nationalsozialistischen Macht." *Das Argument* 10, no. 47 (1968).

Dieben, W. "Die innere Reichsschuld seit 1933." *Finanz-Archiv*, n.s. 11 (1949): 656–701.

Eschmann, E.W. "Wirtschaften auf Befehl und Übereinkunft." *Die Tat* 24 (1932).

——. "Nationale Planwirtschaft: Grundzüge." *Die Tat* 24 (1932): 225–43.

Falkenhausen, Frh. von. "Das Anleihestockgesetz und seine Durchführung." *Bank-Archiv* 34 (1935): 283–90, 365ff.

Fischer, F. "Weltpolitik, Weltmachtstreben und deutsche Kriegsziele." *Historische Zeitschrift* 199 (1964): 265–346.

Focks, P. "Die zünftigen Nationalökonomien." *Die Tat* 24 (1932): 589–93.

Fried, F. [Friedrich Zimmermann]. "Der Übergang zur Autarkie." *Die Tat* 24 (1932): 120–50.

——. "Jugend und Wirtschaft." *Nationalsozialistische Landespost*, Dec. 9, 1933.

Friedrichs, A. "Die Finanzierung der Staatskonjunktur." *Bank-Archiv* 37 (1938): 142–47.

——. "Die Finanzierung der Arbeitsbeschaffung." *Bank-Archiv* 33 (1933–34).

Gossweiler, K. "Der Übergang von der Weltwirtschaftskrise zur Rüstungskonjunktur in Deutschland, 1933–1934." *Jahrbuch für Wirtschaftsgeschichte*, pt. 2 (1968): 55–116.

Guillebaud, C.W. "Hitler's New Economic Order for Europe." *The Economic Journal* 50 (1940): 449–60.

Herle, J. "Unternehmerverbände im neuen Deutschland." *Der Deutsche Volkswirt* 7, no. 48 (1933).

Holtz, A. "Sozialistische Wirtschaft." *Der Aufbau* 4, no. 17 (1936): 6–7.

Kaldor, N. "The German War Economy." *The Review of Economic Studies* 13 (1945–46).

Klagges, D. "Soziale Gerechtigkeit durch Organisation und Berechnung." *Nationalsozialistische Briefe* 5 (1929–30).

Köhler, B. "Wir wollen das Recht auf Arbeit." *Arbeitertum*, Jan. 15, 1933.

——. "Die Mitteilungen nur für Parteigenossen?" *Mitteilungen der Kommission für Wirtschaftspolitik der NSDAP München* 2, no. 1 (1937).

Kollmann, E.C. "Walther Rathenau and German Foreign Policy: Thoughts and Actions." *Journal of Modern History* 24 (1954): 127–42.

Krüger, P. "Zu Hitlers 'nationalsozialistischen Wirtschaftserkenntnissen.'" *Geschichte und Gesellschaft* 6 (1980): 263–282.

Mandelbaum, K. "An Experiment in Full Employment: Controls in the German Economy, 1933–1938." In *The Economies of Full Employment.* Oxford, 1945.

Mason, T.W. "Der Primat der Politik." *Das Argument*, no. 41 (1966).

——. "Some Origins of the Second World War." In E.M. Robertson, ed., *The Origins of the Second World War: Historical Interpretations.* London, 1967, pp. 105–35.

——. "Zur politischen Relevanz historischer Theorien: Die Imperialismus-Diskussion im Schatten des kalten Krieges. *Aus Politik und Zeitgeschichte: Beilage zu Das Parlament*, B 20/72 (May 1972).

Meinecke, F. "Drei Generationen deutscher Gelehrtenpolitik." *Historische Zeitschrift* 125 (1922).

Moeller, M. "Schacht als Geld- und Finanzpolitiker." *Finanz-Archiv*, n.s. 11 (1949).

Petzina, D. "Hauptprobleme der deutschen Wirtschaftspolitik, 1932/33." *Vierteljahreshefte für Zeitgeschichte* 15 (1967): 19–55.

Rathenau, W. "Transatlantische Warnungssignale." *Die Zukunft*, July 30, 1898.

Reinhart, F. "Die volkswirtschaftliche Verwendung der Bankeinlagen." *Bank-Archiv* 35 (1935–36): 56–60.

Roscher, W. "Die romantische Schule der Nationalökonomie in Deutschland." *Zeitschrift für die Gesamte Staatswissenschaft* (1870): 51–105.

Scheunemann, W. "NS-Programm und Wirtschaftspolitik: Brechung der Zinsknechtschaft." *Mitteilungen der Kommission für Wirtschaftspolitik der NSDAP München* 1, no. 5 (1936): 12–15.

Schmoller, G. "Die Wandlungen in der Handelspolitik des 19. Jahrhunderts." *Schmollers Jahrbuch* 24 (1900).

Schweitzer, A. "Foreign Exchange Crisis of 1936." *Zeitschrift für die Gesamte Staatswissenschaft.*" 118 (1962): 243–77.

——. "Organisierter Kapitalismus und Parteidiktatur, 1933–1936." *Schmollers Jahrbuch* 79 (1959): 37–80.

——. "Der organisierte Kapitalismus: Die Wirtschaftsordnung in der ersten Periode der nationalsozialistischen Herrschaft." *Hamburger Jahrbuch für Wirtschafts- und Gesellschaftspolitik* 7 (1962): 36–47.

Sommer, A. "Friedrich List und Adam Müller." *Weltwirtschaftliches Archiv* 25 (1927): 345–76.

Sontheimer, K. "Der Tat-Kreis." *Vierteljahreshefte für Zeitgeschichte*, no. 7 (1959): 229–60.

Stegmann, D. "Zum Verhältnis von Großindustrie und Nationalsozialismus, 1930–1933." *Archiv für Sozialgeschichte* 13 (1973): 399–482.

Stucken, R. "Hände weg vom industriellen Anlagekredit!" *Bank-Archiv* 37–38, 378–80.

Stuebel, H. "Die Finanzierung der Aufrüstung im Dritten Reich." *Europa-Archiv* 6 (1951): 4128–36.

Treue, W. "Hitlers Denkschrift zum Vierteljahresplan 1936." *Vierteljahreshefte für Zeitgeschichte* 3 (1955): 184–210.

Turner, H.A., Jr. "Hitlers Secret Pamphlet for Industrialists, 1927." *Journal of Modern History* 40 (1968): 348–74.

——. "Big Business and the Rise of Hitler." *American Historical Review* 75 (1969–70): 56–70.

——. "Großunternehmertum und Nationalsozialismus, 1930–1933." *Historische Zeitschrift* 221 (1975): 18–68.

——. "Hitlers Einstellung zu Wirtschaft und Gesellschaft." *Geschichte und Gesellschaft* 2 (1976): 89–117.

"Überwindung des Kapitalismus." *Der Angriff*, Dec. 20, 1935.

Vleugels, W. "Die Kritik am wirtschaftlichen Liberalismus in der Entwicklung der deutschen Volkswirtschaftslehre." *Schmollers Jahrbuch* 59 (1935): 513–53.

Vogelsang, T. "Neue Dokumente zur Geschichte der Reichswehr, 1930–1933." *Vierteljahreshefte für Zeitgeschichte* 2 (1954): 397–436.

Wagemann, E. "Zum Thema Geld- und Kreditform: Mißverständnisse und Irrtümer." *Wochenbericht des Instituts für Konjunkturforschung*, Jan. 27, 1932.

Wagner, A. "Finanzwissenschaft und Staatssozialismus." *Zeitschrift für die Gesamte Staatswissenschaft* 43 (1887): 37–122, 675–746.

Wirsing, G. "Zwangsautarkie." *Die Tat* 23 (1931).

——. "Richtung Ost-Südost." *Die Tat* 22 (1930–31).

Index

Index

99, 138, 183, 218
lectern Socialists. *See*
 Kathedersozialisten
Lenin, V.I., 11
Ley, Robert, 120, 123–24, 134,
 151, 153, 192
liberalism, 10, 18, 26, 72, 94, 118,
 223, 243
 classical, 73, 75, 78, 84, 100
 economic, 84
 opposition. *See* antiliberalism
liberalist-Marxist theory, 33
life insurance, 201
liquidity of banks, 61, 208, 210,
 211, 213, 214
List, F., 71, 75, 77–82, 87, 91, 92,
 96, 103–4
living space. *See Lebensraum*
living standards, 149, 188, 222,
 232, 239, 241
Lorenz, Oskar, 29
Lucke, Dr. von, 29
Lurie, Samuel, 17–18
Luther, Hans, 162

MacMillan Report (1931), 65
Mandelbaum, K., 220
marginal gain, 94
maritime policies, 88–89, 236
market
 economy, 67, 145
 mechanism, 4, 10, 26, 100, 170,
  248
marriage loans, 171
Marxism, 4, 10–15, 37, 51, 71,
 117–18, 212, 217, 243
Mason, Tim, 14–15
mass politics, 11
maximalism, 220
medieval tradition, 76, 77, 92, 96,
 117
Mefo-bills, 7, 63, 162, 165–67
Meinberg, W., 142, 151
Meinecke, Friedrich, 84

Mein Kampf, 21, 26, 89, 90, 123,
 147, 203
Menger, Carl, 94
mercantilism, 72, 74, 90
Messerschmidt Company, 240
middle class, 205, 210
 activists, 129, 130
 associations, 120, 203
 ideology, 115–19, 244
 interests, 97, 109, 132–34
 small businesses, 24, 118, 134,
  188–89
migration from villages, 150–51,
 156, 171, 172, 229
militarization, 230
military
 expenditure, 7, 197, 219–20,
  260–62
 power, 78, 80, 83, 171
 service, 171, 218, 229, 231
Milward, Alan, 8, 18, 219, 220
minimalism, 219–20
Ministry of Finance, 28
Mises, Ludwig von, 101
Moellendorff, Wichard von, 91–92,
 104–5
Moeller van den Bruck, A., 94,
 100
monetary expansion, 106
monetary policy, 182, 222
monetary theory, 62, 64, 71,
 77–78, 86–87, 104
money, 87
 commodity concept, 62
 creation, 10, 25, 58–59, 61, 74,
  77, 104, 192–93, 214
 free, 24
 market, 200–201, 211
 paper, 76–79, 86, 103, 166
 supply, 10, 41, 56, 74, 161,
  165–67
monopolist bourgeoisie, 11
monopoly capital, 4–5, 10, 11,
 13–14

Monroe Doctrine, 93
mortgage market, 204–5
Müller, Adam, 75–77, 81–83,
  95–96, 103–4, 105
multiplier, 6
multiplier effect, 63
municipal bonds, 204, 206
Mussolini, Benito, 156, 175
Mutschmann, Martin, 126

Naftali, Fritz, 51–52
Nathan, Otto, 4, 7
National Agrarian Association,
  142–43
National Association of Savings
  Banks, 209–10
National Corporations, 128, 129,
  131
National Credit Agency, 209
National Economic Council, 130
national economy, 35–36, 44,
  81–82, 87, 99, 175, 247
National Groups, 131, 132
national income, 196, 198, 257
National Institute for Economic
  Efficiency, 223
nationalism, 53, 79–80, 84
  DNVP, 68, 107–8, 142, 162
nationalist etatism, 10, 22, 69, 245
  contextual background, 71–75
  founding fathers, 75–81
  historical school, 81–91
  traditional/modern components,
    100–105
  war socialism, 91–94
  Weimar period, 94–100
nationalization, 73, 98
  banks, 43, 46, 86, 208–9, 211,
    216
  land, 23, 141, 143
national labor law, 32, 124
National Liberal party, 85
National Opposition, 68
National Peasant Day, 152

national power, 69, 89
national security, 78
National Socialist Organization of
  Shop Stewards (NSBO), 123–24
National Socialists
  corporate structure and, 116–38
  DAF, 120–21, 123–24
  economic establishment, 107–15
  Library, 55, 72
  Organization of Shop Stewards,
    123, 126, 127
  party (NSDAP), 28, 119, 124,
    190
  Tax Reform, 185
Nationalsozialistische
  Betriebszellen Organisation. *See*
  National Socialist Organization
  of Shop Stewards
Nationalsozialistische Deutsche
  Arbeiterpartei. *See* National
  Socialist party
National Sustenance Corporation
  (RNS), 145–47, 151–55, 231
Naumann, Friedrich, 94
Navy Association, 88
Nazi
  Economic Council, 28, 34, 130
  economic policy. *See* economic
    policy
  economic system, 244–49
  ideology, 9–20, 243–44
  war preparation, 2–9, 20,
    159–60, 172, 218–23, 225,
    233–34, 236–37
neo-conservative methods, 92
New Deal, 2
new economic order, 32–37, 92,
  95, 157, 222, 249
new European order, 18, 99, 183,
  247
"new men," 28
New Plan, 40, 42, 90, 174, 177–81
"noiseless procedure," 201
nominalism, 62, 64